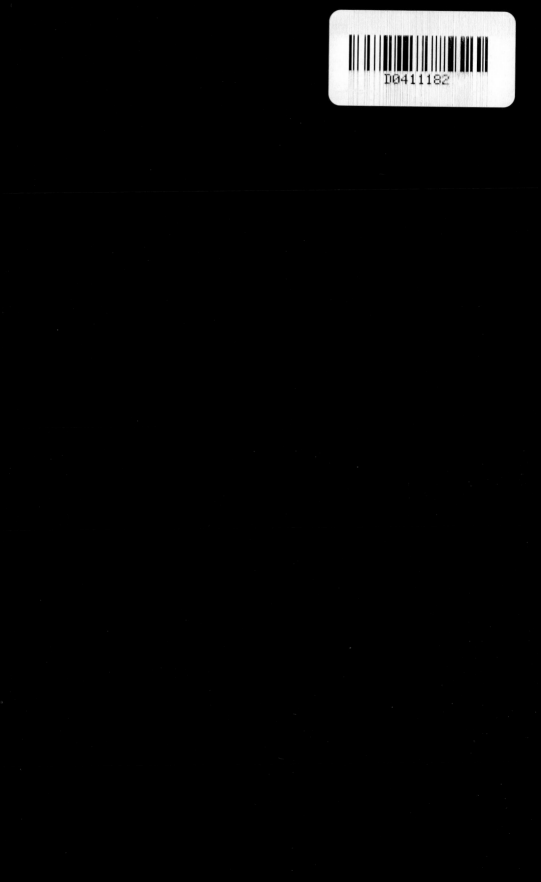

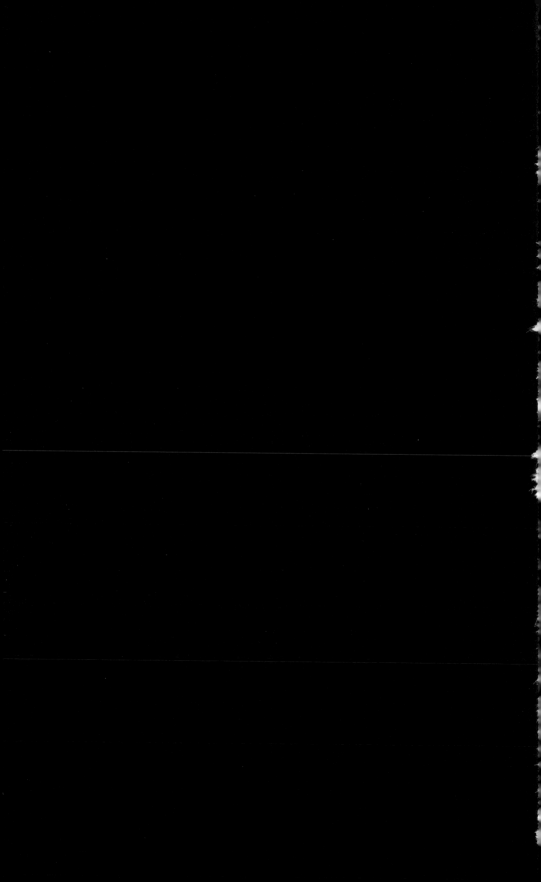

Elsie and Mairi Go to War

DIANE ATKINSON

ELSIE AND MAIRI GO TO WAR

Two Extraordinary Women
on the Western Front

preface
publishing

Published by Preface 2009

10 9 8 7 6 5 4 3 2 1

Copyright © Diane Atkinson, 2009

First published in Great Britain in 2009 by Preface Publishing
1 Queen Anne's Gate
London SW1H 9BT

An imprint of The Random House Group Limited

www.rbooks.co.uk
www.prefacepublishing.co.uk

Addreses for companies within The Random House Group Limited
can be found at www.randomhouse.co.uk

The Random House Group Limited Reg. No. 954009

A CIP catalogue record for this book is available from the British Library

ISBN 978 1 84809 133 7

The Random House Group Limited supports The Forest Stewardship Council (FSC), the leading
international forest certification organisation. All our titles that are printed on Greenpeace approved
FSC certified paper carry the FSC logo. Our paper procurement policy can be found at:
www.rbooks.co.uk/environment

Mixed Sources
Product group from well-managed
forests and other controlled sources
www.fsc.org Cert no. TT-COC-2139
© 1996 Forest Stewardship Council

FSC

Typeset in Sabon by Palimpsest Book Production Limited, Grangemouth, Stirlingshire

Printed and bound in Great Britain by
Clays Ltd, St Ives PLC

For Holly and Daisy

Contents

Prologue

Leaving the Palace of Tears

What a scramble. All the preparing to go off with Dr Hector
Munro's Field Ambulance – buying clothes – rushing through
Selfridge's with the help of one of the assistants. Mrs Knocker
had her work cut out. In the evening Dr Munro gave us our
tickets which were presented *gratis* by the Red Cross . . . In the
evening we packed up our clothes . . . at length we tumbled into
bed about 11 p.m. and went to sleep for the last time in Merrie
England.

Up at 6 a.m. to finish packing . . . it's a wonderful feeling
knowing that one is leaving England, the Island of Peace, and
going straight into the most awful horror. I look round and
try to stamp everything on my memory in case I never see it
again, and I wonder what my fate will be in these next few
months.

Mairi Chisholm

What a rush and muddle everything seems to have been for the
past few weeks, arranging and getting up this big scheme – to
send out nurses and men not only to help the soldiers but to
find them in the outlying cottages and on the ground. At last
this is the eve of departure and everything is ready.

It is now 11 p.m. of the 24th September and I have everything
packed and ready – labels on and in a desolate lodging room –

I am now prepared to go to bed, my last night in England for how long nobody can tell. It seems funny to think that this time tomorrow night I shall be in Belgium – in the midst of all the terrors of war.

Elsie Knocker

Elsie Knocker and Mairi Gooden-Chisholm left for Belgium on 25 September 1914; they had gone to London when war was declared on 4 August. The past six weeks had been giddy; they were swept up in the drama of khaki jingoism. Their days were framed by red, white and blue bunting, surrounded by men and boys signing up to give the Germans a damned good thrashing, and thousands of women determined to do their bit.

Eighteen-year-old Mairi and thirty-year-old Elsie Knocker, divorcée and mother of a young son, were madcap motorbikers who had met while roaring round the Hampshire and Dorset lanes, and had competed in motorbike and sidecar trials for the last year. Elsie was nicknamed 'Gypsy' because of her love of the open road and membership of the Gypsy Motor Cycle Club. She was a passionate biker who wore a dark green leather skirt and a long leather coat buttoned all the way down with a belt 'to keep it all together' designed for her by Messrs. Dunhill of London. She rode two motorbikes, a Chater Lea with sidecar and a Scott.

Mairi Chisholm's elder brother Uailean had an Enfield motorbike and was competing on it in rallies and the Bournemouth Speed Trials in September 1913 when their father, Captain Roderick Gooden-Chisholm, bought Mairi a Douglas motorbike, despite her mother's shrillest disapproval. Instead of the usual round of tennis parties and dances, Mairi spent her spare time in the stables wearing her brother's overalls, stripping down motorbikes and repairing them, and riding hard.

Because of the looming war Elsie Knocker had to cancel 'the ladies' stiff reliability trial over 120 miles of hilly Hampshire and Dorset countryside with plenty of hairpin bends' she had arranged for the middle of August. When war was declared Elsie wrote to Mairi that there was 'work to be done', and suggested they go to London to join the Women's Emergency Corps. Mairi, during a ferocious family row – her father was keen to let her go but her mother was absolutely opposed to the idea, and refused to lend her a box to put her clothes in – crept up to her bedroom, tied a change of underclothes and her dress allowance of ten pounds (equivalent to 800 pounds today) into a headscarf, slipped out of the house and sped off on her motorbike to meet Elsie Knocker.

Elsie and Mairi rode straight to the Little Theatre in John Adam Street, off the Strand, the headquarters of the Women's Emergency Corps. The place bustled with suffragettes, fashionable actresses, a couple of duchesses and a marchioness, and a handful of lady novelists. The Honourable Mrs Evelina Haverfield (who had accompanied her husband when he was serving in South Africa during the Boer War), splendidly got up in a short khaki skirt worn over riding breeches, had launched the corps to provide waged women workers to help the country in its hour of need. Living in lodgings in Baker Street, Elsie and Mairi were hired as dispatch riders and spent their first month whizzing about London carrying messages. One day Mairi was spotted by Dr Hector Munro (socialist, vegetarian, suffragette and nudist), who was impressed with the way she rode crouched over her dropped-handlebar racing motorbike. He tracked her down to the Women's Emergency Corps and asked her to join his Flying Ambulance Corps to help wounded Belgian soldiers. She agreed immediately and recommended her friend Elsie, who was a trained nurse, to Munro. Keen to show that women were as brave and capable as men, Hector Munro selected Elsie and Mairi out of 200 applicants, and also took on Lady Dorothie Feilding, well connected and fluent in French; the novelist May Sinclair, a generous donor to his favourite causes, including the corps; and Helen Gleason, a glamorous American whose journalist husband was touring the Western Front and filing copy for a number of British and American newspapers. Doctors, drivers, cooks and medical orderlies made up the rest of the Flying Ambulance Corps.

Arriving at Victoria Station, the Palace of Tears as Elsie called it, on the morning of 25 September, Elsie and Mairi were tut-tutted at by ladies scandalised by their breeches, leather boots and overcoats: they were the only women in trousers. One of their colleagues in the corps called them 'Valkyries in knicker-bockers'. At first Elsie and Mairi were larky girls in khaki, but six weeks later they were the only women to live and work on the fighting front in any of the theatres of that global war.

'Poor little Belgium' was a condescending catchphrase that came up a lot in conversation, was repeated in parliament and the press, and was used as a fund-raising tool. Sometimes 'plucky' replaced 'little' as if a child who had been bullied was fighting back. However, Belgium was not poor or of little significance in 1914; it was ranked sixth in the world's industrialised powers. It had a population of seven and a half million but its geography made it vulnerable to the ambitions of its potentially greedy neighbours France and Germany. The Treaty of London, signed in 1839 by Britain, France, Russia, Prussia (later to become enlarged and unified as Germany) and Austria-Hungary, had guaranteed Belgium's independence.

On 2 August 1914 the German government had asked the King of the Belgians if he would waive the terms of the treaty, calling it a 'scrap of paper', and allow its troops to march through Belgium to reach France, on whom they declared war the next day, 3 August. In return for Belgian cooperation the Germans promised to honour Belgian neutrality when the conflict was over, but if they refused, would treat Belgium as an enemy. The Belgians knew the offer was not worth much and declined. On 4 August the German cavalry galloped across the border into Belgium. At eleven o'clock that night Britain honoured its promise to guarantee Belgian neutrality, upheld its alliance with France, and declared war on Germany. The streets of London were packed with people waiting for news of the reaction to the British demand that Germany honour Belgian neutrality. Crowds gathered outside 10 Downing Street; toffs in evening dress were driven into Whitehall by their chauffeurs through a blizzard of Union Jacks. The populace was drawn to Buckingham Palace, faces were pressed against the gates, singing for hours and calling for the royal family to come out onto the balcony. Which they did three times, their ears ringing with the national anthem and 'For He's a Jolly Good Fellow'. 'Plucky little Belgium' had been invaded by the brutish German bully and the terms of the Treaty of London and the system of alliances and ententes that had been in place for many years was about to be tested.

The catalyst for the outbreak of war was the assassination of Archduke Franz Ferdinand, heir to the Habsburg throne, on 28 June while on a state visit to Sarajevo. He and his wife were shot by Gavrilo Princip, a Bosnian-Serb nationalist and member of the Black Hand Gang. This led Austria-Hungary to declare war on Serbia a month later, and because of the delicate mesh of alliances and ententes Europe became entangled in a truly global war. For nearly fifty years, since the Franco-Prussian War of 1870–71, peace had been preserved in Europe. Germany, Italy and Austria-Hungary were allies, as were Britain, France and Russia. If one country was threatened its allies were strong enough to deter its opponent from war. This balancing act had worked so far.

The causes of the conflict in 1914 reached back to the nineteenth century and the empire-building of the countries who had signed the Treaty of London. Germany, unified in 1871, was new to the colonial race, afraid of France and Russia's ambitions and resentful of British naval supremacy. The French were still smarting from the loss of valuable Alsace-Lorraine during the Franco-Prussian War. Russia and Austria-Hungary were creaky multinational empires with serious domestic problems. The Balkans were a flashpoint for Austria, which opposed Slav demands for autonomy within its empire, while Russia supported the Slavs' ambitions. Britain had a global empire on which the sun never set, and sometimes awkward diplomatic relations with Russia, France and Germany. It was an explosive brew of economic interests, crude and arbitrary map-making and authoritarian regimes, lubricated by the volatile mood of febrile nationalism.

The German army of three million massively outnumbered Belgium's hundred and twenty thousand. The invasion of Belgium was swift and brutal. The reality of occupation and stories of atrocities, some of which were true, sent half a million Belgians fleeing the country. Between 20 September and 24 October, 35,000 refugees landed at Folkestone and many thousands more would follow. A hundred thousand Belgians were taken to Germany to make munitions. The rape of Belgium had started. Poignant photographs of old ladies clutching gingham tablecloth bundles of clothes and precious knick-knacks, and of young mothers pushing prams full of children and handfuls of possessions, showed the British public what life might be like if

Germany was not defeated. The vast majority were in no doubt that Belgium needed and deserved help.

The three essential reasons for action were spelt out in printer's ink during the summer of 1914. *The Times* set out the case: the British Empire 'had to stand by its friends'; self-interest dictated that if France and Belgium and the Netherlands were over-whelmed by Germany then Britain was at risk; and 'civilised relations between peoples and the utmost regard for the spirit of international law' should be upheld. Britain was apparently a template for the values of loyalty, rectitude and public morality.

Elsie Knocker and Mairi Gooden-Chisholm soaked up the news and went to war.

I

The Shapter Chapter

On 22 July 1890, Elsie Knocker's father, Dr Lewis Shapter, frail and pale, sat down and wrote his will. He had been ill with tuberculosis for the past four years and must have known he did not have long to live. The will was a painful duty that could not be put off any longer. His wife Charlotte, thirty-eight years old, had died at the family home in Exeter on the second of May 1888 after a week-long struggle with meningitis, leaving him with five children under ten years old. John had had a mother for ten years; Una for nine years; Effie was six; Elsie was four and Lewis Henry was less than two when Charlotte Shapter, née Bayly, died.

Three months after writing his will Lewis Shapter coughed and coughed and died at a nursing home in Exmouth. He was forty-two years old. His father, Thomas Shapter, a well-known doctor in Exeter, was with him when he died. The Shapter children were orphans.

The two oldest, John and Una, and the youngest, Lewis Henry, were sent north to be looked after by Caroline Lucking, a house-keeper, at Rosarium Cottage in Uttoxeter, Staffordshire, five miles from their their father's sister Elizabeth Livesay in Sudbury, Derbyshire. She was married to William Livesay, a doctor, and had two daughters, Elsie and Laura. These three Shapters stayed there until legal and financial matters were clarified. Aunt Elizabeth was herself in poor health and this may have been why she did not offer a home to the orphans. Elizabeth Livesay did not have long to live: she died of tuberculosis at Penmaenmawr, near Conway in North Wales, at Christmas 1892.

Eventually John was kept by Uncle William Livesay; Una went to live with her mother's brother and sister, Aunt Georgina and old-soldier Uncle Richard Kerr Bayly in Exeter, and Lewis Henry was adopted by Aunt Frederica, another of his mother's sisters, who lived in Bournemouth with her husband, a retired colonel, Charles Edward Brown. Effie's new parents were a childless couple in Exeter, the Mackeys, a barrister and his wife, perhaps friends or distant relations of Lewis and Charlotte Shapter. Effie and Una were at least in the same town, but not in the same house.

Though there were other Shapter and Bayly aunts and uncles who could have taken Elsie, she was put up for adoption. Many family histories of this time have the ghosts of mothers and babies hovering over survivors' lives. Parcelling up children like bundles and passing them around or placing them in the care of guardians who may or may not have been known to them was often necessary at a time when tuberculosis was a fearsome killer, and childbirth was the most dangerous time of a mother and baby's life.

Elsie was adopted by Lewis Edward Upcott, an inspirational classics master or 'beak' at Marlborough College, and his wife Emily, a talented watercolourist. In 1891 the Shapter family solicitor answered a newspaper advertisement placed by the Upcotts, a childless couple. Elsie's new parents, whom she always called Aunt and Uncle, were educated and arty. Lewis was forty, his classical scholarship and breadth of learning making him a

byword for academic brilliance. Emily Upcott was thirty-five
and the daughter of Sir Charles Robinson, a curator and connois-
seur who had acquired Renaissance paintings and sculptures for
the South Kensington Museum, later the Victoria and Albert.
Sir Charles was Surveyor of the Queen's Pictures for the last
twenty years of Queen Victoria's life, and was knighted for his
services to the arts in 1887.

Elsie's new Upcott 'uncles' had either gone into the family
business of wool manufacture, or had shone at Oxford and
become eccentric and charismatic masters at Wellington College
and Christ's Hospital School; another was a big cheese on the
Indian railways. Elsie's Robinson 'uncles' were: Uncle Gerald,
one of the best mezzotint engravers of his day; Uncle Charles,
a barrister, collector of Old Master drawings, ancient and modern
engraved gems and Chinese bronzes, and a member of the British
fencing team at the Olympic Games in Athens in 1906; and Uncle
Frederick, a sculptor and art master at Uppingham School.

The orphan Lewis and Emily Upcott adopted was a six-year-
old girl whose father had been dead less than six months and
whose mother's face may have been a fading memory. Elsie may
not even have had a photograph of her parents or her siblings
to remind herself of where she had come from and to whom
she was related. Her brothers and sisters were away in Devon,
Dorset and Derbyshire, while her new home was in Preshute,
near Marlborough College in Wiltshire. The Upcotts had Walter,
a fifteen-year-old pupil, boarding with them. One of the school
matrons, fifty-year-old Maria Cane, also lived with them, and
they were all looked after by a cook and three maids.

Elsie was well provided for: her father had left a legacy to pay
for all his children's maintenance and education, also providing
his daughters with marriage settlements, and nest eggs for all
when they were twenty-one. When her Shapter grandfather and

various aunts and uncles died her inheritance was topped up. Life with the Upcotts may have been intimidating; conversations at mealtimes might have been hard to follow when Uncle started reciting poetry in perfect Greek and Latin. His big, black bushy beard brings Edward Lear's limerick to mind:

> There was an Old Man with a beard,
> Who said, 'It is just as I feared!
> Two Owls and a Hen,
> Four Larks and a Wren,
> Have all built their nest in my beard!'

Clever Uncle Lewis only taught sixth-formers. His old boys included J. Meade Faulkner, who wrote *Moonfleet*; E. F. Benson, the creator of *Mapp and Lucia*; Arthur B. Poynton, the master of University College, Oxford; Sir Basil Blackett, who became director of the Bank of England; and Earl Jowitt, a Lord Chancellor.

Here Elsie was an only child – she had been one of a family of five. She entered a largely male world: there were boys of all ages, shapes and sizes, and her childhood and adolescence with the Upcotts may have been where her tomboyish, harum-scarum ways originated. Uncle and Aunt had wanted a boy when they advertised for a child but changed their minds when they saw Elsie at the Shapter family solicitor's office in Exeter. Lewis and Emily Upcott passed on to her their love of sports and made sure she grew up to be a good horse-woman, and took her to boxing and wrestling contests in Marlborough Town Hall: 'It was funny sitting beside this prim couple while, frozen-faced, they watched men twisting each other's limbs . . . they gave barely perceptible tokens of approval and disapproval.'

The Upcotts' cultural and aesthetic interests meant they were

liberal in their sympathies; they were also active in the artistic
and educational life of their town and county. Mrs Upcott's
work as a Poor Law guardian meant they were more aware
than many of their contemporaries of poverty. Elsie's upbringing
was such that she did not grow up to be a typical Victorian
young lady, submissive, delicate and modest.

Elsie's father and grandfather had been doctors, and her
mother came from a long line of army officers. She grew up a
blend of her parents' family backgrounds: medical and military.
Elsie's father, Lewis, who was born in Exeter in 1848, never
knew his mother, Elizabeth, after whom Elsie was named, who
died of pneumonia before his first birthday. His father, Thomas,
did not remarry, instead relying on the help of his unmarried
sister Margaret, a butler and a cook, two maids and two nurse-
maids to look after him and the children. When Thomas was
widowed he had five children: Elizabeth was five; Thomas aged
four; three-year-old Esther; William was nearly two and baby
Lewis less than a year old.

Lewis followed his father into medicine, studied at Gonville
and Caius College, Cambridge and qualified as a doctor in 1876.
He returned to the substantial family home in Exeter, where he
brought his bride, Charlotte Bayly, on 3 September 1877. Quickly
the young doctor started to make a name for himself, speaking
at the sanitary congress in Exeter in 1880, securing a position
as a consulting physician to the Devon and Exeter Hospital and
the Lying-In Hospital in Magdalen Street, and becoming one of
the governors of the harshly named Wonford Idiot Asylum. His
practice enabled him to afford to hire a cook, two maids and
a nurse to look after his young family.

Charlotte was born on the island of Jersey in 1846 (five years
had been lopped off her age by the time she died in 1888), where
her father was a captain in the Suffolk Regiment. The Baylys

had a typically nomadic army life: her five brothers and sisters were born in Dublin, England and France.

Being orphaned at the age of six it is difficult to know how much Elsie knew about her family. There had hardly been any time to get to know her parents or be told about any of her other relations. Sixty years later when Elsie sat down to write her autobiography, *Flanders And Other Fields,* she only mentions a brother and a sister once, suggesting that she had very little contact with her family as they were growing up. The autobiography contains some inaccuracies, perhaps arising from a mix of loss and sadness at having been orphaned and split up from her brothers and sisters, oxygenated by criticism of the way she was treated by her adopted parents, who by all other accounts were delightful. The opening paragraph of *Flanders and Other Fields* is from a tearful shouty six-year-old standing up straight to be inspected in the Shapters' solicitors' office:

> I never knew my parents. They died when I was a baby . . . I learnt later that my mother was very beautiful and that my father was a brilliant and highly respected physician. They were both young . . . I was the fifth child . . . everything had been set so fair . . . Suddenly I and the other children were orphans, suspended in a void. The other four children were taken by an uncle . . . I was apparently too young and our other relatives were scattered about the globe . . . not easily contacted and constantly on the move.

Allowing for the loss of memory of an eighty-year-old, Elsie's recollections of her early years show a degree of hurt that she tries to conceal by making things up when the truth is too painful. She was not a baby when her father died; she was not the youngest child, Lewis Henry was; one uncle did not take the other four children, and their relations were not 'scattered about the globe'. But her account may have been her way of coping with how her life turned out the way it did.

After an unhappy time at a girls' school in Marlborough, where Elsie tells us she was bullied for being a 'charity child' because she was adopted, the Upcotts sent her to St Nicholas's Ladies' School in Folkestone, Kent, where she excelled at sport, dancing and singing, rather than academic subjects. St Nicholas's offered the forty girls the standard curriculum, plus the French and German that would be so useful in Belgium. Elsie's time at the school was scarred by memories of being bullied by one of her teachers, 'who would walk into the classroom and point a long, bony finger at me, and say, "I've got my eye on you," and walk out again. I was frozen with fear and – I did not know any reason why – and the whole class laughed at me. No wonder I grew up with an inferiority complex!'

Elsie left St Nicholas's in 1903 and spent six months polishing her French and German at a finishing school in Switzerland, and then studied at a school for chefs and cooks in Trowbridge in Wiltshire. She got top marks but felt socially awkward when her highfalutin accent was mocked. In 1903 the Upcotts thought it would be good for Elsie to train as a nurse at a children's hospital in Sevenoaks in Kent.

According to Elsie her life went awry in Sevenoaks in 1905, for this is where she met Leslie Duke Knocker, who was 'the first man to take any notice' of her. She was flattered and charmed. He was almost six feet tall, slim, with brown hair and brown eyes. By the time they married on 5 April 1906 Elsie had come into her inheritance, and given their disastrous marriage one wonders if Leslie Knocker, an accountant ten years older than her, married her for the legacy and marriage portion her father had left her in 1890. Years later she would remember feeling rushed into marriage, bewildered and perhaps hurt that her adopted parents appeared to want her off their hands. Elsie may have blamed them for the mess she later found herself in.

The banns were called at Elsie's church in Preshute, a pretty medieval building with a crenellated tower. She and the Upcotts could have walked to the church from their home, the White House, designed by Charles Edwin Ponting, a local architect in the Arts and Crafts style. There was no sign of Elsie's brothers and sisters. Leslie's father, William Wheatley Knocker, was a template for Victorian respectability. A solicitor with his own firm, Knocker, Knocker and Holcroft, he was clerk to the magistrates of Sevenoaks, registrar and high bailiff to the County Court in Sevenoaks and active in local charities. Leslie had been born at Dunmow in Essex in 1875, the middle son of five boys and a girl, two of whom were solicitors and one a doctor.

Leslie was educated at Tonbridge School as a day boy from 1889 to 1892. In May 1893 he went to work as a clerk at the British Linen Company, earning forty pounds a year, less than a pound a week. Leslie travelled by train from Sevenoaks to work at the London branch at 41 Lombard Street in the City of London. When he resigned in March 1899 his clerk's salary had increased to a hundred pounds a year, and his next employer was the Bank of British North America. Before Elsie knew him Leslie had been to New York three times: in 1894, 1897 and 1899, travelling on the SS *Teutonic* on the first two journeys and the SS *Umbria* in 1899. Immigration officials recorded him as a 'gentleman' in 1894; he gave no occupation in 1897 and said he was working in insurance in 1899. Whatever had taken Leslie Knocker across the Atlantic it was not enduring and by the spring of 1901 he was back in England, living in lodgings in Croydon and working for the London City and Midland Bank.

Elsie says her in-laws suggested that the young couple go to

Singapore where Leslie's elder brother Stanley got him a position at the China Mutual Insurance Company. When he was married Leslie Knocker was working in a bank in the City of London earning three pounds a week, the marriage certificate said he was an accountant. Elsie seems to have plunged into her new life hardly knowing her husband and without much thought as to what their future might hold.

A month after their wedding Elsie and Leslie set sail from the Port of London on the SS *Sardinia*. By the time they reached Singapore Elsie was pregnant and Leslie's mood had darkened. Her in-laws, with whom they lived, made it clear they would have to find other accommodation as soon as the baby was born. The divorce papers of 1911 document the four years of her frightening and wretched marriage.

In July 1906, less than six weeks after their arrival, Leslie Knocker was 'very violent and ordered her out of the house and threatened to eject her by force if she did not go'. Elsie was two months pregnant. Things were so bad that her doctor urged Elsie to return to England to have her baby, and her son Kenneth Duke was born at the Upcotts' house on 1 February 1907. Fortunately Elsie had her inheritance to pay for her fare home and her keep as her husband gave her very little money. She and Kenneth returned to Singapore in August 1907 and an uncertain future. Elsie did not tell her adopted parents about her violent and drunken husband and the problems in her marriage. She stuck it out for another sixteen months before her doctor 'insisted for health reasons' that she and her son return to England in January 1909. They went back to the Upcotts; it must have been difficult for her to answer the usual questions about how their son-in-law was. Elsie stayed in England for nine months and then went back to Leslie, but this time she left Kenneth in Malborough.

During the time she was away Leslie Knocker had left Singapore for Java, for the Batavia branch of the China Mutual Insurance Company as resident secretary. Two weeks after she arrived in Java he 'got into a furious passion' and ordered Elsie out of the house, 'threatened her and when she left locked her out'. She had to seek refuge with friends. Throughout the summer of 1910 his behaviour seemed to spiral out of control, with him using 'indecent and disgusting language in her presence and in front of gentlemen who were staying in the house'. Other times he threatened to punch her and 'greatly terrified her'. In July his frequent adultery, sometimes with 'native women', was brought to her attention, and he 'struck her in the face' more than once.

Elsie left the Far East for the last time in December 1910. In the past four years she had made three journeys to the other side of the world, steaming to and from a bad marriage with weeks on end to think. She must have asked herself what was wrong with her husband, wondered if he drank too much and why, what caused the mood swings and violence, and why he was so cruel and detached from their son. Elsie may have compared him with his respectable brothers and wondered if she had married the black sheep. Leslie's flagrant adultery would have been known the small and claustrophobic expatriate community, and this would have been a cause of deep pain.

Elsie was determined to end her marriage. On 10 January 1911 she travelled alone from Marlborough to London and signed a sworn statement at the office of Loughborough, Gedge, Nisbet and Drew's in Austin Friars in the City. It was presented as evidence to the Royal Courts of Justice in the Strand: on 23 October she was awarded a decree nisi. The next day, without mentioning Elsie by name, the *Daily Mirror*'s WIFE SEEKS REFUGE IN STABLES told the grim tale of Leslie Duke Knocker's awful

behaviour and offensive offer to pay any man a hundred pounds
to take her away which had driven her sobbing to a loose box.
On 2 December 1912 Elsie was awarded a decree absolute on
the ground of 'adultery and cruelty'.

Leslie Knocker came to England in 1911 and travelled to
Winnipeg, Canada on 10 August on the SS *Corsican*. In December
1912 the registrar added a final note to the paperwork stating that
the judge had ruled all Knocker's 'rights, powers and interests in
and over both the wife's and husband's funds be extinguished and
that it be read as if he were already dead'. Elsie, having petitioned
for the divorce, was liable for her own costs. This is the last we
hear of Leslie Knocker until the outbreak of the First World War.

Elsie's resort to the divorce court was an unusual one for a
woman of her age and background. She was twenty-seven and
mother of a four-year-old son when she started the complex and
costly legal proceedings. The Upcotts must have been concerned
but they continued to support her emotionally by giving her
and Kenneth a home throughout those difficult years. They did
much of the parenting of their adopted grandson during his
early years. Elsie was able to secure her freedom as her father's
will and various legacies meant that she had funds to pay for
laywers; many women in similar situations had to put up with
sad and bad marriages. Elsie was one of 380 women in England
and Wales granted a divorce in 1912, slightly fewer than the
number of men who were divorcing their wives that year. Her
courage in daring to divorce Leslie Knocker should not be under-
estimated. Divorced women were social outcasts, failures and
pariahs, shunned by respectable society, and the stigma was so
severe that many divorcées said that they had been widowed
rather than admit to being divorced. Looking back at Elsie's
journey to the law courts we see it is an important clue to her
later single-minded courage.

What were Elsie's brothers and sisters doing while she was finishing her education, learning to cook and nurse children, marrying disastrously and divorcing? Living in Derbyshire, Dorset and Devon, the Shapter infants had grown up, come into their legacies and were looking to the future. In 1901 her eldest brother John, who was twenty-two years old, was a gentleman living 'on his own means' with his uncle William Livesay in Sudbury in Derbyshire, cared for by four servants.

Elsie's sister Una was twenty-one and still living with her Aunt Georgina and Uncle Richard Kerr Bayly in Exeter. In 1904 she married Claude Elton Carey, and their first child was born in 1906. By the outbreak of the First World War Una's husband Claude was a superintendent at Chudleigh police station with a sergeant and five constables under him. There is no record of Elsie going to her sister's wedding; she certainly was not a witness to the ceremony.

Effie Kerr Shapter was living with her adopted parents, the Mackeys, in Exeter in the summer of 1908 when she married Alexander Huntly Gordon, a thirty-one-year-old widower who was an officer in the Indian police. The ceremony was at St James's church in Exeter; the groom had recently been bereaved, having married his first bride, Anna Klein, in London in 1904. She probably died in Simla, where Effie and Alexander returned immediately after the wedding and where their son was born in 1909. Elsie was in Singapore at the time of this wedding.

Elsie's youngest brother, Lewis Henry, was fifteen at the turn of the century and about to embark on a military career. He was brought up in Winchester and educated at Stourwood College in Southbourne. In 1904 he joined the 3rd Suffolk Regiment and was promoted to lieutenant a year later. He was a crack shot, won silver cups in 1908 and 1909, and was an instructor in musketry. His adoptive parents (Uncle Charles and Aunt Frederica) were army folk: Charles was a lieutenant colonel in the Royal Artillery who had seen action in Afghanistan in 1880. Lewis Henry's army photograph shows a dashingly handsome young officer with dark hair and a fine moustache. He left the army in 1911 and started a new life in Canada, buying a ranch at Port Washington in British Columbia. Lewis Henry Shapter left Liverpool for New York on the SS *Lusitania* on 25 July 1914 and arrived four days later at Ellis Island. He had hardly started his onward journey when Britain declared war on Germany and he caught a boat back to England.

In the three years leading up to the outbreak of the First World War Elsie's life, according to her autobiography, was packed with adventure and what she felt were thrilling opportunities. Her recollections spill out at a breathless rate, so vivid were her memories that the chronology is difficult to unravel. What we do know is that for first time in her life she was a free woman and eager to make the most of her freedom, at liberty to do what she wanted and to determine her own future and that of her five-year-old son. Lewis and Emily Upcott enjoyed their role as grandparents and, helped by three servants, looked after Kenneth whenever Elsie needed them to.

During this time Elsie rebuilt relationships with her close family. She and Kenneth went to stay with Aunt Georgina at Summerland Cottage in Exeter, ten miles from her sister Una and her husband Claude Elton Carey, who lived at Chudleigh. Elsie went to train horses at a riding school in Alphington, near Exeter. She was a daredevil. Someone bet her five pounds (today worth 400 pounds) that she would not dare ride into Green and Son, the ladies' outfitters and haberdashers in Alphington High Street. Elsie and her horse clattered into the shop, clip-clopped up the stairs into the millinery department, down again and out of the shop, not the most decorous behaviour for a twenty-eight-year-old mother.

Elsie realised she needed a career to augment her savings and decided to train to be a midwife. She left Kenneth with the Upcotts and enrolled at Queen Charlotte's Hospital in Marylebone Road, London. Her duties took her to local slum housing, where families often lived several to a room. Elsie enjoyed the strict training, undaunted by the desperate poverty and the bedbugs she shook out of her clothes at the end of an exhausting day. She looked back on this time as an epiphany, a time when she learned a lot about herself: 'I liked being in a tough spot. I liked responsibility. I liked having to make quick decisions. I had strong nerves which longed to be exercised. I liked the feeling that I was wanted and that other people were relying on me . . . my self-consciousness disappeared, and I found a new self when I was serving others.'

She qualified as a midwife in July 1913 and returned to the Upcotts in Preshute, but her plans were interrupted when her eldest brother, John, got back in touch for the first time since their father had died. He was living in a cottage at Fordingbridge in the heart of the New Forest. He had had a serious accident and asked her to go and look after him. Elsie was delighted to be able to live with a member of her real family and have the chance to make a home for herself and Kenneth. Recently she had received a legacy from an uncle and had bought a Chater Lea motorbike and sidecar: the start of her passion for speed and the open road. She could put Kenneth in the sidecar and go wherever she wanted.

At this time the sport of motorcycling was in its early days, suffering from inefficient machines and social opprobrium; when Elsie bought her machine there were only fifty women riders in the country. All motorcyclists had to be competent mechanics. The oil and the grit and dust and breakdowns, the skids and the crashes, abuse from motorists and dogs and pedestrians were considered by the diehards a price worth paying for the freedom: escape from the claustrophobic constraints of Edwardian middle-class life.

Elsie's name and picture appeared regularly in the pages of *The Motor Cycle* and *Motor Cycling*, offering brisk advice on what 'costumes' lady motorcyclists should wear. Giving Dunhill some free advertising, she extolled the virtues of her snug-fitting leather coat and skirt: 'there is not enough width to flap about, and the leather is heavy enough to keep steady'. She assured readers that she had had no trouble with her outfit 'or any thought of an accident owing to my dress', adding that it had been 'much admired' and, importantly, that 'one can get off one's machine and shop without being stared at'. For Elsie the autumn of 1913 and the first half of 1914 were filled with the roar of the engine and the thrill of the open road. She joined the Gypsy Motor Cycle Club and bought another motorbike and sidecar, a Scott. This was the most thrilling time of Elsie's life up to that point. As soon as her domestic duties were done she could crank up her bike and tear around for wagers. She entered every trial she could, including a twelve-hour non-stop run to Malvern and back to the New Forest, and a 'reliability run' from Exeter to Weston-super-Mare and back. In this there was a maximum speed of twenty-five miles per hour. The only other woman competitor had a bad skid and grazed her arm but carried on. When Elsie was approaching the home straight near Exeter she was in sixth place when the throttle cable on her Scott snapped and she accelerated to sixty miles an hour, flashing past the riders ahead of her. She only had her brakes and the exhaust valve lever to slow herself down, and when she arrived at the garage where the run had started she slammed on the brakes. To the amazement of the mechanics standing around she hit a wall and buckled her front wheel. One of them was heard to say saucily, 'I wonder if she's as red hot as her engine.'

Elsie was keen to try flying, the craze of the day, and went up with Gustav Hamel, the celebrity pilot, in April 1914, a month before he died when his plane ditched in the English Channel on 23 May. His most famous stunts were looping the loop and upside-down flying. Since 1912 the newspapers had run many breathless stories of glamorous society ladies flying with handsome Hamel. In February 1914 he had set a record when he flew Lady Dudley over Worcester racecourse and looped the loop five times just 200 feet above the ground. Reading of his exploits, Elsie was mad keen to have a go and on 8 April she went to Meyrick Park in Bournemouth to see 'several of the most wonderful exhibitions of flying ever attempted even by that exceedingly daring aviator . . . who everyone knows is in the forefront of this new profession'. Several thousand people ooohed and aaahed at Hamel's 'spectacular display':

> He rose quickly and before he had got any distance in the air over the golf links he turned and flew upside down. Coming round again he looped the loop twice in a graceful style and followed with a double loop. The wind was strong and Mr Hamel proceeded higher until 5,000–6,000 feet was reached. Then he performed a beautiful dive lowering the tail and proceeding some distance on his back. Descending a little the feat was repeated amid enthusiastic cheers and after two more graceful loops Mr Hamel came down . . . He had a great ovation on alighting.

After a short rest he was back in the air again, looping the loop closer to the ground and travelling a great distance upside down.

Although the weather had not been considered suitable – the wind was 'tricky'– for him to offer passenger flights, Elsie managed to get on board, up in the air and in the newspapers: 'The arrangements as to taking up a passenger were altered late in the afternoon, before five o'clock Mr Hamel agreed to fly with a lady, the fortunate one being Mrs Knocker . . . She occupied a seat behind him and was taken for a five-minute spin in the air, circling the golf links and Meyrick Park three or four times at a height of two or three thousand feet.'

Hamel and 'the plucky lady' were loudly cheered when they stepped out of the aeroplane. Elsie told the reporter from the *Bournemouth Daily Echo*, 'It was simply gorgeous, and absolutely lovely. I cannot say how delighted I am. I felt absolutely safe and it was a lovely feeling. Down below you all looked like little specks, and I have never experienced anything like it.' From the report, Elsie seemed to be well known in Bournemouth, the writer noting that this was the first time she had been in an aeroplane. Locally she was an 'expert motorist' and drove her own car, and also took a 'keen and practical interest in all outdoor sports'.

Elsie, single mother of a young child, could not get enough of the adrenalin, and she returned to Meyrick Park four days later on Saturday the 11th to see Hamel loop the loop twenty-one times like a swallow, doubling the previous world record. He was full of insouciance and spoke 'quite casually of his great achievement' to the assembled reporters. Prince Maurice of Battenberg, a grandson of the late Queen Victoria, went up with Hamel and flew upside down and looped the loop twice in front of crowd of between five and six thousand people: 'it is the first time I have looped the loop. I felt no sensation as we turned over. It was a good loop.' Intoxicated with the glamour of it all, Elsie talked her way into Hamel's cockpit for the second time in a week. There is no mention in the newspapers that he looped the loop with her on board, although everything we know about her suggests that she would have been longing for him to do so. If anyone wanted her loop to be looped it was the daredevil Mrs Knocker.

On 21 July Mrs Knocker addressed 'Lady Motorcyclists' in the pages of *Motor Cycling* magazine about the event she was organising, 'a test for ladies only' because 'it seems hard that all trials should be organised for men, and there are at present so many good lady riders'. The test would be a tough one because 'lady riders will agree that a difficult test is sure to be more interesting than an easy one'. She hoped there would be plenty of 'good driving, steady heads and good nerves'. The closing date was 6 August and the first of three prizes would be a silver cup.

Meanwhile on 26 July 1914 the Gypsy Club had its most remarkable meeting yet when members attempted the steep climb up Leith Hill, near Dorking in Surrey. The climb was a 'very rough path with pieces of rock projecting above the surface at intervals, gullies two feet deep and a gradient of one in two and a half'. It was difficult to walk up and most of the spectators said it was 'absolute madness for any motorcyclist to try to ascend the appalling gradient'. Predictably, Elsie was in the thick of things on her Chater Lea. She made a 'very lucky attempt' and was 'a great favourite with the crowd who did not expect to see a lady driver try such a dangerous feat'. She nearly made it but 'just failed on the bend'. Elsie was making her mark in the top thirty lady motorcyclists in the country.

An enthusiastic lady sidecarist, Mrs. E. B. Knocker, on her Scott. On another page she describes some of her experiences.

Elsie is at the controls of her Scott motorbike in 1913, wearing dark-green leathers made for her by Messrs. Dunhill.

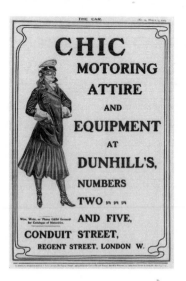

THE CAR.

CHIC
MOTORING
ATTIRE
AND
EQUIPMENT
AT
DUNHILL'S,
NUMBERS
TWO ⋙
AND FIVE,
CONDUIT STREET,
REGENT STREET, LONDON W.

DUNHILL'S MOTORITIES

LEATHER SMOCK

2847. Very useful full length leather slip to be worn under any motoring coat, finished with a strap at neck and elastic at wrists. In green, blue, brown and tan · · · · 6 Gns.

2848. Other styles · · from 3 Gns.

2847

II

The Chisholm Chapter

airi Lambert Gooden-Chisholm was a teenager when
she roared off to war; she was eighteen, not yet old
enough to do as she pleased, but with her father's
approval she ran away to the biggest adventure of her life. She
came from an upper-class Scottish family: her father Roderick,
also Ruairidh, was born in London in 1864, at the tail end of
a family of four girls and three boys, something of a surprise
five years after his sister Henrietta. He was educated at Brighton
and Henley before joining the Royal Engineers but failed to
complete his training. Between 1882 and 1888 he studied farming
and estate management, but the depth of the agricultural depres-
sion persuaded Roderick's father that he should once again enter
the army. In January 1889 he joined the 3rd Battalion of the
Seaforth Highlanders (Ross-shire Buffs, Duke of Albany's) and
for two years was an instructor of musketry in the regiment.
When he was not on duty, from May to December, he would
return to London and organise in south St Pancras for the Liberal
Unionists.

Roderick's regimental headquarters were Fort George, overlooking the Moray Firth near the village of Ardesier in Nairn,
Inverness-shire. This is where he met Margaret 'Nonie' Fraser

while being entertained by her father, Colonel William Fraser of Culbokie, at Redheugh, their home in Nairn. Roderick, by now a captain, was twenty-nine and Nonie Fraser was twenty-four when they married in Nairn 'according to the forms of the Free Church' on 12 July 1893. Early in January 1894 he resigned his commission and with his new bride moved to England.

Roderick had married well: not only was Nonie beautiful with a tiny waist, her family was wealthy and well connected. Roderick's parents must have been happy at the alliance of the Gooden-Chisholms and the Frasers: his father was part of the rich Scottish elite who lived in London devoted to all things Scottish, generously supporting the Highland Society, the Scottish Hospital and the Royal Caledonian Schools.

Known as the Gooden-Chisholms for reasons of inheritance, they had lived in London at 33 Tavistock Square from the middle of the 1830s to the turn of the century in a substantial house whose simple elegance demonstrated the family's status as members of the wealthy merchant class. When Mairi's grandfather James died on the last day of the nineteenth century his estate was worth today's equivalent of fourteen and a half million pounds. Mairi was not a spoilt rich girl who could indulge her whims, quite the reverse; her early years were comfortable not ostentatious. The family money would be nailed down in trusts that allowed its members to live well but not in an extravagant way, although her parents travelled the world when she was a baby, and could move freely in raffish royal circles. Roderick bought a yacht on the Solent and had a car at the earliest opportunity: they enjoyed the good life.

In 1851 Mairi's grandmother Anne Elizabeth Lambert had married the boy next door. Ten years earlier, in 1841 she had been living at number 32 Tavistock Square and had met James Gooden. Both their fathers were merchants. In 1841, in her teens,

Anne was polishing a range of ladylike accomplishments while next door James, who was an artist in his twenties, was painting pictures until it was time to take over the family business. Anne Lambert's father John died in 1844 and she and her mother and brother moved to a villa in riverside Mortlake in south-west London. In the summer of 1851 Anne Lambert and James Gooden got married and she came back to 33 Tavistock Square to live next door to her old home. Charles Dickens, who had recently moved into Tavistock House, wrote *Bleak House* (1852–3), *Hard Times* (1854) and *Little Dorrit* (1857) during the ten years he lived there.

Roderick and Nonie settled in Datchet near Windsor, and on 19 April 1894 their first child, a son, was born. Uailean Hamish McUistean came into the world in a smart mock-Tudor house that concealed a remarkable medieval dwelling from the 1470s. The house looked on to the village green, and so close were they to the River Thames that they were constantly at risk from flooding.

In 1896, on 26 February, Mairi was born at home in Datchet, and she and her brother were extremely close. The family photographs suggest a childhood of ponies, horses and bicycles, holidays in Scotland with their Fraser grandparents and regular trips to Inverness to Mr Whyte's photographic studio. Scottishness was important to Roderick and Nonie. Uailean would be dressed up like a Highlander, in Chisholm tartan kilt, tweed jacket, sporran and a Balmoral, a beret with a pompom and bearing a silver Chisholm clan badge (motto *Feros Ferio*, 'I strike the fierce'); and Mairi's lace dresses would be tied with a Chisholm tartan sash and decorated with a sprig of fresh heather. Wherever they went there were spaniels, retrievers and terriers snuffling about.

By 1900 the family had moved to Dorset. In the summer

Captain Gooden-Chisholm rejoined his old regiment but resigned his commission a year later. They lived in a big house in a little village called Ferndown, not far from Bournemouth. Whimsically Roderick named the house Whin Croft (Gorse Croft), though there was little of the Scottish croft about it. Over the next ten years Ferndown grew rapidly, filling with bungalows and villas christened with Pooterish names like The Bungalow, The Retreat, The Gables, Tanglewood, The Firs, Pine Grange, Forest Glen and Heathery Edge.

Uailean was six and Mairi four when they arrived in Dorset. They were educated at home by a governess until they were old enough to be sent away to school. Theirs was a traditional children-should-be-seen-and-not-heard upbringing: years in the nursery brought up by servants, their mother and father living their lives elsewhere in the house and emotionally even further away. Mairi and her brother were taught 'not to squeal if hurt and never to display emotion, and in all the time I lived at home my mother never kissed me'. Mairi remembered that she and Uailean were once found digging a hole in an aunt's garden and were asked what they were doing. They said, 'We are burying our parents.'

Uailean was seven when he was sent to Knyveton Court School in Bournemouth, run by Miss Euphemiah Bellingham Vernon and her sister Maud. In the autumn of 1907, aged thirteen, he was sent to Charterhouse School in Godalming but only stayed for two terms. The only trace he left behind was a single appearance in the Black Book on 16 November 1907 for 'repeated inattention'. Uailean was not academic; he had been bumping along in the bottom half of the class when Roderick removed him from the school and had him tutored by Eustace Fynes-Clinton, a brilliant classical scholar and an 'inspiring teacher' who had recently retired as headmaster of Wimborne Grammar School.

In January 1909 Uailean arrived at Cheltenham College and we learn that Roderick and his fifteen-year-old son were not getting on. In an astonishing outburst his father wrote on his son's registration form, 'I have left in my will that he inherits only a small sum sufficient to keep him from starvation until he can show that he has been capable of earning £150 per annum for five years.' Uailean was at Cheltenham until the summer of 1911, where he excelled in the engineering class. Then Roderick sent him to Bristol University, where he was an associate member of the Guild of Undergraduates but did not complete the course and left in 1912.

On 17 August 1906 Nonie had given birth to her third and last child, Lucy Margaret Gooden-Chisholm, at Whin Croft. Uailean was twelve and Mairi ten and they were unmoved by the new arrival. Lucy was named after a formidable aunt, Hannah Lucy, her father's sister, who had been a matron at Gorleston Cottage Hospital in the late 1880s, until her marriage in November 1891 to Shirley Baker, a solicitor. Widowed in 1893, she remarried in 1899. Frederick Fitzclarence Goddard, a retired colonel in the Army Drivers' Corps, was her second husband.

When Mairi was eleven she was sent to Redmoor, a school for the 'daughters of gentlemen' on Canford Cliffs in Bournemouth. The owner, Miss Edith M Rudd, who was a vicar's daughter, offered a 'thorough modern education' and 'individual care and attention' for up to a dozen young ladies. As Redmoor was 'close to the sea on the highest part of the cliffs', buffeted by bracing sea breezes and surrounded by breathtaking views across Poole Harbour, it would have appealed to her parents' love of the great outdoors and fresh air. Mairi's French improved under the tuition of Miss Henrietta Asser. Although Mairi was at Redmoor for just two years her ties with the school were strong enough for Miss Rudd to write to her in November 1914: 'I read the *War News* every evening to the girls and when your name appeared you had an ovation. Redmoor is very proud of you and you have the good wishes of us all.' Miss Rudd signed off 'with love from your affec-tionate friend'.

Mairi was sent to St Katharine's School in Hook Heath, Woking in 1909 for the last three years of her education. The owner, Miss Jessie Wight, a sea captain's daughter from Newcastle with twenty years' teaching experience, had opened her ladies' school in 1906. We know little of Mairi's time at this school, but the fund-raising activities of Miss Wight and her girls in 1918, pledging 1,000 pounds (nowadays 40,000 pounds) to the Elizabeth Garrett Anderson Hospital for Women in London, suggests a school ethos that put women and children first. Miss Wight's letter to 'my love, dear Mairi' in November 1914 revealed the warmth with which she was remembered, and the school's pride at the news of her 'plucky doings'.

The Gooden-Chisholms brought glamour and raffishness to their dozy Dorset nook. There are a few clues that the couple moved in high-society circles. Roderick liked to play cards and was known to gamble quite heavily. One school holiday before 1910, when Mairi was about fourteen years old, King Edward VII came to Whin Croft to play cards with Roderick and Nonie, bringing his mistress Mrs Keppel with him. Years later Mairi remembered that Mrs Keppel had 'the Curse' and made a stain on the chair on which she was sitting. When Mrs Keppel noticed the mark she drew everyone's attention to it, shrieking, 'Oh look what I've done.' Apparently the King roared with laughter, which might have made a shy schoolgirl blush.

Mairi's school-leaving portrait in 1913 shows a fresh-faced young girl with long brown beribboned hair and plenty of poise. Her tie has been feminised with tassels and an enamel brooch;

her jaw is set; she looks to the distance. When she returned to Whin Croft, Uailean was at home, his education completed, and this is when brother and sister spent a thrilling chapter of their lives together. Instead of doing what girls of her class were supposed to do, playing lots of tennis and going to dances in preparation for marriage – virtually the only option for girls of her background – Mairi was a tomboy, spending her 'entire time dressed in Uailean's clothes with my nose in machinery'. She had 'absolutely no time for feminine things', preferring to be covered in grease and smelling of oil, stripping down engines and grinding in valves. Mairi should have been polishing her serves and volleys but instead became a very good mechanic. Motorbikes were unreliable and mechanics were few, so owners had to be able to fix their own machines. Mairi was kept busy as Uailean's mechanic in the summer of 1913, and helped him compete in local motorbiking events. They did not have to travel far for spare parts and petrol: like many cycle agents at this time, Percy Goswell in Ferndown also sold motorcycles and spare parts, and the Ferndown Motor Company sold motorcycles as well as cars.

Mairi's father was proud of his daughter's ability but her mother thought it was dreadful that her child was being 'ruined', insisting it was 'no way to bring up a girl'. To make matters worse, Colonel Carey Elwes, a family friend, told her parents, 'That girl of yours is a born mechanic, you should let her have a motorbike.' By the autumn of 1913 Mairi had an open-frame Douglas dropped-handlebar racing motorbike that cost fifty-three pounds (equivalent to £4,500 today). In December 'Miss Chisholm of Wimborne' was snapped following the London–Exeter Run 'riding splendidly in the grease'. She wore 'Uailean's overalls and a red fisherman's cap with a bobble', and years later she remembered feeling at the time that she was 'one heck of a girl'. Taken six months after she had left Miss Wight's school for ladies, the photograph shows that Mairi's horizon had widened considerably.

But this idyllic time did not last, and in 1914 Roderick Gooden-Chisholm relocated Uailean to Trinidad to help him run the estate he had bought in 1912. While their two older children had been away at school, the Gooden-Chisholms had enjoyed the substantial inheritance Roderick's father had left in 1900. There were horses and ponies for everyone, cars to take for a spin, and the yacht *Cygnet*, which Roderick entered in the Solent Yacht Club's regattas. On 24 October 1906, seven weeks after Lucy was born, Roderick and Nonie had sailed from Southampton on the SS *La Plata* to Jamaica, to buy a plantation. Roderick was hoping to make use of the estate management and farming he had studied in the 1880s before he had joined the army. By the spring of 1912 they had settled on Trinidad and bought El Salvador, an estate that included a large cocoa plantation not far from San Fernando, the island's second-largest town. Two years earlier Roderick had also been excited at the idea of sugar-beet farming in Dorset, but nothing had come of it.

In the summer of 1912 Roderick took Uailean to Trinidad to show him the estate he was to manage and could expect to inherit. More modern than his contemporaries, and certainly his wife, Roderick also taught Mairi the rudiments of estate management when she left school. On their way back to England father and son called at New York and their visit left a trace at Ellis Island, where they were processed. We learn that Roderick Gooden-Chisholm was five feet seven inches tall with fair hair and blue eyes, and that his eighteen-year-old blond brown-eyed son was six inches taller than him.

The Gooden-Chisholms' lives were to become transatlantic.

Gentleman-farming on this scale needs attention and supervision. 1912 saw the start of regular trips to the West Indies and a planter lifestyle that was quite different to the cosiness of rural Dorset. Roderick's plan seems to have been to plant his son in Trinidad as the first step to relocating his wife and two daughters there. However, Mairi never visited them in the thirty years they lived there.

During Mairi's last term at St Katharine's change was in the air. When her mother took Uailean and Lucy to Trinidad on the SS *Magdalena* in January 1913 Mairi may have wondered where her future lay. The summer of 1913 was a precious time for Mairi and she would make the most of every minute she spent clattering round the lanes and tracks of Dorset, and Nairn in Scotland.

Uailean was due to sail again for Trinidad at the end of January 1914, but a line through his name on the ship's manifest shows that plans were changed at the last minute. In the *Bournemouth Daily Echo* on 8 April is a story of an accident at Ferndown that suggests that Uailean and Mairi may have skidded into a local man who was walking through the village. Although Mr Cox was 'injured somewhat seriously . . . with a fractured leg among other injuries', the riders of the motorbike and sidecar, 'a gentleman and his sister', escaped with minor injuries.

Eventually Uailean sailed for Trinidad that summer and it soon became clear that he did not care for the life of a planter, preferring to zip round the island on his motorbike and tinker with its engine. He tried to join the Trinidad Constabulary but was too young, and with a little help from his father started a motorbike business, helped by 'one of his numerous best girls'. One day he visited Dr Andre Lange, the local medical officer, and fell in love with his beautiful daughter, Claire, who was helping at the surgery. By the time war broke out, twenty-year-old Uailean was a sub-inspector of the island's police force.

When her brother left, Mairi was already part of another world, with a new circle of friends whom she had met motor-biking, now an all-consuming passion. The most colourful of Mairi's new chums was 'Gypsy', Mrs Knocker, 'an enthusiastic sidecarist', who had ridden into her life in the autumn of 1913. Perhaps inspired by Elsie, Mairi had followed the competitors in the London – Exeter run on her dropped-handlebar Douglas in December 1913. When the colourful and speedy Gypsy asked her to take part in her 'stiff reliability trial' in the summer of 1914 Mairi could not refuse.

DUNHILL'S MOTORITIES FOR MOTOR CYCLISTS.

LADIES' MOTOR CYCLING OVERALLS.

No. 3531.

Double texture, fawn Waterproof Overalls, for Motor Cycling. The coat is cut in shape of cape, with sleeves and pockets. and can be belted in at the waist (as illustration) if preferred. Full skirt knickers, which can be put over a short walking skirt.

Price complete – – – – – – – – – 42/-

No. 3532.

Gaiters, easily adjusted, fastening with spring clips – – 6/-

THE " BIJOU " BONNET

is a Leather Bonnet in various colours, lined with silk and pleated round the face. It is very becoming :—

3447. In Chrome Leather – – 10/6
3447A. In Suede – – – – 12/6

THE " HAREM " VEIL.
For Side-Car Passengers.

Practical and becoming new shape veil, absolutely adjustable to any size hat. Arranged so as to keep the hair and hat perfectly free from dust, and so that the veil can be dropped over the face when required. Invaluable to the lady in the side-car.

4182. In dust-proof silk from – – **5/6**

DUNHILL'S MOTORITIES

2444

THE "AMHERST" MUFF

A UNIQUE and original form of muff, designed by Lady Amherst of Hackney. Made in soft pliable leather, which does not, like fur, become sodden in a shower of rain. A pocket in the back, neat though commodious, is a useful receptacle for the purse and other small articles. Beautifully warm and light to carry.

2114. In various shades of leather, lined satin · **25** ·

Essential for chilly passengers, the Amerherst Muff was designed in 1912 for Dunhill's by Lady Amerherst of Hackney. She was a keen ornithologist, Egyptologist and intrepid traveller.

III

The Cellar-House of Pervyse

Elsie and Mairi began to keep diaries as they prepared to go to war. Each wrote three volumes, in chunks of time rather than as a continuous narrative, recording their experiences when they could, sometime while sitting on the back step of an ambulance waiting to retrieve the wounded. When the fighting was at its most hellish there was no chance to record the events as they happened; these times were often summarised a few days later when they could sit down and put pen to paper.

In the early evening of 25 September 1914 Elsie and Mairi followed Dr Munro down the gangplank of the *Princess Clementine* at Ostend onto Belgian soil. This was the first unit of Munro's Flying Ambulance Corps: Drs Reese and Shaw; two London bus drivers Bert Bloxham and Tom Worsfold, who chauffeured the Daimler and Fiat they took with them; the Reverend Fremlin Streatfeild and his brother Robert; and Eustace Gurney, another driver. Helen Gleason, May Sinclair and Lady Dorothie Feilding completed the team. The four-hour crossing had been calm and no one was sick, and they had not encountered the German submarines at the entrance to Dover harbour or their destroyers and light cruisers in the English Channel. The corps sang its way to Belgium in the 'highest spirits', the words of 'Gilbert the Filbert', one of the popular music-hall songs of the year, floating on the breeze:

> I'm Gilbert the Filbert, the knut with a k,
> The pride of Piccadilly, the blasé roué.
> Oh Hades! the Ladies who leave their wooden huts,
> For Gilbert the Filbert, the colonel of the knuts,
> I'm knuts.

They spent the night at the Station Hotel in Ostend, which had been shelled the evening before but escaped serious damage. Elsie and Mairi shared a room. At 'lights out' at 8.30, despite Munro's warning that the hotel could be shelled again, Elsie went to bed 'feeling quite cheery in spite of it . . . and determined to sleep peacefully'. It was a quiet night. They tried to make an early start the next day but a shortage of petrol meant they could not leave until the afternoon. While she waited, Mairi sent a telegram to her parents and scribbled a note to her Aunt Lucy in London, assuring her that she had arrived safe and sound, and that 'Mum has cut up rough about my coming out. She had wanted me to go out to Trinidad but I had already fixed this up.' She added primly, 'Fancy going out to Trinidad and lolling about doing nothing when there is such a tremendous lot to do here. It's too rotten to think of.'

When they got going, Mairi was surprised that Belgium was such 'a remarkably flat country, with not one hill the whole way to Ghent'. The corps was loudly cheered along the way and at first the party saw few signs that the country was at war, but within a day of arriving in Ghent they were confronted with evidence of the battles and the humanitarian disaster that had been unfolding since the Germans had invaded the country on 4 August.

A thousand Belgians gathered to greet them when they arrived at Ghent, and they made their way to *L'Hôpital Militaire Numéro Un*, where 'all the nurses were most kind in seeing to our wants'. English habits preceded them and they were served with a 'glorious tea' in the hospital kitchen. The beautiful American Helen Gleason slipped away to see her roving reporter husband, Arthur. The corps was billeted at the Flandria Palace Hotel and the next day got down to work. Elsie was sent out in one of the ambulances to the front fifteen miles away and had her first glimpse of a country at war: the area was abandoned and filled with burnt-out ruins, the roads choked with refugees wandering 'along the road in huddles with their children, it is all so sad and pathetic.' She collected fifteen wounded soldiers from a convent. Back in Ghent Mairi was kicking her heels, itching to get behind the wheel of an ambulance, or any vehicle. Her first sight of the war was a captured German car, its radiator riddled with bullets, the interior covered in blood and 'many bloody rags on the ground'.

For the next few days Mairi, Elsie, Helen Gleason and Dot Feilding helped feed the 8,000 refugees crammed into the Palais des Fêtes. When that was done Elsie and Mairi would go to the wards and practise their French by 'ragging with' the wounded soldiers. Shyly, Mairi noted they were 'very cheery and like to see us very much', whereas the more worldly-wise Elsie enjoyed the flirting, realising that it was 'most unprofessional but they love it'. On 30 September Elsie noticed the same handsome Belgian officer for a second time and had coffee with him before he went back to the front. She found him 'so kind and considerate . . . I am falling horribly in love and shall have to be careful if I want to get out of Belgium with my heart whole.' When Elsie was collecting the wounded from twenty miles beyond Ghent the hundreds of panic-stricken refugees on the road warned her that the Germans were coming.

The Munro Flying Ambulance Corps was a motley crew, each member bringing different qualities to the job of bringing in wounded Belgian soldiers from the battlefield to hospitals. Dr Hector Munro was a quirky, charismatic bachelor with a natty moustache, and was rarely seen without his pipe, trench coat and battered trilby. A Highlander living in London, he was in his forties when war broke out, involved in various causes and working at the newly founded Medico-Psychological Society, also known as the Brunswick Square Clinic, which offered the first psychoanalysis and psychoanalytic training programme. He had opened Britain's first nudist camp but it struggled to attract campers.

Arthur and Helen Gleason were a thirty-something American couple, married in New York City in 1912, who had come to London from Paris when war broke out. He was a Yale-educated, left-leaning journalist who had written for the *New York Tribune* and been managing editor of *Scripp's Metropolitan*, *Collier's Weekly* and *Harper's Weekly*. With the publicity value that a pretty American could bring to their activities, plus Arthur's professional expertise and pro-Belgian sympathies, the stories of the work of Munro and his team could be syndicated to the world's press. Helen, a talented pianist, was from Cedar Rapids in Iowa, in the middle of the Midwest. Her 'bright yellow hair . . . like ripe corn in the sun' would light up 'a gloomy room'. After six months Arthur became a driver for the corps and continued to file copy until he was captured by the Germans. He managed to escape and joined another British ambulance unit based at Ypres.

Lady Dorothie Mary Evelyn Feilding, known as Dot to her friends and Lady Dolly in the popular press, was the daughter of Rudolph Robert Basil Aloysius Augustine Feilding, 9th Earl of Denbigh. She was a tall brunette, twenty-five years old and fluent in French. Shortly before she left her home at Newnham Paddox, near Lutterworth in Warwickshire, she had passed an intensive first-aid and home nursing course at Rugby Hospital with distinction. When Dorothie arrived in Belgium her eldest brother, Rudolph, a captain in the Coldstream Guards, was already fighting in France. Lady Dolly's looks and pedigree (EARL'S DAUGHTER AT THE FRONT) ensured that news about Munro's corps appeared on the front pages of British papers soon after they arrived.

At fifty-one years old, the best-selling novelist and poet May Sinclair, full name Mary Amelia St Clair, was the oldest member. She had met Dr Munro through their mutual interest in the suffragettes' campaign for the vote, and her work on the board of the Brunswick Square Clinic. Perhaps Munro allowed her to join because of her generosity and wealth. He knew that she had given five hundred pounds (equivalent to £40,000 today) to the Medico-Psychological Society in 1914. When war broke out she made no secret of her desire to do something and be involved. Despite having no head for figures and no experience as a journalist, she was taken along to help keep the books and write articles about their work, a vital function that helped raise money to keep the corps going.

Money was tight. The Belgian Red Cross was grateful, but the corps received no official funding from either the British, French or Belgian authorities. The British Red Cross eventually donated two ambulances and sixteen pounds a week, but day-to-day running costs had to be met, and from the outset Munro and his team struggled to keep going, members paying their own way. Mairi had sold her beloved motorbike before she left England.

Mairi's diary, which had at first brimmed with schoolgirlish enthusiasm, was by the end of their first week in Belgium starting to show her frustration at not doing enough and not what she had thought she would be doing. Everything took too long for her, and there were all those bits of paper to flourish and passports to show. From a sheltered background and used to servants, Mairi was the youngest member of the corps by at least ten years, so her learning curve was the greatest. Elsie's first week, on the other hand, revealed the years of experience she took to Belgium and the worldly wisdom she had acquired since her divorce. From the outset Elsie was upbeat, a sharp observer of the medical situation that confronted her, and very focused on what needed to be done. In those first few days she showed her emotions and her interest in men – possibly a new father for seven-year-old Kenneth.

From 1 October Elsie had drinks and meals with the Belgian officer she worried about falling in love with. He was tall, blond and handsome, his hair contrasting with his 'well-fitting dark green uniform'. Nicknamed by Elsie 'Gilbert the Filbert', his real name was George Suetens, a member of the Voluntary Motorcycle Corps. His role was to go out on his motorbike at night and shoot as many Germans as he could, and in the last week he had killed forty-eight. Elsie and Gilbert would have drinks and meals with the other members of the corps but sneak off for romantic encounters on their own. 'Gilbert the Filbert' suggests that George was a snappy dresser: 'knut' was army slang for officers so smartly dressed they were dandified; a filbert is a small edible nut. There was a feeling on Elsie and the others' part that their new friend was perhaps vain and a ladies' man, but in a cheeky and affectionate way. (The title of the song lives on as the name of the fanzine of Leicester City Football Club which, until 2006, had been in Filbert Street since 1891.)

One afternoon Mairi 'hastily turned round and beat a retreat' from a tea shop in case Dot Feilding saw Elsie and Gilbert canoodling. Feeling awkward, Mairi told Dot 'there was a great crowd in there' and they went elsewhere. The shortage of petrol meant that sometimes the corps was unable to make many trips to the battlefields to bring in the wounded and they would hang around in Ghent. Mairi grabbed a chance to have her hair washed – for the first time since they had left London – in a little salon in the town and visited a photographer's studio and had her picture taken in a strange mix of European national costumes. They bought postcards and souvenirs and played rounders with the lightly wounded soldiers and orderlies in the yard of the hospital. But on 3 October news came that a train full of badly hurt Belgian soldiers was due to arrive from Antwerp, where the Germans had inflicted heavy casualties.

The survivors were in a shocking state, and this was Mairi's first encounter with serious battlefield casualties. She was upset at the sight of a badly burned young man, perhaps the same age as her brother Uailean, whose face was 'completely smashed up'. At the same time a train carrying British soldiers to the front pulled in at the station and Elsie was moved by the 'very pathetic sight' of the wounded Belgians greeting 'the English with such joy' and waving 'their poor bandaged arms and hands' at their allies. Elsie and Mairi and the others were dealing with the casualties and ferrying them to the hospital until three o'clock in the morning and were up again at half-past five to deal with the eight or nine hundred more victims that arrived from Antwerp that day.

After two nights of almost no sleep, on 5 October Elsie heard that Gilbert had had a 'smash' on his motorbike and she and Mairi rushed out to look for him. They found his wrecked machine in a motorcycle shop in the town and heard that he had not been badly hurt. They were then scrambled to go out in different teams to Zele and Berlaare, towns twelve miles to the east and south-east of Ghent. Elsie was in Berlaare during a bombardment and then went on to Appels, where she, Munro, Dot and Robert Streatfeild left Tom Worsfold with the car by the side of the road and walked four miles over meadows to the trenches by the river Schelde, on the other side of which were the Germans. They found two seriously wounded Belgians, a major and a private who had been shot in the back and had his foot blown off. It started to rain, making it a 'terrible journey': they had 'to sneak back in the dark and under fire . . . with two men so bad'. Tom had been under fire since they left. Berlaare – where Mairi was with other members of the corps – was on fire 'making a great glow in the sky'. It was a cold, bumpy and weary ride home, trying to make the two men comfortable. The major survived his wounds but the young soldier died in the hospital after an operation.

Mairi's night was no less hair-raising. Driven by Bert Bloxham, she was sent out with Drs Reese and Shaw and Eustace Gurney to Zele. This was her first experience of being near the front and at serious risk of being killed. All her senses were fully engaged; she saw hundreds of troops trudging along the road and the sound of German guns filled the air. They walked through the trenches at Berlaare looking for any wounded they could take to Ghent. It was pitch-dark and they came across the Belgians building defences in complete silence. Mairi was only a hundred yards from the front line when they found a badly injured man whom she helped carry on a stretcher. Dr Reese was 'taken very bad' in the car going home. Mairi was 'utterly fagged-out' when they reached Ghent.

At 'brekker' on 7 October Dr Munro and Dr Reese 'had words', suggesting tensions in the corps. There was also news that Mairi's father had arrived. Roderick Gooden-Chisholm had been sent by his wife to bring their daughter back. He caught

a boat to Ostend, hailed a taxi and told the driver to take him
to the front. Roderick arrived with an unhelpful opinion of Mrs
Knocker, whom he had met only once but feared had a powerful
influence over Mairi. In a letter written to his sister Lucy, a
month after Mairi had dashed off to the war, he described Elsie
as 'a very mad woman who is very changeable, and Mairi is
rather chameleon like'. Mairi showed him the sights of Ghent,
caught up with family news and heard about his forthcoming
visit to Trinidad. Despite the Atlantic being haunted by German
submarines and battleships, her father had booked a first-class
passage on 4 November on the SS *Magdalena*. It was typical of
him to be undaunted by danger – if he wanted to go he would.
That evening Elsie had dinner with Mairi and her father and
gave them details of a massacre at Nazareth, a village uncom-
fortably close to the centre of Ghent. Three hundred Germans
had taken twenty-six Belgian military policemen by surprise,
shot them at close range with dumdum bullets and then 'bashed
their heads in'. Elsie had seen the aftermath and been horrified:
'the Germans are truly brutes to mutilate them after death'.

The next day Mairi and her father drove back to Zele, but
she had to leave him there and return to Ghent with eight
wounded soldiers: 'it was pretty hot for a time as some bullets
whizzed over the ambulance'. When they went back to Zele,
Roderick was nowhere to be found, and as the Germans were
advancing they had to get back to Ghent as fast as they could.
Mairi had no time to worry where he was as she was then
sent to Lokeren, eleven miles to the north-east, to take as
many wounded as they could to the hospital in Ghent. On
the way they found Arthur Gleason's car broken down and
being towed by a cart so 'we took it in hand and towed it
home'. Back at Ghent they found Roderick had hitched a ride
there. Meanwhile, Elsie heard that an attack was planned on

Nazareth that day so she and one of the doctors took an ambulance and sat by the road. Nothing happened and they 'fooled around' taking 'silly photographs' before going home. The sight of Belgian troops in full retreat must have filled them with dread. Mairi's father checked out of the Flandria Hotel and went back to England. As he was leaving he told Mairi, 'If it weren't for your mother I'd stay out here with you; you're having the most wonderful time, I wouldn't take you back for anything.'

As soon as he got back to Whin Croft, Roderick wrote a letter to his sister Lucy describing his time in Belgium. Mairi was looking fit and being 'most sensible'. Dr Munro had told him she had been a great help and had a 'remarkably clear head and enormous strength'. Fortunately, Mairi had overcome her squeamishness about 'blood and sights', which made her father very proud. He had had the time of his life and 'lots of adventures', which may have gone some way to assuage his disappointment at being rejected by the War Office on account of his age in the early days of the war. He had enjoyed helping Mairi and the corps, being briefly arrested as a spy and marched at rifle-point to a Belgian officer, being caught up in the middle of hundreds of refugees fleeing the Germans, having to dive to the ground in a volley of machine-gun fire, and walking seven miles to Ghent with his feet covered in blisters. He clearly envied his daughter her starring role.

Meanwhile Elsie's romance with Gilbert continued in the highly charged atmosphere of war. Her diary for October is full of him: teas and coffees, lunches and dinners, anxiety about where he is and if he is safe, and a sense of relief and calm when he returns. She is running two lives in parallel, but her feelings for him do not prevent her from doing her job. Unknown to her, in England her ex-husband, Leslie Knocker, was joining the Army Pay Corps after being rejected as medically unfit for the infantry.

One day Elsie and Mairi were sent to collect a wounded officer from Lokeren, six miles north-east of Ghent and dangerously close to the German lines. As they hurried up to the front they passed the Belgian army in retreat. They opened the door of a cottage, stepped into the gloom and heard 'a horribly eerie sound ringing through the emptiness'. It was the sound of a steady drip 'like the sound of a kitchen tap'. They groped their way down the hall and into a room, where they found an officer lying on a table. He was a new recruit – his uniform was brand new, buttons brightly polished – and his blood was dripping onto the floor, his life 'draining away'. Elsie and Mairi could do nothing for him. As they were leaving the cottage they could hear the Germans pouring into the other end of Lokeren. They drove off.

From the middle of October the corps was on the run from the Germans: Elsie and Mairi had several close encounters with them and heard terrifying tales about what had happened when they captured Antwerp. One day they walked out to the battlefields close to Ghent and noticed a sentry crouched in a ditch. They realised they had strayed through the Belgian lines and had gone 'a bit beyond where they should have gone'. Nonchalantly, they decided to carry on before turning round. Suddenly a car came along with three German officers 'fully plumed in their helmets' driving straight towards the Belgian lines. They looked closely at Elsie and Mairi and went on their way.

A few days later at Melle Elsie and Mairi were caught up in hand-to-hand fighting and had to skulk in a side street when the Germans launched a bayonet charge down the main street. The sound of the blades being plunged into men's 'innards' haunted Mairi for years. German bayonets had a saw at the hilt so that they could also be used to cut up wood, but they inflicted gruesome injuries. Elsie and Mairi filled the ambulance as fast as they could and had 'to scoot' with shells bursting all round them, the air filled with 'screaming shrapnel'.

Although the corps' mission was to help wounded Belgians, all its members risked their lives giving medical attention to wounded German soldiers. Elsie and Mairi made three attempts to rescue Germans lying wounded on the battlefield outside Melle, stumbling over dead bodies and turnips blown out of the ground. The first time they had to withdraw when they came under fire from German snipers, but not before Mairi had managed to cut four buttons as souvenirs from the uniform of a German soldier who had been shot in the mouth. When they tried again they came under shellfire and had to withdraw for a few hours. When they went back for a third time they were defying Munro's orders, so they borrowed a Belgian ambulance and returned at dusk to 'ghastly sights'. One of the soldiers they had been trying to save all day had died, but they brought two men back to Ghent, barely alive. Elsie spoke to the men in German, one of whom suggested she remove his coat and crawl underneath it, telling her, 'I'll guard you with the remains of my life.' There was criticism when they got back for taking such a 'frightful risk'.

Elsie described it as 'the greatest day of all in my life . . . never shall I forget that turnip field . . . I got all my German trophies that day.' Modern readers might feel squeamish about war souvenirs but at the time it was normal. Later Elsie and Mairi would donate their mementoes to auctions to raise money to pay for the work they were doing.

The 'pretty hot scrap' at Melle and worsening news from every direction were the prelude to Munro ordering the evacuation of the corps from Ghent in the early hours of the morning of 12 October, taking the wounded to Ostend. It was a bitterly cold night; there was no time to collect much clothing and the patients were evacuated wrapped in blankets and little else.

Before the war Ostend had been known as the 'queen of watering-places', but it had become a funnel for refugees fleeing Belgium and the home of a sprawling ad hoc military hospital. The smart hotels and grander houses quickly filled with casualties and by the time the corps arrived there were no spare beds and little floor space on which to lay a straw pallet, and so they drove to Malo-les-Bains, a pretty seaside town just over the border in France, a mile from Dunkerque, a vital revictualling centre and 'cram jam' with British, Belgian and French troops. The wounded were taken to any hospital that could take them and Elsie and Mairi and Dot and Helen and the doctors and drivers hung around having a bit of a break while Hector Munro rushed back to England to 'collect funds'. May Sinclair was also sent back to England ostensibly to get funds, but she had a difficult time in Belgium, finding it hard to cope with the conditions. She had been looking for an intense physical and spiritual experience, but found the work hard and mentally gruelling. There was also a fair bit of jostling for roles, even seats in a vehicle, and more than once May felt useless and inept and was left behind on the roadside. She did not return to Belgium, and the following year described the events leading up to her departure in *A Journal of Impressions in Belgium*. It seems Elsie, whom she fictionalised as 'Mrs Torrence', was particularly high-handed with her more than once. May continued to write about the war in her poems and novels, wistful that her active role had ended.

The corps stayed at the Ocean Hotel, wrote postcards and letters, sent spare clothes back to Blighty, had tea at the casino and waited. Extracts from their letters often appeared in their local newspapers. The *Bournemouth Daily Echo* was proud that Mairi was their DORSET LADY AT THE FRONT, and extracts of a letter to her Aunt Fraser in Nairn appeared in the *Nairnshire Telegraph* describing the THRILLING EXPERIENCES OF A NURSE AT THE FRONT. Elsie, Mairi, Dot and Helen's ladylike appearance and coolness under fire often dominated the wide coverage given to Munro's work. The presence of pretty women in such a masculine world could not be ignored, and war correspondents could not help being bowled over by their beauty. In his mid-thirties, the swashbuckling Ellis Ashmead-Bartlett, the *Daily Telegraph*'s man on the Western Front, was smitten when he met them 'arrayed in the most up-to-date khaki uniforms', believing their names 'should enjoy an immortality associated with the greatest heroines in history'. He described Munro's 'daring enterprise' as 'the most remarkable and useful voluntary organisation I have ever seen in any campaign'. When Philip Gibbs, another war reporter, met Elsie, Mairi, Dot and Helen, his initial impressions remind us of how resistant the authorities were to having women close to the fighting, but seeing them in action his mind was changed. 'They did not seem to me at first the type of women to be useful on the battlefield or field hospital. I should have expected them to faint at the sight of blood, and swoon at the bursting of a shell. Some of them were at least too pretty to play about in the fields of war among men and horses smashed to pulp.' However, Gibbs was humbled to see them holding their nerve when helping the wounded 'without shuddering at sights of agony which might turn a strong man sick'.

While Hector Munro was fund-raising in England Gilbert the Filbert reappeared. Elsie and Mairi were strolling around Dunkerque when they spotted him in the crowd: there was no mistaking his 'gait and gay insouciance'. They flew towards him with 'outstretched hands'. He was dusty and weary from his adventures but unhurt. Mairi remembered him flirting with them: 'You won't have the pleasure of nursing me, I believe you're disappointed,' he chaffed in his quick French, but she quickly spotted 'the tender, quizzical looks he gave her friend and tactfully left them alone. She started to wonder if Elsie would marry Gilbert. Mairi was impressed by Elsie, almost star-struck by the older woman, believing she was 'so good-looking, so high-spirited, so charming, that many, many men would want to marry her; and . . . she did love to be loved'.

Gilbert returned to the hotel with them feeling despondent at the state of his country, and Mairi helped Elsie prepare his bath. Mairi's parents would have been shocked: it may have been the first time Mairi had drawn a bath and certainly the first time she had done such a thing for a strange man. Lives and manners were in a state of flux, not least eighteen-year-old Mairi's.

The corps would spend hours in the Gleasons' room talking about politics and the war, and this was fascinating for Mairi. She was mixing with people older than herself from different backgrounds and places; she had to do a lot of running to keep up. Arthur Gleason had just returned from spending five weeks in the trenches, and relief over him being safe added to the atmosphere. To Elsie's delight Gilbert was asked to join the corps, and for her 'things were going swimmingly'. Most nights there were romantic walks along the beach 'with the revolving searchlights sweeping it all the time and all lights out all along, no café lights'. She would take his breakfast to him and get his motorbike ready. But Mairi, who had palled up with the novelist Sarah Macnaughtan, a new member of the corps, had enough of the holiday mood and was itching to get to their next destination: Furnes.

On 21 October the corps drove in convoy to Furnes, where the main hospital, hurriedly converted from a boys' college, was in 'a terrible muddle' and struggling to cope. Many of the town's 6,000 inhabitants had fled in advance of the German push, and Dixmude, Pervyse and Nieuport were being pounded in an attempt to break the line that the British, French and Belgians were struggling to hold. Towns and villages, houses and woods blazed for days on end and Furnes was quickly overwhelmed with hundreds of casualties, many of them serious. Those for whom there was no room at the hospital and were likely to survive the journey, would be taken to the railway station and sent off to military hospitals in Calais or England. There was not enough of anything: when the beds ran out men were laid on stretchers on the floor or propped against the wall. There were so many men dying and not enough male orderlies to remove the bodies from the wards, especially those who had died in the night, that as soon as Elsie and Mairi got there they were told to remove all the bodies they could find to the mortuary and the convent, which Elsie called a 'horrid job'.

Mairi witnessed her first death on her first day at Furnes, a young man with a serious head injury. It became obvious that he did not have long to live and she sat with him until he died. Then the nurses laid him out and Mairi and Elsie carried his body on a stretcher to the convent. They also helped in the operating theatre, carrying away amputated limbs and returning the men to the wards. The days at Furnes were shocking and bewildering for Mairi: 'no one can understand . . . unless one has seen the rows of dead men laid out on a stretcher, the majority wrapped in a winding sheet but here and there one is uncovered who has been left as he died'. The wards were hellish places: 'one sees the most hideous sights imaginable, men with their jaws blown off, arms and legs mutilated and when one goes into the room one is horrified at the suffering . . . which is ghastly. I could not believe that I could have stood these sights.'

Gilbert was placed in temporary charge of the corps when another new and senior member, Robert de Brocqueville, the son of the Belgian minister of war, was called away to Dunkerque. The involvement of such a well-connected Belgian, also a family friend of the Feildings, would be invaluable to Munro's work. Elsie happily took orders from Gilbert when he sent her and Mairi to collect his wounded countrymen from Dixmude, a town eleven miles south-east of Furnes, along an exposed road with shells raining down on either side of them. It was a terrifying and bumpy ride. Forbidden to use headlights, it was hard to avoid the shell craters in the road. They almost drove into the carcasses of mutilated horses and saw vehicles crashed off the road or pitched into the craters. Elsie wrote, 'Mairi and I felt extremely lonely in our little motor ambulance . . . we were the last of the column, so if anything happened to us no one would have known.' The next day Gilbert sent them out again, even closer to the action, to Oudecapelle, six miles away, where they retrieved wounded Belgians and German soldiers. Both women quickly become battle-hardened and found the exploding shells around them 'a wonderful sight, the flash of flame in mid-air, then a big boom'. Gilbert did not send an orderly with them to collect the German prisoners, who apparently had no thought of trying to overpower the women and take the ambulance.

On 23 October the corps, by now sixteen in number, moved into an empty house in Furnes, a ten-minute walk from the hospital where they were based. They were taken there by their newest member, a Belgian driver who was a cousin of the house owner, a doctor, who had fled with his family a few days before. There was a half-eaten meal on the table, children's toys on the floor and the doctor's wife's 'dainty clothes' had been left. Most nights Elsie and Mairi, who shared a room, slept fully dressed, desperately trying to keep warm. They continued to work at the hospital, where the wards were 'simply fearful'. It was worst at night, when the men gasped for air, cried and moaned in pain. Much of their time was spent going out in the fleet of cars, ambulances and a recently donated limousine on roving missions to collect the wounded wherever they could be found. Without field telephones, the corps relied on messengers, mostly on bicycles as petrol was so scarce, to bring information and local intelligence to tell them where they were most needed. Collecting the wounded at night stretched nerves to breaking point and Elsie broke down one night after bringing in eight wounded men in an ambulance constantly threatening to skid into the muddy tracks on either side of the cobbled roads. She was an excellent driver but snapped and 'fell forward on the wheel and burst into tears'. After a good night's sleep she was back on the road.

Certain male attention was tiresome. One day Elsie was whisked off by a 'little French commandant with an ugly red face and scarlet hair' looking like 'the giant in Jack and the Beanstalk' who, with the help of his well-thumbed French-to-English phrasebook, insisted she go and have a bowl of soup with him. It was disgusting, swimming in grease. She was handed a spoon that someone else had just finished with. As if that was not bad enough she was given a 'very decrepit' bit of beef that somebody else had hacked at before it was offered to her. When Elsie refused to wrestle with it he reached for his phrasebook: 'I am stung to the quick'. He then danced about like an 'infuriated rooster'.

There was a bit of bother with Gilbert. Elsie felt he was ignoring her, treating her like 'dust' and spending too much time with Mrs Winterbottom, a driver with the British Field Hospital, also based at Furnes. Newspaper photographs of Mrs Archibald Dickson Winterbottom, a good-looking American divorcée with a colourful past, show a lady used to male attention, and it sounds as if Gilbert was dancing to her tune rather than Elsie's, but the situation resolved itself. Her rival makes no further appearance in Elsie's diary, although sparks fizzed off the pages of Mrs Winterbottom's diary when they had to work together briefly in 1916.

Everyone in the corps was working long hours under pressure and in danger. The living arrangements at the house were not easy: it was crowded, ill-suited to sixteen adults and smelly, as the drains were often blocked. Mairi and Helen Gleason had to unblock them. Dot, an earl and countess's daughter, described it as a 'piggery . . . the first night we had no blankets to speak of and Helen Gleason and I slept in our clothes, and hugged each other like babies for warmth. I remember thinking how funny it was when we woke up and found we were still tightly locked together in the morning.'

There was very little food in Furnes, and they foraged and 'riffled' what they could get. Their diet consisted of porridge, fried potatoes, biscuits, jam, bully beef and claret. There was a party when they found three bottles of champagne in the cellar. But they made the best of what they had and gathered round the pianola for a sing-song to keep their spirits up.

One day there was a Goldilocks and the Three Bears moment when they returned to the house and found that it had been broken into, but nothing seemed to have been stolen. Some time later a French soldier appeared at the back door and asked Elsie and Mairi if he had left his revolver in their bed. They found his gun and cartridge case at the bottom of their mattress. While everyone had been out in the ambulances he had broken in and slept in the bed, forgetting to take his gun with him when he left. It emerged that other French soldiers had been sleeping at the house when Goldilocks and her team were at work. Elsie 'gave him what for on the landing' and they did not return.

On 1 November Elsie, Mairi and Gilbert and several others in the corps were caught up in fighting at Oudecapelle and had to spend the night in an abandoned cottage as it was too dangerous to drive back to Furnes. They had been inches from death. Standing around deciding on what to do next a bullet had 'whizzed' past Gilbert's ear and another 'whistled' between Elsie and Mairi as they chatted. That night they bedded down on straw on the floor with a party of French soldiers. Mairi took it in her stride but Elsie found it odd: 'it is a funny life – never did I expect . . . to sleep a whole night under heavy shellfire in a room with common soldiers and all of us sleeping on straw'.

Tensions within the corps, perhaps exacerbated by lack of sleep, uncertainty and the danger they were in, started to show. Elsie challenged Hector Munro when he arrived with a group of newcomers at their house in Furnes. Munro told her to take the party to Dixmude and she refused, saying she had been out all night. Words were exchanged and 'they all got very annoyed with me and Munro had fits'. She told her diary she thought he was an 'idiot' and that she 'loathed him'. Dot Feilding confided later that she thought he was a 'silly little man', and Mairi was indignant at the arrival of Georgie Fyfe, sister of the well-known *Times* journalist Henry Hamilton Fyfe, and her group of volunteers. Elsie despaired of Munro's muddled organisation; her challenge and rejection of his authority would be the start of Elsie and Mairi extricating themselves from the corps to run their own show at Pervyse.

Momentous decisions were being made at the highest level to try to hang on to what was left of Belgium and give some respite to the exhausted Belgian army, which was struggling to keep the Germans back along the line between Nieuport in the north and Dixmude eleven miles away to the south-east. The River Yser, which had been canalised in the nineteenth century, flowed from France through Belgium to Nieuport, where it was embanked for the last forty miles before it emptied into the sea. The Belgians decided to use the embankments as fortifications, in effect trenches *on* the ground, to prevent the German army reaching the prize of Dunkerque and Calais, from which they would surely launch an invasion of England. But the French, already supporting the Belgians, could spare no more men, and the British were bogged down at Ypres twenty miles to the south and unable to divert any troops. It was decided to open the sluice gates and locks of the Yser to inundate the land. There was a frantic search for lock operators and engineers to perform this vital job, and, after several attempts, on 29 October the sluice gates were opened, the tide roared in and the locks were closed. After taking Dixmude, the Germans were forced to pull back behind a lake eight miles long and five miles wide, waist deep and impossible for troops or animals to cross on foot. The Germans would be pinned down behind the inundations for the rest of the war trying to take Pervyse. The Belgians had spent hundreds of years controlling the waters and keeping their country drained, but this was their last chance to halt the German advance.

During the first two weeks of November the focus of Elsie and Mairi's work in Belgium started to change. They made a five-mile journey east to Pervyse, where they would spend three and a half years. Despite their doubts about the newcomers they had stayed. Dr Munro would not reject anyone who could bring a Rolls-Royce and several other cars with them. The house now bulged at the seams with the extra half-dozen volunteers, who were unhappy and apparently disgusted at having to rough it. Elsie fumed about having to cope with sightseers who were not strong enough to lift a stretcher and who 'just liked to stand about and look on and get in the way . . . and are a nuisance'. Most days were spent on roving missions to collect wounded soldiers for the hospital at Furnes, and the new lot were given a baptism of fire when they saw what had happened in the towns and villages within range of Furnes. In Dixmude they saw trees festooned with the mangled bodies of people blown out of their houses, and Nieuport was like a 'city of the dead'. In Dixmude Elsie bought a German helmet from a French soldier and at Nieuport looted some 'quaint trophies' including a 'very pretty soup ladle' from somebody's house, and was almost killed by a shell when she went back for a salt cellar she had spotted in an empty shop. On her way back to Furnes Elsie drove through Pervyse, close to the inundations, and noticed 'there was not a house in which one could pig it, it is just one huge fallen mass. The road to and from Pervyse was littered with over a hundred broken-down or burnt-out vehicles, and there was the poignant sight of a hasty roadside burial of the driver: it all seemed so sad and just what might have happened to us.'

Despite the generally frenetic pace there were periods when Elsie, Mairi, Dot and Helen had time on their hands. They would chat to reporters, have photographers take their pictures – a sign of the growing interest in them – and went to one of the last photographers in Furnes to have their portraits taken. Elsie and Mairi had admirers; one gave Elsie a German rifle, bayonet and a pair of gloves, and Mairi got a German lance.

On 9 November 1914 there is the first hint in Mairi's diary that Elsie was planning to break away to 'try and get a job at one of the outposts'. Driving through the little town of Pervyse, seeing its strategic importance, in places just a hundred yards away from the watery front line, had given Elsie the idea to relocate to the heart of the battle. Uncertain petrol supplies and the amount of time they spent hanging around was deeply frustrating, and they disliked not having a defined role at Furnes Hospital. But it was driving the wounded from the battlefields to the hospital and seeing many of them die of shock and exposure in the back of their ambulance that goaded Elsie into action. It was surely better to give the men basic first aid and perhaps a night's sleep before taking them anywhere. Today we know this as the 'golden hour', and it is standard practice for doctors and paramedics at an accident or medical incident.

The next day another development helped them to make their move to Pervyse: Dr Irénée Van der Ghinst, a heroic Belgian doctor – he had been at the siege of Dixmude and was held in awe by Elsie and Mairi and the rest of the corps – was posted to the ruined village. Later that day Miss Macnaughtan, known as Naughty, suggested Elsie and Mairi go with her for a short break to Malo-les-Bains, and as there was 'little doing', they agreed. They packed their belongings, Mairi proudly taking her German lance with her. They bumped into Munro in the Rolls-Royce in Dunkerque and he spoke about his plan to open up a soup kitchen 'for the lads in the trenches'. Elsie and Mairi went to see the arrival of the SS *Invicta* at the docks and were offered a free trip to Dover, a 'terribly tempting offer'. They raced back to Malo-les-Bains to get their luggage (and lance) and just caught the boat in time. The weather was awful; they had a 'fearful crossing' and Elsie was extremely seasick. When they reached Dover they were soaked by waves breaking over the sea wall as they hurried to the station to catch the train to London. After a night at the Great Western Hotel at Paddington, sleeping in their first comfortable beds for eight weeks, they went their separate ways: Mairi to Dorset to see her mother and sister Lucy (Roderick was on his way to Trinidad) and agreeing to meet up again in three days' time. We do not know how Elsie spent her time as she did not keep a diary during her stay. Perhaps she went to Marlborough to see her seven-year-old Kenneth, who was with the Upcotts.

When Mairi arrived at Waterloo Station to catch her train to Bournemouth, where her mother, Lucy and Miss Arnold, her governess, had gone to stay at the Princes Hotel 'for a change', she caused a commotion. The sight of her in grubby breeches, dusty boots and coat, carrying that lance, brought the place to a standstill: 'all the porters flocked round and I had difficulty in moving about with it as a crowd followed everywhere'. The sight of a young girl dusty from the battlefield, like Joan of Arc, brought the war to the heart of London in the same way as the sight of hundreds of soldiers. Her fellow passengers on the train to Bournemouth were fascinated by her stories of the war. When she told them that blankets and pillows were urgently needed at Furnes Hospital they gave her fifteen shillings and wished her well.

The last time Mairi had seen her mother there had been a row and she had run away to the war. She had then refused to return to England with her father. Now Grandmother Fraser was gravely ill in Nairn, and Mairi's mother was 'not fit to travel' to see her. But during that weekend Mairi was pampered: a hot bath every day was the greatest luxury; a visit to the hairdresser; luncheon; tea at the Rink; shopping for warm clothes and visiting friends. In one place she visited she was given a standing ovation, a sign that her growing celebrity was preceding her. Also she received a letter 'from all the girls' at Redmoor School bursting with pride at all her 'daring exploits and splendid work' and assuring her that her name 'will ever be remembered'. The girls felt that their bandage-making and sock-knitting was 'very poor work compared to yours'. But the weekend was also spent waiting for telegrams, each one gloomier than the last until they heard that 'the Ma', Grandmother Fraser, had died in the early hours of Saturday morning, 14 November. Mairi felt 'dreadfully cut up that I had not been there'.

The next day Elsie and Mairi met back at the Great Western Hotel. Elsie looked 'very fit': the brief break had done her good. The kindly May Sinclair saw them off at Victoria Station. While the journey to Dunkerque was uneventful, the ride they hitched to Furnes was anything but. A British officer offered to take them and on the way turned round to see shellfire falling behind the car and ran a soldier over: 'the car caught him a fearful whack and knocked him spinning'. Elsie and Mairi jumped out and got him into the car to make sure that nothing was broken, but he was 'very much knocked about'. They left him at a nearby first-aid post and continued their journey. When they got to the house they found that Dr Joos, the owner, had taken his bed away and Elsie and Mairi had to sleep on the floor.

Mairi now had a hacking cough and cold and had to rest, feeling wretched and miserable. Meanwhile Elsie, Dot and Helen bustled about organising the soup kitchen they were opening at Pervyse. With Dr Van der Ghinst's help they found a cellar under a ruined house and moved all their belongings out of Furnes to the blitzed village on 20 November. Mairi followed as soon as she got better.

The cellar room in which they lived, made soup and patched up the wounded was less than six feet high. Ventilation was minimal and a smoky stove provided their only source of heat. There was a little table in the corner and straw was strewn on the floor to sleep on although there was a rickety bed with a rock-hard mattress. Some light filtered into the room from a grille in the pavement above. In the earliest days going to the lavatory could be unnerving as it often meant going out at night to a shell hole or 'a bit of ruin'. Two soldiers from the trenches wondered why the women left the cellar for short periods at night and then realised what was going on. They scouted around the village and brought them a commode which was placed in a cubbyhole at the bottom of the bit of staircase that remained. They put a sheet up in front of the commode and insisted: 'Do not think of trying to empty it by yourself; we will attend to it and we will tell the others when we change trenches that they must look after it.'

The day started at six o'clock in the morning, when the ladies got dressed (put their boots on and brushed their hair), lit the stove and made cauldrons of soup or hot chocolate, which they kept warm all day. They served it to the wounded soldiers they were looking after and others who called in, and also took it in enamel pails at breakfast and in the evening to the men on the sodden front line. They walked in the dark in the 'icy freezing stillness' without a light and in silence, whispering the password to the sentries, knowing the Germans were not far away. Sometimes German sentries called out, asking Elsie and Mairi who they were and what they were doing. Cheekily Elsie would reply, 'Do you want a cup of hot chocolate? There's one going spare.' It was a moving moment when the war and real life collided: 'There we were, with the Belgian sentry, and the German sentry imbibing chocolate, right out in No Man's Land. I mean it was just too silly for words.'

The women scoured nearby houses for cutlery, crockery, chairs, towels, bedding and any food they could find, and harvested any vegetables growing in gardens and on outlying farms. They managed to make their 'quaint tumble-down house' cosy and 'comfy'. When they ran out of food they had to make the dangerous drive to local towns to buy supplies out of their meagre funds. Mairi, Elsie, Helen, Dot and Dr Van der Ghinst slept on the straw while their driver braved the hard bed. Mairi wrote, 'it is a funny old life to be sure. To think of all the things we are doing here. I am now writing in the cellar by the light of a candle.' This summed up her topsy-turvy life.

During the autumn of 1914 Elsie and Mairi got to know Lieutenant Robert de Wilde, a Belgian army officer who became a regular visitor to the cellar. He was the same age as Elsie and married with children. When they met him he had recently been made a Chevalier de l'Ordre de Léopold for his bravery as an artillery observer in the first hectic weeks of the war. He kept a diary of the first year and was a fan of the work they did. 'The cellar is both a kitchen and a dormitory. They make chocolate, broth, tea, and everything that is comforting for those in the trenches. They are so devoted, they go to the trenches . . . to distribute socks, cigarettes, sweets, all of this gives great moral support to the soldiers since they feel they are sharing their dangerous situation.'

Geographically and militarily the town of Pervyse was vital to the Allies and one of the most dangerous places to be on the Yser Front, the northern section of the Western Front. Because of the boggy soil, the road that ran from Nieuport-Bains on the coast to Dixmude and Ypres in the south was raised on an embankment, and Pervyse was the midpoint of the road. If Pervyse had fallen to the Germans the Yser Front would have been lost. Its jumbled ruins had to be held at all costs. Although knowing they would not be welcomed by the English high command in Ypres, the Belgians were happy to have Elsie and Mairi in Pervyse for the practical help they could give, and also to remind the French that Belgium had other allies.

Dr Henry Souttar, chief surgeon at the British Field Hospital at Furnes, drove out to Pervyse soon after the women moved there, and found the village almost wiped off the map. Nearly a thousand bodies had been brought in from the surrounding fields and interred in mass graves in the churchyard or put into shell craters all over the village, but further shelling had resulted in many grisly sights. On the day Souttar visited Elsie and Mairi, they were above ground, dealing with the wounded among the rubble of what had been the living room of the house. He was impressed by their high spirits and sense of humour and admired them for their courage, which he thought was as contagious as fear: 'I think that the soldiers watching through the night in the trenches nearby, must have blessed the women who were waiting there to help them, and must have felt braver for their presence.'

In the dusty ruins of the soup kitchen and first-aid post Elsie, Mairi, Dot, Helen and Alexandre, a lightly injured soldier who helped with the cooking and the wounded, tried to have a good time. A piano had been found and placed in the corner of what was left of the room. Strange sights and sounds floated through the watery landscape: they had sing-songs, and the walking wounded would dance with each other and the women. Belgian officers would call in for tea when there was a lull in the fighting.

For the ordinary soldiers the cellar was a haven in a land-scape of mud where trench life was fiendishly uncomfortable. Until pumps and duckboards were installed men were often knee-deep and sometimes waist-deep in water for days at a time. Injured men had the comfort and basic care that the women could provide: infected wounds could be swabbed with iodine and boils lanced. A visit to the post was a semblance of the care they might have received from their womenfolk at home, a reminder of their lives before they were marched into a water-logged hell.

Within a week of the post opening the women started to receive visitors, including top-brass Belgian military, who were grateful for the help they were giving to the soldiers of the 3rd Division. Hector Munro would bring influential patrons and would-be patrons to have tea and talk about the work they were doing. When Dot's mother, the Countess of Denbigh, arrived they 'tootled about' with her and walked her out to the trenches. On 26 November the grandest of all their visitors turned up, King Albert of the Belgians, who was 'very nice and charming' and thanked them for what they were doing.

A steady stream of young officers visited the women. Two Belgian lieutenants of the *Génie* (engineers) invited Elsie and Mairi to dinner one night; a cook and an orderly were left in charge while the ladies were out being wined and dined. The officers had persuaded one of their cooks to prepare a meal in the smashed-up house where they were billeted. It took Elsie and Mairi an hour to make themselves presentable, but some of the stains on their battered clothes were impossible to remove. The young officers produced handwritten menus and rustled up Scottish anchovies, tomato soup, asparagus, chicken, *petits pois* and dessert, washed down with claret and champagne. It was a 'very jolly evening': one of the officers played Liszt's Hungarian Rhapsody on the piano and the evening ended with a rousing sing-song. Walking the women home, one of the lieutenants proposed to Elsie three times before they reached their particular ruin. Mairi called her the 'Infant Snatcher' as the officer was only twenty-three years old. This proposal of marriage is missing from Elsie's diary, where she called the young officers 'such dear things who are so good to us'. Gilbert had been missing from its pages for quite some time.

Headlines in *The Times* during December explain the deteriorating conditions at the cellar house. The 'cosy cave', in which they had 'snuggled down' would become increasingly dilapidated as THE BATTLE FOR FLANDERS raged around them; in places the countryside had been turned into a HUGE CHARNEL HOUSE. A reporter from *The Times* stood among the ruins of Pervyse, 'which for all human purposes now only exists upon a map'. Nightly bombardments to soften up the relatively lightly armed Belgians and French were followed by small forces of Germans wading through the inundations waist-deep on desperate and hopeless missions to take the village. These attacks were 'repulsed at once'.

Despite the fact the best wash they could manage was to fill a bucket with hot water and keep guard for each other, Elsie and Mairi – who of all the corps spent the most time at the cellar house – never complained about the privations. Not once did they moan about the food, the bully beef and pickles, meat paste and biscuit rations; they were realistic about their situation and grateful for what they could lay their hands on and what was donated by well-wishers, including the Belgians, who often called in with treats. They got on with patching up the wounded and driving them to Furnes Hospital, chopping vegetables and stirring the chocolate. Any improvement made by the ever-willing *Génies*, such as repairing one of the rooms above ground to give them a little extra space when there was a rare lull in the fighting, was an excuse for a tea party. There was 'much swank' about their cellar post.

There were also reminders of their past in England. After serving breakfast one morning Elsie decided to go to the part-ruined L'Espérance Hotel in the village for a proper bath and borrowed a horse from a cavalryman. She met an English photographer who had come to take pictures of the war-torn village. By a startling coincidence he had seen her six months before at that Gypsy Club event, trying to climb Leith Hill on her motorbike. They had to cut their chat short when shells started to fly over their heads. Elsie made a dramatic exit, telling him she had to 'scoot back' to help Mairi. She returned the horse and was starting the dangerous walk back to the cellar house when she saw one of their drivers, Woffington, known as Woffy, motoring towards her hell-for-leather. She whistled to him to stop and turn round and take her to the post. After several journeys taking the wounded to Furnes the day ended when the fighting stopped and half a dozen officers called in with champagne to celebrate two comrades' birthdays, one of whom presented Elsie with a twelve-inch shell, 'a nice keepsake'.

The strain of the work and the forced intimacy of their situation caused tension from time to time. Mairi is diplomatic about the rows, calling them 'discussions'. As a girl working with an older woman who was more experienced in every way, Mairi had to defer to Elsie and do as she was told or risk being sent back to England. In the first week of the difficult and dangerous December of 1914 Mairi tells her diary that the young Belgian lieutenant who had proposed to Elsie had brought in an injured colleague. While Mairi was bandaging his head wound Elsie walked in, and when the soldiers had gone 'we had a discussion about familiarity but made it up afterwards'.

Although Elsie was running the show at the cellar house, Dr Munro would call in from time to time to introduce new corps personnel and bring various supplies from Dunkerque. None of the tensions of the past resurfaced. Elsie proved herself to be much happier in charge, and she made the post her project and no one else's. On the day of the 'discussion' about familiarity Munro arrived with Mrs Hilda Wynne, the formidable widow of a general and a new driver to the corps. They fussed over

Mairi, wanting to take her back to Furnes for a rest, but she refused to budge.

On 4 December Dr Van der Ghinst brought his wife Marianne to see the work the women were doing at the cellar house, and to his dismay his wife insisted they spent the night there. He left in the morning to go back to his post at the L'Espérance but was clearly unhappy and sent a group of *Génies* to patch the place up and try to make it safer. There was a two-hour disagreement between the doctor and his wife which left Madame Van der Ghinst feeling 'very annoyed'. He returned to his post and she stayed to help with the wounded and slept with the women in their 'cave'. The next morning Madame Van der Ghinst asked Woffy to drive her to her husband. Mairi went along too and carried on to Furnes, where she 'muddled around for a bit' at the hospital, where Georgie Fyfe was helping relocate refugees to England.

Mairi called in at the corps' house to collect her own and Elsie's luggage and found that four of Dr Joos's female relatives and a little girl had taken up residence with Munro and the other corps' members. One of Joos' relatives told her off about the state of the place. Mairi was disappointed to find that two precious souvenirs, a German rifle and a leather belt, were missing, and saddened that 'one can't trust one's little things to one's own party'. Dr Munro returned unexpectedly and cheered her up with the gift of some beautiful books and clothes, which may have been sent from England or looted from empty houses. When Mairi got back to the cellar Elsie was there, and Gilbert. This is the first sighting of him in their diaries in over a month. Clearly, he was still part of the corps – Mairi mentions him being there with a carload of people including two nurses – but not close to Elsie.

There was plenty of politicking within the corps and Elsie was possessive about the cellar house:

I am very very sick and tired of various people poking their noses around and wanting to have a look. Everybody is jealous of the work we are doing out here and wants to come out and do the same but they don't want to take the trouble to start one of their own . . . Now they want to come out and shunt us on elsewhere while they enjoy the comforts we have searched the village for.

The *Génies* were devoted to making them as comfortable and as safe as it was possible to be in such a place, looting anything they could, installing a bath above ground in a room they virtually rebuilt. But on 7 December Elsie decided that she should not let Belgian officers come round quite so often, including the *Génies* who had improved their 'cosy cave'. Dr Van der Ghinst arrived that day and 'fussed around', saying it was far too dangerous for them to be so close to the trenches that night because they had received intelligence that the Germans were moving big guns to Pervyse for a bombardment. This put Elsie into a 'fluster'. As head of the team and responsible for the post, should she evacuate them to Furnes or not? Eventually, after supper she and Mairi walked in the pelting rain and howling wind, avoiding the shell holes, to the house where the *Génies* were living. They insisted the two women stayed the night with them, so Elsie and Mairi trudged back to the cellar, placed Alexandre the cook in charge while they were away, and took Woffy back with them to spend the night with the *Génies*, sleeping at their feet.

The next morning the *Génies* handed their house over to Elsie, as they were being sent to Ypres. Dr Van der Ghinst visited, bringing the local priest, who rode a white horse, and a local bigwig to persuade them that it was too dangerous to stay at the cellar. Eventually Elsie agreed that they would continue to run the post but sleep in the relative safety of their new billet a quarter of a mile away. The women knew the cellar was dangerous but were afraid that if they left it would be for good, and grudgingly agreed to compromise over their sleeping arrangements. The wounded would be treated as usual, and the soup and chocolate kitchen would open every day. If there was an emergency at night, Woffy was to drive into the village and collect them.

Pervyse was taking hold of Elsie emotionally, and her attachment deepened daily. Her diary reads like a love affair with the place and the people with whom she was living and working:

> I love little Pervyse and shall be very very sorry to have to leave it altogether. I have got so used to everyone up here and every soldier knows me . . . I don't think I shall ever forget my life at Pervyse, it is all so strange and weird and at times so lonely, and yet there are moments when you forget everything and laugh and giggle like children.

Once they were established in their new quarters life took a domestic turn for Mairi and at times she sounds like Cinderella, sweeping, tidying up, making 'brekkers', ensuring the place was 'spick and span' before trudging off to the cellar house. When the weather was 'beastly' and there was 'nothing doing' she read *The Crimson Azaleas* by the popular Horace De Vere Stacpoole, taking herself off to Japan in an exotic and romantic tale of an Englishman and a Scotsman racketing about in a world that was as different to hers as it was possible to be.

There were more visitors. The controversial Labour member of parliament for Leicester, James Ramsay MacDonald, a pacifist considered by many people 'a rank traitor', was expected on 10 December. He had been introduced to the work of the corps by Munro, but they were embarrassed by MacDonald's presence, not wanting to sit down and eat with the politician when he arrived in Furnes. Elsie was introduced to him by Georgie Fyfe and was not perturbed when he announced he would visit the cellar post the next day. But Ramsay MacDonald was arrested by the Belgian police and accused of spying before he could see them. Subsequently formal apologies were made. Two weeks later he was allowed to continue his visit to the trenches, and made a flying visit to the cellar two weeks after that.

Having sent the Belgian policemen looking for Ramsay MacDonald on their way, Elsie and Mairi were busy treating badly wounded soldiers when the double Nobel prizewinner Madame Marie Curie and her daughter Irene, whom she had trained as an X-ray technician – and was the same age as Mairi – arrived at the cellar. Instead of offering to help they went to inspect the trenches. This rankled with Elsie, who called them a 'nuisance'. However there were very good reasons for the Curies' preoccupation: the mobile X-ray units Madame Curie had recently developed were being used to help treat fractures, bullets and shrapnel wounds near the battlefield, and a visit to Pervyse gave them the perfect opportunity to see a first-aid post in action on the front line.

Many days were grim, and the breezy schoolgirl language of Elsie and Mairi's diaries – 'ripping', 'beastly', 'horrid' and 'plucky' – cannot disguise the awful reality of their work. The women had to make men who had been shot in the chest as comfortable as possible as they wheezed their last breath; head wounds from shards of molten shrapnel were impossible to treat, and the sheer volume of blood and gore they had to cope with was overwhelming. On one of many days, Mairi rushed to the cellar post to find Elsie covered in blood and struggling to cope with the wounded. They patched them up as best they could and Elsie drove them in an ambulance flat out to Furnes. Mairi stayed behind and carried out 'the bloody things in to the garden, my hands were dripping in gore'. She washed her hands in a puddle.

No sooner had the Belgian *Génies* been posted elsewhere than British officers from Dunkerque were calling in for tea at Pervyse. They were members of the Royal Naval Air Service, whose work involved patrolling the Channel and North Sea for German ships and submarines, and attacking enemy-held coastline. When Commander Harry Delacombe and Captain Tom MacKie were not on duty they would take a car and go sightseeing along the front down to Ypres, delivering parcels and stores that had arrived at Dunkerque. Delacombe was a starry new acquaintance for Elsie and Mairi, especially the intrepid Elsie, who had been up with Gustav Hamel before the war. He had been *The Times* aeronautical correspondent and was the author of *The Boys' Book of Airships and Other Aerial Craft*. Yorkshireman Tom MacKie, ten years younger than Delacombe and also married, was the manager of the Albion Chemical Company in London. Elsie and Mairi's diaries reveal they took every opportunity to have a good time, lark about, drink tea and sup champagne with Harry and Tom.

There was a feeling of the lull before the storm in the middle of December, Elsie and Mairi were told that the Allies were preparing a push against the German line. Belgian reinforcements were pouring into Pervyse and the surrounding villages: 'from all accounts we may expect a very great movement very soon'. Colonel G. T. M. 'Tom' Bridges, who had been at the reliefs of Ladysmith and Mafeking in the Boer War and was the head of the British mission to the Belgian army, 'had the shrieks' when he heard that Elsie and Mairi were still working at Pervyse. It was decided that Dot, an earl and countess's daughter, was the best person to discuss their situation with

Colonel Bridges and tell him that they were determined to stay at Pervyse.

While Dot was explaining the situation to Colonel Bridges in Furnes, all was quiet and Elsie and Mairi strolled up to the trenches to chat to the machine-gunners and play with their dogs. When they returned to the cellar post Mairi was rummaging around in the devastated garden looking for wood for their fire when a shell whistled past her. She had to dive to the ground, then rush down into the cellar. The next shell that came in took a corner of their house off. A soldier who was standing at the door was wounded by shrapnel in both arms so they bundled him into the cellar, called their driver Tom to get the badly damaged Daimler ready, and told him to drive them all as fast as he could to their other house. The car was peppered with thirty-six shrapnel holes and the front tyre was 'riddled with bullet holes' but they arrived in one piece. With classic under-statement Mairi confided to her diary: 'we certainly had a bit of luck in coming through unscathed'. When things quietened down they returned and picked their way through piles of roof tiles and bricks to get into the cellar.

The next day Captain MacKie and a friend called in for tea and told them that there was going to be a big push to force the Germans back. Elsie and Mairi were excited rather than afraid at 'the great news'. According to Elsie, Tom MacKie was smitten with Mairi's 'limpid blue eyes', and when they left at midnight Elsie noticed that he was 'very lovesick' and 'went home with a fluttering heart torn in twain'.

Ahead of the anticipated push Munro brought Brigstock, a new driver, and Dr Henry Jellett to Pervyse. At times Brigstock proved more of a hindrance than a help. He was 'highly agitated' by his new job, often begging Elsie and Mairi to evacuate the cellar post when the situation got hot. But Dr Jellett, known as

'Jelly' in Mairi's diary, was well used to working in a tight spot: he was an eminent gynaecologist and the master of the Rotunda Hospital, a famous maternity and midwifery training hospital in Dublin. He had driven over an ambulance donated by Sir William and Lady Chance, was calm under fire and adept at plugging holes in their roof, which leaked like a sieve. Elsie, who was a qualified midwife, had a great deal of respect for him, finding him a 'great addition to the family' and 'most amusingly calm'. She was tickled by the fact that he insisted on undressing completely for bed and putting on his pyjamas. It was going to take more than a war to change Jelly's night-time rituals. A *Times* report of Pervyse at this time puts his routines into context, describing families standing among the jumbled ruins of their homes, trying to salvage anything they could as 'one of the most pitiful commentaries of the war'. Meanwhile Jelly was climbing into his pyjamas as usual.

Munro made arrangements for Elsie to go home for Christmas on 22 December; Mairi, Dr Jellett and Dot were to stay behind and run the post. Mairi packed up all their war souvenirs, including the hands of Pervyse's church clock, for Elsie to take back to England. Elsie was given a tremendous send-off by 'all my dear little soldiers and the girls', and Jelly drove her to Furnes, where she spent the night with Georgie Fyfe and had a 'long business talk' before visiting Naughty, Sarah Macnaughtan, who was running a soup kitchen at the railway station. The last sight she took with her to England was a stream of 'limping, bandaged figures covered with mud . . . and the poor stretcher cases trying to be so brave'. Elsie went to Dunkerque with Munro, who was returning to England with Ramsay MacDonald.

She spent Christmas Eve rushing about London: trying and failing to see Dot's uncle the Honourable Everard Feiling, who was the corps' treasurer, and seeing Arthur, Helen Gleason's husband; lunching with May Sinclair; shopping in Selfridges, where she bumped into 'some dear naval drivers' whom she knew. They 'rushed across Selfridge's and shook hands with me and were so charming' and took her to tea at her hotel and presented her with chocolates and magazines. Elsie's train pulled in at Marlborough station at eight o'clock, in time to hang up a Christmas stocking for son Kenneth and swap news with her adopted parents. Compared to what Elsie was now used to, her Christmas at Marlborough was relaxing, even dull. She tells us in her diary that after a brief round of social calls she 'felt the pull of Pervyse', to which she excitedly returned on the last day of 1914.

Things were different for Mairi, Jelly, Dot and Helen. They festooned the house where they slept with Belgian and English flags and hung up the mistletoe presented to them by Harry Delacombe and his fellow officers, to remind them 'what time of year it was'. Mairi was sure it would be 'the strangest Christmas we may ever spend'. Dot and Jelly drove back from Furnes 'simply laden with parcels and goodies for our meal'. On Christmas morning Helen and Mairi were giving out socks to soldiers who had walked down from the trenches – the joy of a new pair of dry socks was worth the risk – when the Germans shelled them, injuring the men as they queued outside the door. Two shells hit the house and went through a wall. Shrapnel landed at the front door, where the men were sheltering. Mairi called it 'a nice Christmas present for us . . . it was certainly hotter than I have known it'. Once they had treated the wounded and swept the rubble away, they sat down to their 'cheery little Christmas dinner' of oxtail soup, cold fowl, fried potatoes, plum pudding, mince pies, nuts, crackers and champagne.

On the last day of 1914 some of the big subjects of the year before the declaration of the war were talked about as Mairi,

Helen and Jelly waited for the Germans 'to plump [*sic*] in some shrapnel'. They had some 'quite interesting discussions' on divorce, Irish Home Rule and the suffragettes. Such was the stigma of divorce, if Elsie had been there she would not have been able to share her experience of the courts as she had told everyone she was a widow. As an Irishman living in Dublin, Dr Jellett would have had something to say about Home Rule, and Helen may have been interested in the campaign for the vote in Britain as her home state of Iowa had given the vote to some women in 1894, but full suffrage for British women would not come until 1928. Mairi had been a schoolgirl when the suffragettes were smashing windows and burning down empty buildings, and had left school around the same time as Emily Wilding Davison made her fatal dash onto the course at the Derby in 1913. Whether or not Mairi was interested in votes for women, no one could ignore what the suffragettes were doing, and she had worked alongside many suffragettes when she was a dispatch rider for the Women's Emergency Corps in London in the first weeks of the war.

Towards the end of the afternoon Elsie returned to Pervyse, and Mairi wondered what 1915 would hold in store for them: 'Death to many I am afraid and it remains to be seen which ones.'

Mairi and Elsie were deeply affected by the number of men who died in the back of their ambulances or shortly after reaching hospital. The sights at Furnes hospital haunted Mairi, who would have known that her brother Uailean would enlist as soon as he could. The wards devoted to head injuries were the worst: they saw men lose their minds, regress to childhood and sometimes take days to die. If Elsie had known that her youngest brother Lewis Henry had already enlisted she would have been even more afraid.

IV

When Elsie Met Harry

The ringing words and sleek promises of the politicians that the war would be over by Christmas proved hollow. The rhythms of life at the cellar post were unchanged. On the first day of 1915 Commandant Georges Gilson of the 9th Regiment of the Line called to see Elsie and Mairi, took 'lots of cheery' photographs of them and painted a watercolour in Elsie's war album of Pervyse's glowering sky and stumpy trees surrounded by sheets of glinting water. They sat down to a lunch of 'champagne, tongue and sweets'. Gilson, who spent as much time as he could at the post, invited Robert de Wilde to join them the next evening, and told them 'many queer things' including that 'he could foresee many things'. He did not mention a calamity in Elsie's life that would occur at the end of the month.

Under orders from Munro, the next day Elsie took six wounded soldiers from Malo to the Feildings' house at Newnham Paddox, near Lutterworth in Warwickshire, which had been turned into a convalescent home; Dot gave her money for the journey. When Elsie collected the four 'sitters' and two stretcher cases she found they had no clothes to travel in and had to dash to the nearby Duchess of Sutherland's hospital for apparel. It was a major logistical endeavour to get the men to England even with the help of a doctor and two orderlies. There was a howling gale and a rough passage which made the wounded men very seasick. On the boat she met Major A. A. Gordon, British attaché to the military household of the King of the Belgians, and they talked about the work she was doing at Pervyse. The boat was late arriving at Dover, where Helen Gleason's husband, Arthur, was waiting to meet them in an ambulance. Elsie telephoned the local military hospital for beds for the night but they refused to take them in. They had missed the last train to London and Elsie managed to get rooms at the King's Head Hotel in Clarence Place. Once the wounded men were tucked up for the night she and Arthur went to the smoking room and talked mostly of Gilbert's 'skunky behaviour'. This is the last we hear of Gilbert the Filbert.

The next morning Elsie helped the doctor wash and dress the men's wounds and the final leg of the difficult journey began. Arthur drove them to Dover railway station for the train to Victoria, where they took four taxis to Euston and waited five hours for the train to Rugby. One of the men was 'taken bad' on the journey and 'crumpled in on himself'. Elsie had to give him an injection of morphine, and had the train stopped to get boiling water for the poultices to dress his wounds. Another man was in a bad way by the time they arrived at Rugby, in agony from gunshot wounds to the buttocks. They were exhausted and frazzled when Dot's mother, the Countess of Denbigh, and a team of doctors met them at the station. Once the wounded and the orderlies were settled for the night Elsie had supper with Lady Denbigh. Set in parkland, Newnham Paddox was a grand seventeenth-century house remodelled. Elsie was surprised at how dark and shabby the place looked and thought 'they seemed very poor'.

After breakfast she gathered up several Belgian convalescents she was escorting to London and the care of the Salvation Army. They travelled with some very eager, fresh-faced Tommies, volunteers who were desperate to get to the front: 'Poor dears they little know what that means.' In London she had lunch with Arthur Gleason, who had driven up to London that morning, and Everard Feilding. On the boat returning to Dunkerque Elsie was surprised to be 'confronted' by a detective from Scotland Yard and questioned closely about the work of the corps; she was clearly suspected of being a spy. When she reached Pervyse the others were agog to hear about her being interrogated by a detective, and Mairi noticed how 'fagged out' Elsie was by the 'rotten time' she had had taking the sick men back to England.

While Elsie was away life at the post had run smoothly. One quiet day Mairi, Helen and Jelly went out with their cameras to take pictures of the trenches and the ruined town. They took grim grey snaps of the vast sheets of water that kept the Germans away vanishing to the horizon. In the foreground were higgledy-piggledy heaps of wrecked houses and chewed-up gardens. Mairi and Jelly were nearly hit by a shell: 'I ducked my head and the bally thing just passed over me and we scarpered off.'

On 6 January, the morning after Elsie got back, an unnamed artist turned up at the house to paint a group portrait, doubtless prompted by the articles and pictures of them appearing in the press. It was tricky to get them all together for long enough to be able to sketch them for the picture; Mairi found the posing 'at fearful angles' arduous and was glad when it was all over. Later that day Mairi dashed off a note to Aunt Lucy asking her if the letters she sent from Pervyse were censored, and promising to write to her cousin Jim Trinder, a solicitor who had joined the Northumberland Fusiliers, although with some foreboding: 'I hate to hear of people coming out – it makes one feel blue.'

Elsie's return to Pervyse certainly changed the mood of the place. In her absence Jelly had been in charge and on her second day back Elsie resented him telling her that as the Germans were shelling the area of the cellar post she should not go there until it had stopped. Elsie responded by defying him and taking Mairi with her. During the next two weeks the number of meetings Dot and Munro – whom she increasingly calls 'Father', perhaps sarcastically – have with Elsie suggests that there were worries about the long-term future of the post. What was left of it was increasingly dilapidated – there was only so much the *Génies* could do to make it watertight and shell-proof – and the logistics of resources being split between two sites added to their increasing difficulties. Elsie may have guessed that the cellar post would close and be relocated to the house where they lived, and the uncertainty may explain why she and Mairi had a 'big quarrel', Elsie taking Helen and going 'off in a huff' up to the post. Elsie found it hard to give things up: she had made a home for herself and surrounded herself with an extended family – the corps and wounded soldiers. She perhaps recalled her feelings of abandonment as a child. Elsie brought a visitors' book back from England to collect the autographs of people who came to see them.

The British press was fascinated by the female members of Munro's corps, and Elsie and Mairi's names start to appear regularly in the newspapers early in 1915. The *Daily Mirror*'s man in Paris reported 'the splendid devotion' of the BRITISH NURSES WHO RISK THEIR LIVES. The *Daily Express*'s ENGLISH WOMEN UNDER FIRE told readers about the lady 'cave-dwellers' of Pervyse, whose work exposed them to 'terrible sights' and 'not the least part of their heroism is the stoic manner in which they face gruesome, blood-chilling situations'. The article ended with a plea for readers to donate 'cigarettes, balaclava helmets, thick mufflers and warm socks' for the Belgian soldiers the women were helping. French and Belgian newspapers also sang their praises, purring at their 'excellent French', and were impressed that the women, whom they called valiant Amazons, received journalists into their 'miserable room as if it were a salon, and have as much modesty as courage'.

Elsie, Mairi and Helen were excited on the morning of 17 January. They had been invited by Robert de Broqueville to a concert at Guines, a dozen miles south of Calais. Rare treats were anticipated for days, with anxiety about how to get clean and 'vainly trying to make ourselves tidy'. They left Dr Van der Ghinst in charge of the cellar post for the day. They were driven in a Rolls-Royce ambulance which 'flew like a bird' to Calais, where they were hit broadside by a tramcar. Luckily little damage was done and they continued on their way unperturbed. De Broqueville took them to his 'dinky little cottage' at Guines, where they tidied themselves up and had veal and peas, hot roast beef and apple pie for lunch before setting off to the concert. They walked past lines of Belgian soldier-cyclists and cavalry on their way into a hall awash with Belgian, British and French flags and took their seats in the second row. A string of generals and colonels arrived, resplendent in ribbons, medals and dress uniforms that made the women feel very grubby in their battered leather coats, breeches and boots. It was a 'toppingly good' programme and ended with hearty singing of the three national anthems. On the way home they called in to see their friend Commander Harry Delacombe at the Royal Naval Air Service base in Dunkerque.

On 19 January Elsie could no longer avoid the closure of the cellar post, admitting that she could not 'be in both places at once . . . the cases are never properly seen to unless I do them myself'. Dr Jellett, to whom she was referring, might have disagreed with her. Tactfully, Jelly left Pervyse for two weeks to do ambulance work while the women moved the contents of the post to the house where they were all living. (When the American novelist Mary Roberts Rinehart visited she called it 'the sick and sorry house'.) On 21 January, ten minutes after Elsie and Mairi left the post for the last time with a load of furniture and the sign that had hung on the door, it received a direct hit and was completely destroyed; they had been moments away from being 'pinked'. They went back to see the damage and were horrified by the carnage. In an outhouse, in what had been the garden, were six horses: three had been killed outright and the other three were horribly injured, riddled with shrapnel. There was blood everywhere. Elsie's time at Jack Allen's stables in Devon came in useful but it was hopeless. One of the horses was spurting blood and it took seven attempts to apply a tourniquet to staunch the flow. A vet was called to shoot two of the horses, which were beyond help. Elsie and Mairi spent hours picking pieces of shrapnel from the third horse, trying to save its life. Mairi recalled, 'it was a queer sight by lamplight, two dead horses with the poor fellow watching them and awaiting his turn.' The next day Elsie was extremely agitated and asked one of the *Génies* to shoot the horse and put it out of its misery.

Mairi was breaking the heart of Captain Lejeune, a Belgian officer, leaving Helen, who also had her admirers, to entertain him. She confided in her diary, 'it is really funny to see the number of broken hearts one has left behind'. Lejeune wrote a note in Elsie's visitors' book that may describe his unrequited feelings for Mairi. He sounds love-struck, feels like an 'uncouth old soldier, even clumsier in wielding the pen than the sword', and is helpless in the face of his emotions. He says he struggles to: 'express the unforgettable charm of the hours passed with you', 'convey the melange of extraordinary feelings I've felt during them' and describe the 'emotions that stirred me to the depths of my soul when your agile fingers made the keyboard sing, while outside the dull boom of shells hummed their accompaniment to your songs'.

Commandant Georges Gilson called at the post on 25 January. Even though he brought worrying news of an imminent German attack, Elsie was intensely happy to see him when he 'appeared in the doorway in his usual frank way'. Tall and dark with a bristling moustache, Elsie said they all felt 'as if our big protecting brother had come back' and 'talked like tea-pots'. He told them a big German offensive on Pervyse was about to begin and stayed with them that night. Helen played the piano he had scavenged for them, and they kept their spirits up by singing loudly. Outside the ammunition wagons rattled over what was left of the cobbled streets, bound for the trenches. There was a strange party mood in that 'silent ruined' place. In the early hours of the morning they watched the men walking past in silence and then noticed signalling coming from somewhere behind their house. They deciphered the signals and to their dismay realised that a spy was warning the Germans that the Belgians were reinforcing themselves with more men and ammunition.

Early the next morning Gilson left for the trenches nearby, and Helen set off for Dunkerque and a few days' leave in England. Shelling began in earnest and several badly injured men staggered to the post, while others were brought in over their comrades' shoulders. Gilson brought one of his men in with a severed artery in a state of severe shock, and he would have bled to death if Elsie had not positioned his head and feet to slow down the flow of blood. Then she gave him a saline injection and with Gilson's help put him to bed, surrounded him with hot-water bottles, gave him an injection of morphine and patched up his wound. Elsie's theory about shock and the danger it posed was vindicated: later in the afternoon the soldier was taken to hospital in a much better condition that when he had arrived. 'I think it's a bad plan when a man is suffering from shock and is taken over these roads . . . for a serious operation. He cannot withstand the strain . . . I like them to have a good rest before they go on.'

On 27 January General Jacques arrived at the house when Elsie and Mairi were padding splints with the startling news that King Albert of the Belgians had made them Chevaliers de l'Ordre de Léopold. Albert, who had been king since 1909, led his army throughout the war; his wife Queen Elisabeth was a nurse, and he allowed the eldest of his three children, fourteen-year-old Prince Léopold, to enlist in the army and fight as a private in 1915. With their medals ribbons sewn on their coats Elsie and Mairi were now entitled to a salute from any soldier they met. In the midst of their cluttered first-aid post the general's formal speech must have sounded extraordinary. Mairi called it a lot of 'pow-wow and bow-wow' and Elsie felt a bit silly: 'I never felt so foolish in my life. I stood like a stuck pig and gazed at him too dumbfounded for words.' When they got over the shock they drank their health in Horlicks. Gilson sent Elsie a note asking if she was safe and well: 'it is nice to have him back and to feel that every man in the trenches is interested in us'. She sent a message back with news of their award and within half an hour he sent her a Cross of Léopold that he had acquired from a German who had taken it off a Belgian officer. In a playful mood, Elsie christened Mairi 'Albert' after the music-hall star Albert Chevalier. Gilson called in for a few moments at six o'clock that night when the troops in the trenches were

being changed. There were tears in his eyes when he congratulated them and he was more delighted than they were: 'dear G.
G., he is such a buck'.

But with the awards came a sour note and the start of a split
in the corps that would never truly heal. The next day Munro
visited the house with Dot's Uncle Everard, and Elsie and Mairi
did not tell them about the decorations straight away. Gilson
called in and invited the women to a 'dinner of felicitations'
that evening at Avecapelle, five miles west of Pervyse, where he
was billeted. Munro and Everard were intrigued and Elsie teased
them by pretending that she did not know what Gilson meant.
Eventually Gilson told the men the news. Elsie noted that Munro
'seemed very taken aback . . . and Feilding did not seem at all
pleased'. It is odd that Elsie should have behaved in this way,
needlessly needling her boss. But her diary reveals prickliness
and feelings of being an outsider: 'It was so funny that after all
the huge advertisement that Dorothy and Father [Munro] have
had and flinging titles about that little Mairi and I should have
come on a long way first . . . that is what pleases me most.'

Diplomatically Gilson also invited Munro and Feilding to
dinner, and they set off in convoy leaving two orderlies at the
house. Elsie and Mairi beat the dust out of their clothes and
set off into the 'gorgeous' moonlit night in a different car to
the two men, who had a lot to say about Elsie and Mairi's
medals. Gilson took the women to the house he lived in and
they met the family: father, mother, a fifteen-year-old daughter,
a son and a baby boy. They waited for Munro and Lord Leigh,
another bigwig interested in the corps, and then walked round
to where dinner was served in a tiny room in a tiny house. The
soup, sardines, meat, chocolate shape (blancmange), fruit and
champagne were served on a red and white gingham tablecloth.
As if Munro had not been irritated enough, Gilson made 'a very

nice speech' and two soldiers called and said in excellent English, 'We have been sent to represent our company to thank you from the bottom of our hearts for all that you have done for our soldiers and also to congratulate you on the great order which you have won and so honestly deserve.' It was a marvellous drive home under a 'perfect moon', but ominously there were German planes circling over Pervyse.

At the house the next day Mairi's admirer Lieutenant Lejeune was hanging around and 'joking in his mad fashion'. Gilson, who came with some of his men and told them of an imminent bombardment, was tinkling away on the piano. Then Munro, Dot and Jelly arrived. Strings had been pulled and a wrong was righted (as far as Munro and the Feildings were concerned): Munro announced that Dot had also been awarded the Cross of Léopold. After all, Dot and Helen (who was still in England) had been at the heart of the corps and had done the same kind of work as Elsie and Mairi, but Elsie, in a temper, sounded almost tearful in her diary: 'they made a great yarn about Dorothy and said that she had also been decorated and I cannot understand how anyone can have the audacity to say a thing which is not true . . . of course she may be some day but she is not now'. We can hear a foot being stamped in frustration. Whether Elsie liked it or not, Dot was awarded the order some days later – as was Helen Gleason, about which Elsie and Mairi were delighted.

The visitors left and Gilson remained at the post with them all day, staying the night in Jelly's room. Everyone went to bed fully dressed in case they had to retreat. At four o'clock in the morning Gilson woke them, saying that the Germans had taken the Belgian forward post and he had to go with his men to recapture it. Elsie and Mairi watched the soldiers march past in silence in the brilliant moonlight, many of them walking to

Elsie stands to the left of Mrs Emily Upcott, her adoptive mother, in the garden of their house in Marlborough in the early 1890s.

Mairi, her mother and brother Uailean, outside their home in Ferndown, Dorset in 1903.

Mairi's school-leaving photograph. She had an oval face, brown hair, blue eyes and was five feet five inches tall.

Mairi's father, Ruari, in the 1880s. He was an officer in the Third Battalion of the Seaforth Highlanders.

Before it was reduced to rubble, Pervyse was a bustling Belgian village with its own railway station. By November 1914, 'not a house had gone unscathed … often enough in the case of cottages there was nothing left but a tumbled mass of bricks, rafters and tiles.'

In 1914 Elsie and Mairi's first-aid post was in the cellar of this house, seen here from the back. Their friend Captain Robert de Wilde described Pervyse: 'Dead cows lie with their legs in the air … The gunfire, sporadic during the day, is continuous during the night … sometimes the thundering cannons from Ypres can be heard from a distance.'

Helen Gleason, Lady Dorothie Feilding, Mairi Gooden-Chisholm and two unknown British officers standing outside the cellar house, the first post they opened in Pervyse in November 1914.

Elsie taking photographs with Commandant Georges Frederic Gilson of the 9th Regiment of the Line, perhaps a romance. A strong man in his forties, who could support the weight of two men standing on his shoulders, Gilson was a Belgian veteran who served in the Congo three times between 1896 and 1908. Evacuated from Pervyse with typhoid in 1915 and 1916, he was gassed twice in 1918 and survived the war.

Helped by Joseph, their Belgian orderly, Elsie and Mairi gardening at the third and last first-aid post they ran in Pervyse. Food supplies were so uncertain they grew vegetables to feed themselves and to make soup for the men.

Elsie looks relaxed enough for a holiday snap as she lies against the sandbags.

Elsie takes a swig from a bottle of wine, reminding us what an ad hoc life they had in Pervyse. The women foraged in the ruins of the town for food, drink, blankets and clothing for their wounded soldiers. Because the water-table was high and local springs could be contaminated by decomposing bodies, clean drinking water had to be brought from England in barrels. Fortunately there was wine.

They had not been at Pervyse for long when Elsie, who could speak German, struck up informal relations with the Germans in the opposing trenches. One day they were sent a message by the enemy that if they wore head scarves the Germans would never fire on them, but if the women wore their tin-hats, from a distance they would look like soldiers, and might be shot.

Mairi posing in a shell hole. Her eyes were described as having: 'the glint of a man who knew no fear. They are so limpid and so candid, no one could dream of the horrible experiences and revolting sights which have bitten deep into the life of this brave little Scot.'

Mairi kept a portrait of Commander Henry 'Harry' Halahan, who was in charge of the naval guns at Nieuport, on her desk for the rest of her life. Elsie remembered him as a 'kind elder brother to us, who often came over for a scratch meal in the dug-out. He brought the food and we heated it up.'

Captain Francis Mourilyan, Butler of the Royal Field Artillery, drew this pretty portrait of Mairi when he visited in 1915. Butler died at the Battle of Passchendaele in October 1917.

Baron Harold de T'Serclaes in front of a Maurice Farman MF11 aeroplane at Coxyde airfield in 1916. He was an observer who gathered intelligence about the position and movement of German troops and armaments, and also acted as gunner.

Elsie and Harry on their wedding day, 19 January 1916. 'The bridegroom is renowned for his splendid pluck, he has twice been decorated for his daring deeds. He is a man without fear and one that is loved by his many friends … The bride looked charming in navy blue *crepe de chine*, with a becoming hat in black velvet, trimmed with a large white feather.'

Elsie and Harry's marriage was a holiday romance in a war-zone. They cuddle up on boulders just a few yards behind the lines. Elsie had to beat the caked mud off her coat and boots and jam on a woolly beret instead of a nurse's veil.

When Elsie and Mairi were delayed on a fund-raising trip to England in May 1916, Harry, Baron de T'Serclaes, wangled some leave to come to London and escort them back to the Front. He looks uncomfortable in the sidecar of the motorbike of Gordon and Rosa Fletcher, Elsie's biker friends, who stand at her shoulder. Mairi is the outrider.

Squadron-Commander John Joseph 'Jack' Petre of the Royal Flying Corps leaped straight out of a boys' adventure book into Mairi's life in 1916. He was a brilliant sportsman and a nifty dancer and ice-skater. His brothers were mad about flying and even built their own aeroplane, the Petre Bus, which they took up before they had properly learned to fly.

Mairi with Jack Petre and Teddy Gerard, also a pilot, in front of the recreational tents she and Elsie ran at Steenkerke, near Pervyse. The people of Liverpool donated money for the tents where British soldiers sent down from the line could have some rest and recuperation. There was beer, boxing, cards and dominoes.

their deaths. The stillness of the bright night was filled with the crackle of machine guns and sniper rifles; this was the most dangerous situation they had been in. Their driver sat in the ambulance with the engine running, ready to make a dash for it. Gilson returned with grave news, that 150 Germans had taken his post and another one and that he and his men had to counter-attack. By ten o'clock in the morning the Belgians had shelled the Germans into retreat and had retaken the two posts, but it had been a close thing. Dr Van der Ghinst called in later on for 'a serious talk' about the future of the corps. It seems that Elsie was not the only person who felt ambivalent about the way Munro was running the show: the highly respected doctor confided that there was 'great dissatisfaction amongst the [Belgian] officials on the subject of Munro's Ambulance Corps and the way it is run, except the Pervyse branch which is satis-factory'. Dr Van der Ghinst expressed unhappiness at the youth and inexperience of some of the members, saying that there was a perception that some of them did nothing but 'joyride'. Elsie may have felt a little smug. Her weeks of muttering about the man she cheekily called Father seemed to be shared by others whose opinions mattered.

On 31 January they were in a spin. A messenger announced that King Albert would present their medals the next day at Wulveringhem, seven miles away. They had 'absolutely no clothes' to wear. Having sent all their washing to be done at Furnes, they had lost everything when the town was evacuated on 23 January after a night of heavy bombardment. They rummaged among the piles of clothes sent over from England for wounded soldiers and cobbled together two blouses from two old flannel shirts. They brushed their dirty breeches, wiped the mud off their long leather coats, polished their boots and jammed on their khaki woollen caps, as spruce as they could get under the circumstances. In the midst of their hurried needle-work a stream of visitors arrived including a reporter from *The Times*. When the last of their visitors left they managed to have a much-needed bath but had to share the water. Elsie was in a 'perfect turmoil of emotions' all day.

February 1 was Kenneth's eighth birthday, cause for a double celebration. In their excitement they spent the morning falling over everything and getting in each other's way. A Belgian army driver collected them and took them to Wulveringhem. Elsie and Mairi stood in line for an hour as the king made his way along the line of soldiers waiting to be decorated. He was 'very kind and shook hands with us' and thanked them for their work at Pervyse. The ceremony was over by four o'clock and on the way home they called in on the British Royal Naval Air Service officers to show off their medals. English and Belgian news-papers rushed to tell the story of Mrs Knocker: 'neither shrapnel nor shell can shake her,' and 'God only knows the number of wounded men their motherly hand has bandaged,' said *L'Indépendance Belge*. The women kept themselves in the public eye by writing to their local newspapers, telling the *Marlborough Times* that they had felt 'horribly squirmy and nervous' when the King approached, but found him to be 'just a dear'. The *Bournemouth Graphic* cooed about their LOCAL LADY IN THE TRENCHES being decorated by King Albert. A *Sunday Times* jour-nalist who went to interview them was taken aback by their reticence: 'Mrs Knocker gets really annoyed when anyone reminds her that she has on several occasions attended the wounded under heavy shellfire and it is just the same with her friend . . . both ladies seem to think they have only done their bare duty.'

The weather was dreadful. *The Times* headline THE FROZEN WASTE OF FLOOD paints a picture of life in Pervyse during the first week of February. Although the rain kept the floods deep, making it harder for the Germans to cross, it was grim for the soldiers not far from the corps' front door. Because the ground was waterlogged they could not live in the trenches as in other parts of the front, but on the boggy surface between banks of earth in little wooden huts.

On Sunday 31 January 1915 Elsie was interrupted while she was writing her diary – the diary she had been keeping since 24 September 1914. The entry was about 'scooting' round with Mairi to have a precious bath, but she stops in mid-sentence and that is the last note in the three mossy-green journals. Mairi wrote hers briefly that day and continued until 24 March, then there is a six-month gap until October, when she resumes until the first week of March 1916, and there her diary ends.

When Mairi came to write up the week after the medal ceremony, starting on 2 February, a dark cloud had settled on the post. 'I am going to skip very lightly over this week because it has been too full of unpleasantness and sorrow to be talked about.' The trouble was caused by an article in *L'Indépendance Belge* that seemed to credit Dot with being in charge of the work at Pervyse and having taken the wounded Belgian soldiers to England, which left Elsie feeling miffed. Mairi was hurt that they had 'received no kindness' from the corps about their medals, and wrote and told her Aunt Lucy that 'the whole thing has been a nightmare'. Gilson had visited many times 'to try and pacify matters'.

Then on 7 February Mairi wrote that Elsie had opened an English newspaper and read that her youngest brother, Lieutenant Lewis Henry Shapter, had been killed in action near Ypres on 31 January. Although he had been attached to the 1st Battalion of the Hampshires when he rejoined the army, he was fighting with the 2nd Bedfordshires, who were dug in near Fleurbaix, a town four miles south-west of Armentières, when he was killed. Arriving early in the new year, he would have heard about the extraordinary Christmas Day the Bedfordshires and the 55th Field Company of the Royal Engineers had at Fleurbaix. The Germans had come out of their trenches first and British officers had followed suit. They chatted about the weather, the local beer, and 'feminine fashions' like lifelong friends. They were also able to bury their dead and then the grisly business could start all over again. Lieutenant Shapter was the only soldier of the regiment, officer or other rank, to be killed on 31 January, probably by a sniper.

It was relatively quiet in Fleurbaix during January 1915 and casualties were correspondingly light, but conditions were tough as the weather was awful. Snow and driving rain compounded the misery of the thousands of men in agony with trench foot and frostbite. Duckboards and gumboots were a rarity in the trenches at this stage in the war, and the troops had to man the trenches whether they were half-full of water or not. Trench foot was caused by standing for long periods in waterlogged tight-fitting boots. When the agony of their swollen feet drove the men to take their boots off they were unable to get them back on again and the worst cases would bind their feet with puttees and hobble through the mud in search of medical attention. Feet turned a marbled red and blue colour and toes and sometimes the whole foot became gangrenous and had to be amputated. Twenty thousand men were treated for trench foot during the winter of 1914 and the spring of 1915. Eventually duckboards, gumboots, changes of socks and rubbing the feet with whale-oil grease would help to avoid the dreadfully debilitating condition.

Also included in the 2nd Bedfordshires diary at this time is a copy of an anonymous letter from an officer to his wife. Not a typical love letter, it sketched a sanitised picture of what life was like at Fleurbaix. Without mentioning Lieutenant Shapter by name, and sparing the reader the horrid details of trench foot, it revealed something of what Elsie's brother's life must have been like during the month leading up to his death. The writer did not mention the thick glutinous mud and water that filled the 'trenches . . . the boots . . . the thoughts . . . the days and horizons' of the men in the 'God-awful' cold, sodden conditions. He was delighted with the men's enthusiasm: 'the keenness of it all is quite marvellous', despite the chronic shortages of essential equipment: 'we have got no machine-guns . . . but I believe however, that guns will be to hand shortly'. He thought his officers 'were a first-rate lot'. He ended his letter by apologising for letting his pen run away with itself, explaining that he was 'keener about this show than anything I've ever had to do with my life so you must forgive me'.

Lieutenant Shapter was buried at the Military Cemetery at Château Rosenberg, near Ploegstreete, fifteen kilometres south of Ypres. He was twenty-eight years old and promoted to captain posthumously, his new life on his Canadian ranch never to be. The announcement of the death in *The Times* of a 'dearly loved adopted son' was a reminder of the time when the Shapter orphans were split up a quarter of a century before. Mrs Frederica Brown, who was his aunt and then became his mother, was his next of kin.

Mairi wrote that the first week of February had been a 'very very sad week and I do not care to speak about it because it is written on my mind'. Munro tried his best in his well-meaning but sometimes bumbling way to help and comfort, hoping that tea in Nieuport with some of the French doctors they had met in Melle would restore morale and improve the atmosphere in Pervyse. He arranged for a Rolls-Royce to collect Elsie and Mairi and brought Dot with him in his car. Nieuport was one vista of desolation after another and there were plenty of relics to add to their collection. Tea was taken and champagne popped, and on the way home the Rolls' back axle got stuck in mud and the car had to be pulled out by horses. But feelings were still hurt when two days later Munro called in with Mrs Clitherow, a bossy-sounding member of the corps, and there was a row over the medals and 'remarks that had been made concerning them'. In the afternoon they all trooped off to the trenches and took pictures of the inundations: 'a wonderful sight'. Water covered the railway line and the trenches were now 'little islands' in the dreary, soggy landscape. Mairi took some 'very fine photographs', but her description reveals the impression the floods made on her, because the photos are only of stretches of dirty-looking water with what look like twigs – telegraph poles or trees shorn of their leaves – standing bleakly in the distance.

Financial worries did not help matters: shortage of money was a constant strain. The Feilding family paid for classified ads to be placed in *The Times* about the work of the Hector Munro Ambulance Corps, which had brought in 'thousands of wounded French and Belgian soldiers'. Dot's Uncle Everard, who was chairman of the London Appeals Committee, made an 'urgent appeal for funds' and may have planted a piece on his niece in *Country Gentleman* magazine. Singled out for particular praise in the corps was Lady Dorothie, 'a pretty girl who has an infinity of pluck and courage', and eye-witness reports of her going out under fire to bring in the wounded were included. The last time the reporter had seen her was at Ascot races, looking 'very attractive'. The landed gentry were being nudged to put their hands in their pockets to help the work being done by one of their own.

While the torrential rain helped keep the Germans at bay, it made life very difficult. Happily Helen Gleason and Marianne Van der Ghinst, the doctor's wife, were there to assist Elsie and Mairi. Their pals, the *Génies*, worried about the women's safety in the rising water and urged them to be ready to evacuate at a moment's notice. It was clear that if they were not bombarded out of the place they could be flooded out of their beloved 'little Pervyse'. Elsie dashed about to see where they might open up a new post, and Mairi told her diary that she felt 'really C D – seedy', and was unable to eat for three days.

Mairi's letter to her Aunt Lucy on 15 February 1915 did not mention how poorly she was but concentrated on how lucky they had been to escape so many close encounters with shells. She also wondered about her future, when the war was over, and seems to have expected it would include Elsie.

> I think it will be impossible for me to settle down in an ordinary slack life again. I hope to be able to set myself to work on some definite thing . . . Naturally the thing I am <u>really</u> interested in is Motor Cycling, so that I should very probably take that up – go into partnership with Mrs K and get the agency from some firm to sell and demonstrate their bikes. It might do quite well but of course it is difficult at the start because I don't quite know how I shall manage it . . . we may get taken on by a firm. I should like to make a little money of my own in case of accidents and I have no other talent at all, or nothing that in the least appeals to me.

On one of her dashes to Dunkerque Elsie made arrangements for herself and Mairi 'to go for a hol' at Wimereux, near Boulogne, and to have a cinema show at the post on 18 February. The *chef d'activité* was the Honourable Lieutenant Philip Wodehouse, who was deputy assistant censor at the Australian hospital at Wimereux. Elsie and Mairi invited their friends from the Royal Naval Air Service, and also Colonel Edward Maitland Maitland, and the Honourable Mrs Ward, at whose villa in Wimereux they would be staying. Early that morning Elsie went to see General Jacques to ask his permission to invite some Belgian soldiers to the show, but he refused. When she returned all four women started to get the room ready and 'of course we all had a fight and wouldn't speak to each other for some time'. Helen and Mairi made the sandwiches and cut up the cakes and made themselves presentable for the afternoon's entertainment. Before the entertainment began Elsie took Mrs Ward, Edward Maitland Maitland and Philip Wodehouse up to the trenches, where they were very nearly 'pinked' by the German bombardment, which smashed all the windows of the post, 'which was most annoying of them'. As soon as the glass was swept up, and after a hitch with the projector, Wodehouse's cinema show began. One of the Belgian officers then gave an impromptu performance, singing and acting, adding 'much to the amusement of everyone present'. The evening ended at half past nine and Mairi packed for their week-long seaside holiday with mixed feelings: sad to be leaving Pervyse but also glad as she felt 'rather run down'. Before leaving, Harry Delacombe, also known as 'Grandfather', wrote three limericks to the hostesses:

After nursing for weeks at Pervyse
Midst shells and squalor and flyse
Knocker, Gleason and Feilding
To cleanliness yielding
Said, 'A bath at Dunkirk, if you plyse!'

At the Public Baths of the Town
In hot water they laid themselves down

And the dirt of Pervyse
Which encrusted their knyse
Soon coloured the water deep brown.

Though this anecdote may not quite plyse
Girls at home midst their comfort and eyse
Who can ever compare
With those heroines fair
Facing death night and day at Pervyse?

The next morning Elsie and Mairi started off, handing out cigarettes to soldiers on the roadside, making the journey to Wimereux 'in style' in a car loaned to them by Maitland. The town was a vast hospital, every house and school filled with the wounded, temporary wooden huts occupying the gaps in between, and canvas bell tents nestled in the sand dunes, buffeted by brisk sea breezes. They were delighted to see that Mrs Ward's villa stood on the clifftop 'all by itself' a mile outside Wimereux. It was 'too gorgeous for words, we revelled in the peace'. After lunch they had their first visitors, three Royal Army Medical Corps doctors from the Australian hospital, Captains Bertrand Edward Dawson, Mark C. Gardner and Walter Rupert Reynell, and the inevitable tea party.

Situated in the clifftop Golf Hotel, where on a clear day one could see the white cliffs of Dover, the Australian Voluntary Hospital had been started in the first week of the war by Mrs Ward's mother-in-law, Lady Dudley. It was funded by Australian subscriptions and a donation of £10,000 from Sir Robert Lucas-Tooth (the equivalent of £830,000 today), an old Etonian and brewer now living in England, and staffed largely by Australian doctors and nurses. The doctors were 'exceedingly kind'. Bertrand Dawson, who was physician extraordinary to King George V and the king's consulting physician in France throughout the war, was fifty years old, handsome and urbane. Walter Reynell was a thirty-year-old Australian doctor working at Guy's Hospital in London when war broke out, and Mark Gardner had qualified in Melbourne before coming to England.

The only drawback for Elsie and Mairi in staying with Mrs Ward was having to share a small double bed 'which rather disturbed our rest', otherwise the holiday 'passed like a dream'. They felt 'entirely spoiled', and for the first time in months got up late in the morning and 'lolled about' a lot. It was a free and easy time. Mrs Ward, two years younger than Elsie, was a 'dear' and ran an open house, and Reynell and Gardner visited a lot and were 'most attentive', taking Elsie and Mairi for long walks. Mrs Ward's mother-in-law, Lady Dudley, and Elsie had one thing in common: they had both been up with Gustav Hamel in 1914.

Before her marriage to Cyril Augustus Ward, fifth son of the Earl of Dudley, Irene Ward was Baroness Irene de Brienen. Her father was from the Netherlands and her mother was Canadian. She was married in 1904 and had three daughters. The Wards lived the high life of an earl's son and his wife: trips to the races, game hunting in Kenya, and he dabbled in politics. Elsie and Mairi became very fond of their new friend.

Lady May Ponsonby came to lunch at the villa, and Lady Hatfield 'buzzed up' to tea. Bertrand Dawson was a 'jewel', took great care of them and showed them 'all there was to see' at the hospital. They were having such a good time that they extended their holiday by a few days. The women played tennis in their breeches and rubber boots, and went to a concert at the barracks given by the orderlies to commemorate the first six months of the war. Starved of feminine company and impressed by the work Elsie and Mairi were doing, British officers twice invited them to their mess for lunch. Mairi says they 'gadded about like anything'. They were celebrities and after the ill feeling about their medals they enjoyed the fuss that was made of them.

Philip Wodehouse was twenty-nine and 'a scream of laughter' who loved dancing and dressing up. He was the second son of the Earl and Countess of Kimberley of Wymondham in Norfolk. While he was at Eton he joined the Cat Club, exhibiting his cat at a show in Westminster to raise money for the Children's Hospital in Great Ormond Street. After Trinity College, Cambridge, he stood as a Liberal in the general election of January 1910.

On 26 February Mairi was nineteen years old. Mrs Ward gave her a silver cigarette case, a symbolic gift that conferred adult status; Philip Wodehouse gave her a torch, and there were two silk handkerchiefs from Captain Gardner. Philip drove Elsie and Mairi to Boulogne, where Elsie bought a birthday cake for the party. Reynell and Gardner were invited and their pals Captain Paterson and Captain Rudolph de Trafford. Rudolph was the second son of a baronet, Humphrey de Trafford, and the same age as Mairi's brother, Uailean. His family lived at Trafford Hall, a stately pile in Manchester, and there was a London house in Park Lane.

Elsie placed a decoration on the cake in the shape of a baby, meant to be Cupid, holding a fork with the names of 'many men to rag me'. Captains Reynell, Gardner and de Trafford stayed to supper. The next day Mairi and Elsie dashed about the beach and behaved 'like mad things' until it was time for tea with Reynell at the hospital. Later they piled into Philip's car and gave a cinema show at the Soldiers' and Sailors' Home in Boulogne.

One day Elsie dressed up in Mrs Ward's London clothes and

pretended to be 'Lady Rathmore'. So convincing was she that when Philip arrived he was completely taken in, and spoke to her at length about her 'poor son who had been wounded'. Mrs Ward enjoyed the joke hugely but could not keep a straight face to introduce Reynell and Gardner when they arrived, and Mairi was sure she had given the game away, but Philip still did not realise who she was. Philip and Mairi left to give a cinema show at one of the hospitals in Wimereux and on the journey Philip was still concerned about Lady Rathmore. The next day, the first of March, Elsie and Mairi were due to return to Pervyse in the car Philip had promised them, but eventually had to rush around Boulogne to find another to take them back to the post. Perhaps feeling hurt by Elsie's practical joke, he 'suddenly got it into his head to say that he wanted his car'. It all sounds like a handful of bright young things having a long weekend party; the horror of the trenches and their fast-dilapidating home must have seemed an awfully long way away. Elsie, aged thirty, was the oldest by a year, and the people they mixed with were playful, clever and well off.

On 2 March Elsie and Mairi returned to the war. When they got back to 'dear Pervyse' they noticed that 'things had been running a bit loose': the place was not how Elsie liked it. They had been away for two weeks and had to adjust to the mood. Hector Munro came to supper, and their friend and ally Dr Van der Ghinst came too.

At dusk the next day one of the corps drivers brought bundles of letters – fan mail. While they were reading, Belgian soldiers clattered past, and a shell whistled into the middle of the men and 'all was turmoil'. Soldiers ran in all directions to get shelter. A mangled boy was brought in. Mairi had never seen anyone in such a mess. A shell had burst in front of him and his wounds were terrible, his legs smashed to pieces and both hands badly mutilated. Elsie and a Belgian doctor treated him while Mairi and Marianne Van der Ghinst dealt with a soldier with a piece of shell lodged in his arm, both soldiers 'as brave as brave can be'. When the bombardment ended nearly five hours later the men were driven to the hospital at Furnes. Mairi called their return to work a 'baptism of fire'.

There was more shelling the next day, 4 March, and three very bad cases were brought to them. While Elsie was dealing with a dreadful head wound, two more soldiers were carried in but they were beyond help: their 'brains were hanging out'. When they died one of the orderlies helped her carry the two bodies into the yard as room was needed for the arrival of more wounded. When things quietened down Mairi went out to the yard to search the clothing of the 'poor fellows' to find their identity tags so their relations could be told of their death. She discovered that one of them was nineteen – her age – and a volunteer who had only been in the trenches for two days. Searching through the pockets of his overcoat she made the gruesome discovery of someone else's brains, blown in there by the force of the explosion. Mairi called it 'a very curious incident'.

Dr Munro arrived in the afternoon, was 'very much agitated' about the gruelling time they were having and wanted to evacuate the post. Elsie would not hear of it, but urged Marianne Van der Ghinst to leave as she had promised her husband that she would quit in the event of 'great danger'. The Germans started shelling again and they tried to persuade the doctor's wife to go, but she refused to leave until the evening. It was decided that Munro would stay the night and that if there was another big bombardment they would have to leave Pervyse the following day. Shortly after this was agreed, Elsie sat down to write a letter to General Jacques explaining the situation when there was a massive explosion and the whole house seemed to rock. Their two orderlies and two chauffeurs staggered from the badly hit kitchen, where they had taken refuge. The house filled with suffocating fumes and they all stumbled round blinded by the smoke caused by the blast. Mairi's first thought, almost a mantra, was not to evacuate.

Munro ordered everyone to put their hats and coats on and make a dash for the nearby brasserie. Mairi yelled back, 'Don't be a fool; it's madness to go out there.' A chauffeur was ordered to go out and turn the car round, thereby risking his life, to prepare to take them down the road. Even at this stage Elsie and Mairi wanted to 'stick by the post until the last'. They jumped into the car and reached the brasserie. Mairi called it 'a ghastly business'. A Belgian doctor helping out at the post was following them down the road on foot when he was struck by a shell. Their friend Georges Gilson's boy François ran through the thick of the shelling and carried the doctor to the brasserie. The doctor only had superficial wounds but would die later of gas gangrene caused by bacteria from the soil-infected wounds, the cause of many deaths and amputations all over the Western Front.

At five o'clock, when there was a lull in the shelling, they dashed back to the post to pack their things up 'helter-skelter'. The kitchen had been destroyed and the 'poor dear bodies' of the two soldiers Mairi had helped carry into the yard were buried under debris, 'a pitiful sight and one I will never forget'. All the windows were smashed and the façade of the house was riddled with bullets; there was a big crater where the garage had been, and Mairi found the body of a soldier who had been sheltering there. Once their luggage was piled into an ambulance they left the place that had been their home for fifteen months and were driven to La Panne.

The seaside resort of La Panne was ten miles away, and home to the King and Queen of the Belgians and their entourage. Elsie, Mairi, Dr Van der Ghinst and the orderlies and chauffeurs arrived at the Hôtel du Kursaal 'the most miserable-looking objects you could find, covered in mud and blood – too horrible . . . and tired for words'. Mairi felt guilty and filled with 'disgust' at their 'shameful evacuation from Pervyse'. The experience was so vivid that she struggled to tell it, even though it was 'deeply engraved on my mind'. The corps stayed at the Hôtel du Kursaal for a week, during which time they reorganised their roles and received the vital paperwork that confirmed in writing that they were properly attached to the '3DA', the 3rd Division of the Belgian army. A note from headquarters spelled out that 'the presence of female personnel in medical units on the military front is no longer permitted' but because of the 'services rendered by Mesdames Knocker and Chisholm, an exception may be made in their favour'. This was crucial if they were to be allowed to carry on their work and not be bundled out of the way back to England. It was agreed that Helen and Marianne Van der Ghinst would be responsible for organising clothes for wounded soldiers – who often had to be cut out of their uniforms and had nothing else to wear – and that Elsie and Mairi would carry on with their nursing work at the front. Elsie also arranged for them to go to England to collect funds for the new post, wherever it would be, and while they waited for the passes and papers to come through they saw some young Belgian officers whom they had met at Pervyse. Elsie had taken the visitors' book with her and they signed their names, star-struck when they wrote their thanks: 'with the modesty of the courageous, you seem, dear lady, not to doubt the sublime nature of your mission. You scorn praise, you deserve admiration, but you ought to know how much you deserve them.' Another chap remembered Elsie: 'in the cold and the mud, calm and peaceful under the iron rain of German shells . . . surrounded by a few companions she bandaged the most ghastly of wounds, gathering in the last words of the dying'. These women of Pervyse were 'charming, pretty angels and perfect beauties'. When the weather permitted, Elsie would borrow a horse and gallop across the beach, while Mairi 'mooched about'. While they were in La Panne Georges Gilson was evacuated from Pervyse with typhoid fever and would not return until August.

On the morning of 13 March they boarded the SS *Princess Victoria* at Dunkerque and sailed to Dover, knowing that when they returned they would have to start all over again. They had made their minds up that they must control their own funds, have their own cars and run their own show. Ten days were spent in England, dashing about seeing 'all kinds of impossible people' begging for cars and money. Fortunately the eldest son of the Earl of Abingdon, Lord Norreys, gave them three cars, one of which was a sixteen-horsepower Wolseley ambulance presented to the St John Ambulance Brigade by the people of Sutton Coldfield. Elsie and Mairi also bought a two-seater 9.5-horsepower Standard. They made a flying fund-raising visit to Dorset and Wiltshire and had a 'squint' at their families. The *Bournemouth Daily Echo* asked readers to send money for a new dressing station to the Devonshire House Hotel in Bournemouth, where Mairi was giving personal interviews to anyone who wanted to help.

While they were in England Elsie told her audiences, large and small, the theory behind their practice of treating the wounded for shock by making them as comfortable as possible and letting them rest before sending them to the nearest hospital. It was a novel and sensible idea that people could understand,

and soon the collecting plates started to rattle with cash. Elsie insisted, 'The effects of shock are worse in many cases than the wounds.' She told of a remarkable case of a soldier who had been wounded in the lung and was grey with the cold, unconscious and 'apparently lifeless' when he was brought to her and Mairi. Elsie put him in front of their stove, wrapped him in hot blankets, tucked hot-water bottles all round him and 'rubbed his extremities to get him warm'. After two hours he was 'roused up' and asked for a drink, and was convalescing in England by the time Elsie told his story. Their whirlwind visit raised £200 cash (now £15,000) and pledges of more.

The second diary of the three Mairi kept during the war ends on 24 March; she leaves us with a breathless sentence about dashing up to London and meeting many 'interesting' people – perhaps they were more generous that the 'impossible' ones they had had to beg for cars and money. She did not start another until 6 October, when she opened a black notebook, took up the narrative again and started by summarising the key events of the six months that had elapsed. During that time 'so many things have occurred, and there has been so much to do that writing has been quite put to one side'. She tells her diary that she does not intend to 'write up all our experiences, they have been so many and in many ways so momentous'. We can find clues to Elsie and Mairi's lives during the spring and summer of 1915 in the brittle newspaper cuttings of their scrapbooks, in Elsie's visitors' book and other people's memoirs, in Elsie's pacey autobiography published in 1964 and in the taped interviews they gave in the 1970s.

When news of Elsie and Mairi's medals reached May Sinclair she was moved to write a poem, 'Ave!', dedicating it to them 'with love'. Still overwrought by her hasty departure from the war, she wrote with raw feelings of personal inadequacy and admiration.

> I dare not call you comrades,
> You,
> Who did only what I dreamed.
> I dare raise my voice to speak to you,
> Calling you by your names,
> As you pass for ever in the glory and the beauty of my dreams.
> Though you have taken my dream,
> And dressed yourselves in its beauty and glory,
> I think you will pass me by with your face averted.
> I am afraid of you,
> For I have done no more than dream . . .

Back in Belgium by 26 March 1915, Elsie and Mairi were buoyed up by their productive trip to England, returning with cash and cars for their exclusive use. They moved into a tiny cottage, grandly named Villa Espagnole, on the other side of Pervyse, not far from their old home. Opposite stood a shrine to the Holy Virgin. The place had been squatted and was filthy. Mairi mopped and scrubbed to get the place ready for the arrival of wounded soldiers, and Elsie drove to La Panne to collect their belongings. Mairi was sickened by the smell of death and broken drains that clung to the house and felt afraid to be there on her own. The cellar was full of stinking water, and no matter how much coal and wood she put on the fire the place stayed ice cold. Elsie and Mairi bedded down on straw in sleeping bags, their new driver nearby, but no one slept that night. Unwilling to spend another night in a place all three of them were convinced was haunted, they left early the next morning, telling the Belgian military authorities the place was 'unsuitable and insanitary'.

Driving round the villages close to the front, Elsie and Mairi could find no building that could be used as a first-aid post; everything was too dilapidated. After meetings with the 3rd Division it was decided the women needed a portable hospital, a wooden shed that could be dismantled if necessary, so they could travel to the wounded rather than have them carried in on stretchers or over comrades' shoulders like sacks of potatoes. In the first week of April Mairi wrote to the editor of the *Nairnshire Telegraph*, appealing for contributions towards the five-bed shed. He admired her 'unique work' and felt sure that her many friends in Nairn and elsewhere would want to help. Readers learned the gravity of their financial predicament. At pains to point out that they were still part of Hector Munro's corps, Mairi explained that they had been seconded to the 3rd Division of the Belgian Army and for that they needed their own funds. They were 'most awfully keen on this work, and would not have it stop for worlds'. If they did not get help 'we shall have to "close down"'. So far they had funded their work themselves, but their 'personal funds cannot last for ever and I regret to say that that we are both "broke to the world!"' Money could be sent to the newspaper office or to Mairi's mother at the Devonshire House Hotel in Bournemouth; cheques and postal orders were to be made payable to the 'Pervyse Poste Account'.

A week later the *Nairnshire Telegraph* printed the amounts the people of Nairn had donated, including Mairi's uncle Admiral Robert Grant Fraser, who lived locally. Tradespark Sunday School and Friends, the hairdressers and the booksellers had each collected more than twenty pounds (£1,500 today). Elsie and Mairi were also given a great deal of help by a Harrods representative, Mr Costa, who was building hospitals in La Panne.

The hut, which looked like a cowboy's log cabin, was set up in a field near Steenkerke on 11 April, not far from Pervyse, apparently beyond the range of German artillery. They had two fairly large rooms: one with five beds for the wounded, the other for Elsie and Mairi and Helen Gleason, who had joined them. There were two 'wee cubicles', one for François, the new orderly on loan from the Belgian army, the other for stores and dressings. Parked snugly against the door to the hut was a mobile kitchen, where they cooked for the wounded and made soup and hot chocolate for the men in the trenches. But this cosy camp only lasted for three days until 14 April. As Mairi was doing the accounts and Elsie was massaging one of her patients, a shell landed with a 'thunderous crash' close by. The ground shook like an earthquake. They evacuated the men to a farmer's shed near by and Elsie ran into the road and flagged down an army motorcyclist and told him to take her to Steenkerke to get their new Wolseley ambulance. They evacuated the wounded to the nearest hospital; the next day they returned to patch up the hut.

By the end of April they had run out of money and Mairi had to make another urgent appeal for funds, telling Nairnshire newspaper readers some of the difficulties they faced. The hut had cost more than they had expected, and they did not feel they could be spared from their work to come to England and Scotland to raise the money in person. She explained that the hut had not proved the best accommodation given their circumstances. While its virtue was its prefabrication, making it possible to put up and take down wherever it was needed, it was too flimsy to use close to the kind of artillery fire they were experiencing. Everything had been 'in splendid order' but their hut proved no protection against German shells. Mairi and Elsie decided to stay in Belgium to look after their patients and 'trust to the infinite kindness of our friends at home . . . We must have more money, and we badly want another car.'

On 30 May Elsie and Mairi's bravery was mentioned in the Belgian army's dispatches. Five days earlier they had taken their driver, Paul, and headed east to Oostkerke to see if there were any wounded who needed their help. As they approached the village it was being shelled. It was a bright sunny day and on that flat-as-a-pancake landscape they must have been visible to the 'Boches', as Mairi called them. Elsie, who was driving, realised how conspicuous they were and drove towards the nearest farm buildings for shelter. An army captain emerged, telling them where a wounded soldier was hiding in a dugout. Paul took the wheel and they raced back into the village, found the man and bundled him into the car. As they 'tore out' of Oostkerke, 'the shells came crashing in', and one burst just behind the car, causing it to swerve violently. The captain who had spoken to them sent a report of their 'extraordinary bravery' to his headquarters. Elsie and Mairi were later told by a Belgian artillery observer close to the German line that the Germans had had the women in their sights, and 'had made a deliberate mark' of them.

It soon became clear that the hut would have to be moved closer to Steenkerke where it was safer, and Mr Costa was called on again to supervise the move. A dugout was built next to the hut to which they could quickly evacuate patients if they were shelled again. Once they were settled at Steenkerke the situation was helped by the Belgian authorities supplying them with rations for the wounded, but these were not enough for Elsie, who wanted to 'feed them up', and they needed money for coal, laundry and food for themselves, their orderlies and drivers. Elsie made several successful appeals for cigarettes, chocolate, puzzles, cards and French books for the soldiers. A benefactor arranged for Harrods to send them a hamper of food every week to Dunkerque, and a Douglas motorcycle, which they knew well from their pre-war lives, had also been donated. At last the weather improved, and this boosted morale. There are snapshots of Elsie and Mairi sitting in deckchairs outside the hut on sunny days, chatting to off-duty British officers, the Red Cross flag fluttering overhead in the breeze. Everyone looks relaxed; they could be on a camping holiday.

In June Elsie had to go back to England for money, and Mairi ran the hut at Steenkerke on her own. One of their supporters, journalist Raymond Blathwayt, wrote a begging letter on their behalf to readers of the *Daily Telegraph*. Theirs was a story of devotion, courage and self-sacrifice, and he warned that their 'gallant work' was 'in danger of extinction for want of funds'. Mrs Knocker needed a thousand pounds to be able to continue their work for the next two years, and he hoped readers would help the women 'to their utmost power'. No one could conceive 'the horror and the tragedy in which they had been enveloped' for the past ten months, he insisted.

On 22 June Elsie and Miss S. Carey, who had collected money for the hospital at Furnes and was the founder of the Belgian Soldiers' Fund, made a joint appeal for money at a gathering hosted by Mrs Neville Chamberlain, whose husband became lord mayor of Birmingham in November. Miss Carey was in the middle of a fund-raising tour to buy sterilising equipment to provide clean water for Belgian soldiers and civilians, warning they were being driven to drink stagnant water that was some-times contaminated with 'unutterable horrors'. Elsie told the audience that water supplies in Pervyse were so bad – their source had been a stream that ran through the local cemetery, now a mass grave – that water had to be brought in barrels from England to Dunkerque and then boiled. Often it was a choice between having a drink or a wash. Elsie may not have divulged to her audience of mostly ladies that when the fighting was at its fiercest, she and Mairi and Helen Gleason had slept in their clothes and not bathed for three weeks, and that Helen had had to cut Mairi out of her vest, dampening it first to stop the skin coming away.

Mairi felt tired and glum while her chum Elsie was away; she had five wounded men to care for and was exhausted speaking French all the time. She missed 'the companionship of another woman; I long to see her back again – she is always so cheerful and gay, that now the place feels like a tomb'. To add to her gloom, a couple of days before Elsie returned Mairi received the sad news that her cousin Jim Trinder, who had been fighting with the Northumberland Fusiliers, had been killed in action on 16 June at the tiny hamlet of Hooge, two miles from Ypres. Before the war the Trinders and the Gooden-Chisholms had attempted some tentative match-making between Mairi and Jim, but she had not been keen.

Elsie's trip was a success. She brought back some money and a seventy-five-horsepower Mercedes. She had launched a new scheme she hoped would motivate people to send cigarettes and tobacco for the soldiers: donors would be sent souvenirs such as rings, hearts and crucifixes made by men in the trenches out of the aluminium heads and copper fuses of shells. However, she told their friend at Wimereux, Mrs Ward, that she had only collected a fraction of what was needed as there were many other good causes asking for money. So Irene Ward wrote to the *New York Tribune* about Elsie and Mairi's work 'on the Belgian Firing Line', explaining that they were the only women allowed by the British, French and Belgian authorities to work near the front line. It was 'tragic to think that two women, who hold such unique positions, should have to give up their work and all the good they have done through lack of funds'. She was sure that the Americans, who had already been so generous, would want to help such hard-working and gallant women, and felt 'miserable to think of these two women struggling so hard'.

The women had the odd half-day off, sometimes visiting Helen Gleason at St Idesbald, near the coast at Furnes, and Georgie Fyfe and Sarah Macnaughtan, who were working with Belgian refugees in La Panne. One day that summer Lieutenant Ivor Mackenzie Bellairs, of the Royal Naval Air Service seaplane base at Dunkerque, collected them at Steenkerke and drove them to lunch with Major Charles Edward Henry Rathborne, a twenty-nine-year-old bachelor from Dublin who was a fluent German speaker. In February, in a heavy snowstorm, the Irishman had taken part in an air raid on the German-held Belgian coastline, in an attempt to stop the Germans building submarine bases. After lunch Bellairs took Elsie and Mairi along the coast in a motorboat, where they watched Rathborne land his seaplane on the water. The sea air 'came like a vivifying blast', and Mairi called it a 'topping day'.

At the beginning of July Elsie drove to Pervyse, three miles from Steenkerke, and felt nostalgic for the old days. When she heard how 'terribly their poste was missed' she started to plan their return. It seemed that Pervyse was a magnet for Elsie and Mairi's hearts, towards which they could not help but gravitate. Their homesickness for a ruin reveals what a special place it was for them. Elsie found a place opposite the brasserie from where they had been evacuated a few months earlier that looked promising. The outer walls were standing but the roof and most of the interior walls had gone. There was one room intact and the cellar was sound. After a great deal of coaxing of the authorities and stubbornness on Elsie's part, they were allowed to move into their new home.

Their Navy friends at Nieuport loved pranks. Behind the post they built Elsie and Mairi a gigantic see-saw and it was a regular ritual to ask visiting staff officers, who spent a lot of time at headquarters and were rarely shot at, to get on it.

> They willingly agreed, not realizing that the plank was so long that the man who was off the ground was fully exposed to rifle-fire from the German trenches. The Germans knew all about this game and would let fly a few shots, well wide, but near enough to put the wind up some of those important visitors. It was fun to watch this comical game, and to see and hear the various expressions that ensued.

Their old friends the *Génies* came round at night to stabilise the building as soon as their day-time duties were finished. Meanwhile there were swarms of flies, 'too horrible for words', attracted to the decomposing bodies around about. The only way they could get rid of them was to hang up arsenic-coated flypapers. The *Génies* had not quite finished the job when they were ordered further up the line, and Elsie and Mairi sand-bagged the building themselves as soon as their work at Steenkerke was finished. Collecting and treating the wounded by day and preparing the new post at Pervyse at night wore them down, especially Elsie, who became overwrought.

She had been having trouble with their driver Paul, who had been 'getting on her nerves' for weeks, constantly challenging her authority. One day Elsie and Mairi went in two cars to collect supplies at Dunkerque. Elsie's Mercedes stopped, and was 'boiling its head off' because there was no water in the radiator. It was Paul's job to see to the vehicles, and she was furious at his carelessness. Mairi got some more from a nearby canal, and siphoned off some water from her vehicle and they continued their journey. When they got back to Steenkerke Elsie boiled over like the radiator, 'blazing up to a white heat' and 'went for Paul and as usual he answered back'. Mairi did not follow Elsie into the hut, but stayed outside to explain to Paul what was wrong with the Mercedes.

Elsie took this badly. Mairi realised later that perhaps she should have been more supportive and followed Elsie into the hut, called herself a 'bally ass' for not doing so. Elsie stormed out and said 'many nasty things to me and ordered me to come in at once'. Mairi boldly accused Elsie of losing her temper and making an unnecessary scene, and then jumped on her motorbike and went to St Idesbald to tell Helen Gleason what had happened and ask her what to do. Arthur Gleason was also there and advised Mairi to go back to the hut, hoping that Elsie might be feeling better. When Mairi returned Elsie was lying outside on a deckchair 'in a state of exhaustion'. Mairi went over to speak to her. As soon as Elsie saw her she started screaming and tearing at her hair so Mairi turned round and started the engine of one of the cars to go to Helen to help sort things out. Elsie forbade Mairi from leaving, and another 'awful scene' followed. After a while Mairi and François, one of the orderlies, were able to get Elsie to bed, and eventually she quietened down, even shaking with cold though it was a summer's day. Elsie agreed to see Helen, so Mairi dashed off and 'raked her out of bed'. Helen spent the night with Elsie, in Mairi's bed.

The next morning Elsie looked 'ghastly ill and in a rather apathetic mood'. On the verge of a breakdown Elsie was obsessed with the idea of getting some civilian clothes to wear, so the three of them went to Dunkerque to do some shopping. Elsie was clearly suffering from exhaustion and a good night's sleep had helped her forget her 'fearful dislike' of Mairi. Elsie and Mairi spent the weekend at La Panne, and were visited by a Belgian officer they had recently nursed for two weeks after a bad fall from his horse. But it was clear that Elsie needed a break, and because their doctor refused to allow her to travel alone, Mairi also had an unexpected trip to England.

On 20 August they arrived at the Devonshire House Hotel in Bournemouth, where Mairi's mother and sister Lucy were staying. Lewis and Emily Upcott brought Kenneth to see his mother for a few days. Elsie and Mairi stayed for more than a week and then returned to London for a few days at the Great Western Hotel at Paddington Station. Somebody tipped off the *Tatler* that they were in the country, and the magazine carried photographs of them in their big coats and boots, proudly wearing their medals and with 3DA badges on their woollen hats. When interviewed by golfer Miss Eleanor E. Helme for the *Ladies' Pictorial*, Elsie was keen to point out that she was only half of the story and praised her partner Miss Chisholm: 'She is only nineteen; she hadn't even been trained for a nurse; but she is just the noblest, pluckiest girl on the earth! I can't say enough about her.' Time away from the stress of nursing the wounded and working on the new post seems to have given Elsie the time and space to see what a grand job Mairi was doing.

The *Bournemouth Daily Echo*'s readers were told about the constant danger Elsie and Mairi faced, their 'primitive life' and their medals from King Albert, as a preamble to an appeal for money to buy a stretcher on wheels. Every penny raised so far, they were assured, had been spent on 'the gallant little Belgian soldier – whom we have learned to love and respect for his splendid pluck and courage'. Money was also always needed for petrol, spare parts for vehicles, repairs, camp beds, blankets, hot-water bottles, coal, food and laundry.

While Elsie and Mairi were in London they saw a friend, the famous actress Eva Moore, who asked 'Mrs Gossip' of the *Daily Mirror* to write about their work in the hope that readers would send cigarettes and money to Eva Moore's home in Chelsea. Mairi had been Eva's dispatch rider when the actress had worked as a volunteer for the Women's Emergency Corps during the day and performed at the Vaudeville Theatre at night. She and her actor-manager husband Henry V. Esmond were one of the most successful couples on the stage. Two of Eva's sisters, Jessie and Decima, were also actresses, and all three had been high-profile campaigners for the vote before the war.

On 10 September they returned to the new post in their beloved Pervyse and were given a rousing welcome by the soldiers. Mr Costa and a Mr Colby had arranged for the heavy building work and sandbagging to be finished while they were away; the walls had been coated with concrete and there was a new front door made of steel and painted with a red cross. There was still plenty to do when they got back, whitewashing the walls and turning a reinforced wreck into a miniature hospital. Mairi called it 'not such a bad little hole considering all things'. They continued to use the hut at Steenkerke as an evacuation station. There was also news that another Trinder cousin, John, a captain with the 18th Battalion London Regiment (London Irish Rifles) had been wounded at the Battle of Loos on 15 September and awarded the Military Cross.

Mairi's visit to England and the events leading up to it left her feeling exhausted and relieved to get back to normality. She had had 'her hands full' with Elsie and poured her heart out to her aunt in a letter:

Mrs Knocker had been very seriously ill out here, and naturally all the responsibility fell on me . . . we were in the midst of constructing our dug-out [the post] and had twelve men working on it, so that I had to see to that as well. It was a terrible strain – the doctor ordered me to look after her as she did not want me to leave her. I know she would have hated being with strangers,

and I should have felt miserable if she had gone off by herself . . .
We know each other so well now, that we understand each other's
wishes . . . I am glad it is all over, it was an awful time . . . Mrs
Knocker is ever so much better.

During the autumn of 1915 Elsie and Mairi continued treating
the wounded and soldiers suffering from cuts and boils and
other ailments, and making soup and hot chocolate for the men
in the trenches. Sometimes they were taken out to lunch by
Colonel Joostens of the 1st Lancers.

Back in England Eva Moore wrote to editors of dozens of
newspapers and magazines, including the *Ladies' Pictorial*, the
Gentlewoman, the *Post*, the *Exeter and Devon Gazette* and the
Evening Dispatch; she gave interviews to reporters, and would
come out in front of the curtain at the end of her performances
in Birmingham, Newcastle, Glasgow and Edinburgh, and tell
the audience about the 'bitter cold and privations' her friends
would face in the coming months. She appealed directly to the
women of England and Scotland to contribute towards the four
hundred pounds 'the Heroines of Pervyse' needed to 'get through
the winter'. Moore confided that Elsie had written to her telling
how 'terribly cold' they were, especially when they had to rush
their patients out of the hut at Steenkerke and into the draughty
dugout, which had no windows. Money was needed for comforts,
such as tobacco, cigarettes and chocolate, and also warm clothing
for the men, 'who are so wretchedly equipped'. Many soldiers
arrived wet through after falling into the inundations while out
on patrol, and until Elsie and Mairi could dry their uniforms
in their tiny oven the men only had blankets to keep them warm.
A month before Christmas Elsie wrote again to Eva Moore,
appealing for a thousand knitted balaclavas and a thousand grey
or khaki mufflers, for the men in the trenches who were 'suffering
very much in their ears'.

Mairi may have heard from her mother that her brother Uailean had resigned from the Trinidad Constabulary in the middle of October and enlisted as a second lieutenant with the British West India Regiment and was on his way to England to do his training at Seaford in Sussex. At the same time, unknown to Elsie, her ex-husband Leslie Duke Knocker was serving in the Army Pay Corps at Rouen in France.

Flying around in the skies over Pervyse that autumn was Baron Harold de T'Serclaes. Dashing, handsome, posh with a pedigree and, most important of all, Belgian and brave, he had everything Elsie could want. It is hard to pin down when in 1915 Harry dropped into Elsie's life, but as soon as he is mentioned in Mairi's diary she adds the words 'enter romance'. Harold Job Antoine Hubert Jean de T'Serclaes de Rattandael was born in Antwerp on 5 January 1889, so was five years younger than Elsie. In 1909 he joined the 1st Regiment of the Guides, and within two years he had made the rank of *maréchal-des-lois*. Harry left the army early in 1914, but with the German invasion looming, rejoined his old regiment on 31 July.

Harry was fighting in the Yser area prior to the opening of the sluice gates at Nieuport at the end of October 1914. Trench life did not suit him and in March 1915 he joined the more glamorous Belgian Military Aviation, near Furnes, and trained to be an observer at St Idesbald. His first flight, on 15 April, was with Sergeant Willy de Roy, who crashed the plane on landing, but they escaped unhurt. Many of the sorties Harry flew were aerial reconnaisances to plot German positions and monitor their artillery and troop movements. In September he had his first taste of combat flying, firing at an enemy aircraft, and later he and Willy de Roy forced a German seaplane to land.

By the time Harry met Elsie, he too was a Chevalier de l'Ordre de Léopold, decorated in September 1914 for showing 'very great courage and great audacity during expeditions in an armoured car with which he had some bloody encounters with the enemy'. In December he was given a knighthood for his 'composure and courage during the defence of a trench attacked by a superior adversary'.

In 1916, after Elsie and Mairi's life in Pervyse had been turned into a book by Geraldine Mitton, *The Cellar-House of Pervyse: A Tale of Uncommon Things From The Journals and Letters of The Baroness T'Serclaes and Mairi Chisholm*, the moment when Harry met Elsie would be described breathlessly. One morning Elsie was alone in the cellar, there was a knock at the door and someone came slowly down the stairs. As her eyes scanned him from the bottom up, from his shining boots up to his crimson breeches, his green tunic and peaked cap, Elsie knew they had not met before. He was taller than the cellar, and could not stand up straight. She felt shy, 'suddenly aware that she was in soiled clothing, sitting in a heap of straw in a most unbecoming way'. There was something about him that was 'very remarkable' and it made her want to giggle, not realising 'that with him had entered her Fate!'

He saluted her, handed her a message from Colonel Joostens and turned to leave, and as he left 'he smiled a smile that lit up his face and indeed the whole cellar'. This 'seemed to linger and irradiate everything in a remarkable way,' gushed Miss Mitton. Curiously, Elsie did not tell Mairi what had happened, until one day they passed him on his way to the trenches, when he smiled again and saluted. Mairi asked who he was and Elsie blushed as she explained what had happened. A week later Harry turned up with a box of marrons glacés for Elsie, supposedly from the colonel.

Miss Mitton wrote that Harry was fighting in the trenches,

when in fact he would have been airborne in 1915; perhaps she thought it sounded more romantic, or was unclear about the details and filled in the gaps as best she could, but whether he was on the ground or in the air, his smile made Elsie feel 'secure'. They did not see much of him but, knowing he was in the vicinity, 'Pervyse seemed in a miraculous way to have become a safe and singularly happy place.' When he was transferred a few weeks later, leaving without saying goodbye, it seemed as if 'Pervyse had been laid bare, and the Germans might sweep in at any moment!'

One day Elsie set off on her motorbike for the headquarters of the 3DA to give someone a ticking-off, and had to stop to tweak the engine. A car 'careering along from the opposite direction' pulled up beside her and 'with a start which thrilled right through her' she saw Harry. He flashed her one of those smiles, but they did not speak. She got back on her motorbike and 'involuntarily looked back' as his car drove off. Harry turned round at the same time, and all of Elsie's irritation with Belgian army bureaucracy and 'nerves' at seeing him again disappeared. She 'noticed how the larks were singing in the battered fields around' and decided to abandon her visit to headquarters, no longer in the mood to 'bully them' or anyone else that day, and rode back to Pervyse 'in a state of serene bliss'.

One day Lieutenant Delfosse invited Elsie and Mairi to tea at the aviation camp at Coxyde. They were formally introduced to Harry, who came from one of Belgium's oldest families. They had only spoken a few words to each other but love soon 'blossomed'. Mairi and Elsie gave two dinner parties at the Villa Chrysanthemum at La Panne, where they had spent two nights in the summer because of Elsie's collapse, and invited all the people who 'had been kind' to them. It is likely that Harry's crimson breeches made an appearance. He became a frequent visitor to Pervyse when the weather was too bad for flying; his 'wonderful smile irradiated the most dismal days'. On 8 November Harry came on his motorbike to ask Elsie to marry him, and she agreed. At first they decided to wait until after the war, but as 'the days went on and love grew apace' they found it hard to be engaged 'in anything like a satisfactory manner and amid such extreme publicity' and brought the day forward. Like many couples when every day could have been their last, it made sense for them to get married as soon as they could, and the wedding was planned for 19 January 1916.

Mairi was very happy for Elsie but also sad to be losing the pal she had spent almost every minute of every day of the past fifteen months with, often sharing a bed and a bath: 'sometimes when there isn't much water we get in to the tub together and share what water there is . . . we have to rough it but it does one a lot of good, especially one's character. I shall miss Mrs Knocker. She has been such a very good friend to me. However I feel sure she is going to be awfully happy, so that is all that counts.' Mairi told her aunt Lucy that Elsie and Harry were 'devoted to each other and it's just the sweetest purest love I've been allowed to see – it does me good to see them together, because it makes one feel that life is worth living where such happiness exists'. The baron was charming and 'ever so good looking' and an 'excellent match for dear little Gypsy', and Mairi promised to take them to meet her aunt.

Early in December, John Redmond, an Irish Nationalist member of parliament, visited Elsie and Mairi at Pervyse and made special mention of Miss Chisholm in a vivid account of his tour of the Western Front. The *Bournemouth Daily Echo* picked up the story from the big boys in Fleet Street, puffed up with pride that a local girl was a heroine of the war and 'the central figure in some of its most stirring romances'. The name by which they came to be known, the 'Heroines of Pervyse', dates from the winter of 1915.

When Elsie and Harry announced the date of the wedding it was decided that when they were married she would live at La Panne and direct the work at Pervyse from there. So Mairi wrote to ask her father if he would come and help her run the post. It was not going to be easy for him to join a foreign army, which, because of his daughter's attachment to the 3DA, was what he would be doing, and it proved a bureaucratic nightmare. Elsie waded in and took the matter up with Major du Roy, equerry-in-chief to King Albert of the Belgians. That made no difference, and it was thought that Elsie would have to stay at Pervyse after she was married until the winter was over, and then they would try again to get the necessary paperwork for Mairi's father. When Dot Feilding heard about this she telephoned Mairi on 18 December to invite her to lunch and offered to ask Robert de Broqueville's father, the Baron de Broqueville, Belgian minister of war, to pull some strings. All the unpleasantness over the medal business had been forgotten.

In the weeks leading up to Christmas Mairi's aunt Lucy was kept busy sending out boxes of Nestlé's Café au Lait for the men in the trenches and comfort boxes bulging with 'gorgeous woollies . . . such lovely fat scarves and socks and mittens that the men *can* wear, instead of a thing one wouldn't give to one's worst enemy!' Mairi looked forward 'tremendously' to the hamper her aunt was preparing; the monotony of their diet was getting on her nerves but helping keep her waistline trim: 'very often we are so tired of seeing the same tasteless things that we just don't eat at all . . . but we are both much thinner now'.

There is an intriguing reference in the same letter to her family having made tentative plans for Mairi to marry her cousin Jim Trinder, who had been killed in June. Much older than her –

he was sixteen when she was born – before the war he had been made a partner in the family firm of solicitors, Trinder, Capron and Company, in the City of London. 'I am afraid poor Jim and I weren't over-suited. I don't think that a marriage between us would have ever been successful . . . it seems to me that I should always be very difficult. I have knocked about such a lot . . . I don't think I am quite like the ordinary girl of 19. I have seen too much of life.' All the talk of wedding plans, and the recent engagement of her brother Uailean to Claire Lange, was making Mairi introspective about her own future. She felt it was 'risky' to marry a foreigner: 'I am too Scotch and stolid to appeal to the foreign temperament.'

Mairi's diary does not record the febrile atmosphere that smothered and almost suffocated them in the weeks leading up to Elsie's marriage, but a frank letter to her aunt gives an account of the 'Dirty Work' that was going on behind the scenes. In Belgium an officer's wife was not allowed to be with her husband at the front, and Mairi wondered if this rule was being used by the 'snake', an unnamed, possibly English man or woman, as a way of levering Elsie and Mairi out of Belgium.

> The 'snake' (you'll know who I mean) has again interfered and for the present broken up our plans. Everything was arranged for Dad to come out – when the said snake said poisonous things to the officials and stopped everything. 'They' are trying to force our hands and push us out of Belgium through Gypsy's marriage . . . but she wants special permission to remain with her husband and direct the work and have Dad out to join me. If Dad can't come out, either Gypsy must continue up here, or if she gives up the work then she has no excuse for staying in Belgium. By refusing permission for Dad they tie Gypsy's hands behind her back – either she must postpone her marriage and go on working here – or else marry and go to England. Natu-

rally at such a time she is keen to become the Baron's wife, but at the same time she *hates* giving up the work . . .

It is such a pity that these minor jealousies should crop up, or spoil one's work . . . as you know throughout this year we have been viciously attacked by our enemies out here, and they have done everything they can to push us out of Belgium.

Elsie went back to England for three days at Christmas while Mairi held the fort at Pervyse. Harry spent Christmas Day with Mairi, their friend Robert de Wilde and the Belgian army doctor who worked at the brasserie across the street. It was quiet and frugal as none of the Christmas parcels had arrived from England. Elsie woke up to a frosty Christmas morning in Marlborough, having arrived late the night before. Kenneth 'dashed wildly' into her bedroom and later in the day she tramped through the frosted country lanes with her son and the dogs; presumably she told Kenneth about his new daddy, and the Upcotts about their future son-in-law and the imminent wedding. The next day Elsie left for Belgium and her beloved Harry. As she waited for the train to Dover she was struck by several emotions: relief at being away from the 'chaos and medley of sound beyond the barriers, and touched by the sight of couples strolling to and fro sometimes in silence and sometimes with uncontrolled laughter – sometimes with tears wetting quivering cheeks'. She noticed a young woman clinging to her husband's arm, 'gazing fixedly at the high white-faced clock, watching, waiting, fascinated as the big black minute hand jerks forward . . . within her brain is the overflowing desire to hold back that menacing hand'.

Elsie was back in Pervyse a few days before the new year. She was to be married; she had found a new father for her son, and they were still in the thick of a war that had made no progress since she returned from her last Christmas trip. This would be her second new year in Pervyse and life looked very agreeable.

V

The Madonnas of Pervyse

The year 1916 started with a frenzy of planning and a blizzard of paper, rubber-stamping and the impatient stamping of Elsie's boots. It took all of the days leading up to the wedding to get the papers and passes in place and there were moments of hysteria when it seemed that nothing would be ready. Elsie had gone to war to do her bit but also to find a new man and a father for Kenneth. Strings were pulled, and when the day came it was like any other wedding day – excitement and last-minute nerves – but there was a war going on.

On the first day of the year Mairi remembered 'how glibly we talked of an advance' and that they should have reached Brussels months ago, but although they were all a year older, 'we are still in exactly the same position as we were last year'. In the morning Elsie sent her to collect some stores and post from Dunkerque and she called in to see Dot and Dr Jellett but was disappointed to hear that the Baron de Broqueville had not been able to get permission from the Belgian military for her father to help at the post. The weather was miserable, lashing rain and a very high wind, and she had the sniffles. When Mairi got back to Pervyse Harry was there having lunch with 'Winkles', Mairi's latest pet name for Elsie.

Elsie and Jelly were now at loggerheads, and on 2 January Elsie went to see Prince Alexander of Teck, in charge of the British mission at La Panne. Teck explained that Elsie and Mairi were still members of the corps and that Dr Jellett had seniority, which meant that 'there was nothing to do but sit and grin and bear all [Jelly's] cheek and rudeness'. Elsie was incensed to learn that she and Mairi were not allowed to leave Pervyse, even to pick up stores, without writing and telling Jelly where they were going. Having turned in for the night they were woken by Dot and a new friend, Commander Halahan, who was in charge of the naval siege guns at Nieuport, bringing the good news that Mairi's father could come to work at the post. Elsie, Mairi and Dot were friends again and enjoyed 'several very good giggles together'. Then talk turned to Arthur Gleason's 'impossible book'.

Young Hilda at the Wars came out in the summer of 1915 in New York and was already in its second edition by September. May Sinclair had mentioned it 'vaguely' to them but it was not until Christmas 1915 that Mairi had a copy in her hands. It was a bombshell, as incendiary as anything the Boche had lobbed at them. So incensed was Elsie that she wrote to her lawyer in England.

The Gleasons had been good friends from the very beginning of the war: Helen had travelled with Elsie and Mairi and the rest of the Munro corps to Belgium in 1914 and Arthur became a chum too. They enjoyed Helen's piano playing and had all stood around singing the night away many times. All that was undone when the book, with a female silhouette in white within a garlanded frame on the cover, was opened and the contents devoured. The first thing they saw was a photograph of 'Hilda' – Helen – looking pensive in her leather trench coat, big boots, muffler and woollen hat proudly wearing her *Ordre de Léopold* medal. The dedication was to 'Chevalier Helen of Pervyse'. It was virtually all about Helen while her comrades in the corps were thinly veiled: 'Mrs Bracher' was Elsie, Mairi was 'Scotch' and Hector Munro became 'Dr McDonnell'.

Mairi could not understand 'what he can possibly have been thinking when he wrote it'. During the first week of January her diary quickly becomes angrier, as she rereads it, calling it 'the most astounding bit of brazen cheek' and full of 'rotten lies'. It was a 'gross betrayal' of their friendship. Mairi was dismayed that Helen had allowed Arthur to publish a book which credited his wife with opening the cellar post at Pervyse and being in charge of it, for saying that Helen was the bravest of all the women of the corps and insinuating that Elsie and Mairi had not deserved their medals. 'Old wounds' were opened and recriminations flew around like shrapnel. Mairi felt that she had been bamboozled by the Gleasons. She had written to Aunt Lucy less than a year ago, 'You would, I think, like her immensely – also her husband . . . they are very sweet and very well read which is a very great pleasure as one can sometimes get away from the war.'

Mairi tells her diary she does not want to go into detail about the last night they all spent at Pervyse, before they were evacuated from the cellar for the first time to 'the sick and sorry house', but she writes that Helen made a 'great nuisance of herself' when she nearly fainted at the sight of a badly wounded boy. Mairi had to look after Helen and leave Elsie to deal with the boy on her own. Nor could Helen speak any French or drive, and Mairi could not remember ever seeing her dress a wound. Mairi reduces Helen's role at Pervyse to that of a 'charming companion'. Her final swipe was about Helen's concern for her looks rather than the task in hand: Helen refused to cut her hair, 'swearing that she wouldn't ruin her appearance for anybody'.

A sample of *Young Hilda at the Wars* shows why Elsie and Mairi were so cross.

One morning the Doctor entered the cellar, with a troubled look on his face. 'I am forced to ask you to do something,' he began, 'and yet I hardly have the heart to tell you.'

'What can the man be after,' queried Hilda, 'will you be wanting to borrow my hair brush to curry the cavalry with?'

'Worse than that,' responded he; 'I must ask you to cut off your beautiful hair.'

'My hair,' gasped Hilda, darting her hand to her head, and giving the locks an unconscious pat.

'Your hair,' replied the Doctor. 'It breaks my heart to make you do it, but there's so much disease floating around in the air these days, that it is too great a risk for you to live with sick men day and night and carry all that to gather germs.'

'I see,' said Hilda in a subdued tone.

'One thing I will ask, that you give me a lock of it,' he added quietly. She thought he was jesting with his request.

That afternoon she went to her cellar, and took the faithful shears which had severed so many bandages, and put them pitilessly at work on the crown of her beauty. The hair fell to the ground in rich strands, darker by a little, and softer far, than the straw on which it rested. Then she gathered it up into one of the aged illustrated newspapers that had drifted out to the post from kind friends in Furnes. She wrapped it tightly inside the double page picture of laughing soldiers, celebrating Christmas in the trenches. And she carried it out behind the black stump of a house which they called their home, and threw it on the cans that had once contained bully-beef. She was a little heart-sick at her loss, but she had no vanity. As she was stepping inside, the Doctor came down the road.

He stopped at the sight of her.

'Oh, I am sorry,' he said.

'I don't care,' she answered, and braved it off by a little flaunt of her head, though there was a film over her eyes.

'And did you keep a lock for me?' he asked.

'You are joking,' she replied.

'I was never more serious,' he returned. She shook her head, and went down into the cellar. The Doctor walked round to the rear of the house.

A few minutes later, he entered the cellar.

'Good-bye,' he said, holding out his hand, 'I'm going up the line to Nieuport. I'll be back in the morning.' He turned to climb the steps, and then paused for a moment.

'Beautiful hair brings good luck,' he said.

'Then my luck's gone,' returned Hilda.

'But mine hasn't,' he answered.

Hector Munro was caught in the crossfire. According to Mairi, he had 'no use' for Helen and thought of her as 'only an extra, useful for filling in gaps at times'. Mairi was fiercely loyal to Elsie. 'I only speak like this because I am angry and bitter that Helen should have played Elsie false – the last thing on earth she should have done.'

On 6 January the pass for Mairi's father arrived and 'great excitement prevailed'. Elsie and Mairi drove over to see Dot. Mairi was dismayed to hear that her father would not be working at their post in Pervyse, but driving for the corps and based at Nieuport. They were driven to Dunkerque by some Belgian officers, where Mairi posted the pass to her father in London in a registered letter, explaining the new 'beastly arrangement'. As she closed the envelope she doubted he would agree to it. In the town they met Captain Charles Coney, who was with naval transport, and he warned them about the threat of German spies. Elsie agreed to discuss matters with him and Henry Maitland Maitland, an intelligence officer, over lunch in La Panne a few days later.

Elsie and Mairi were still making soup and hot chocolate for the troops, trudging over to the trenches at night and feeding the wounded at the post during the day. Although they do not describe the foraging, the peeling, chopping and stirring, it was an important element of their theory and practice of the care of soldiers, wounded and otherwise.

What was left of Pervyse was more desolate than ever. It had turned into a ghost town. In the past twelve months the few locals who had managed to remain in the shelled buildings had given up and moved away; Elsie and Mairi and their orderlies and the sentries were the only ones left. The town was ringed by vast lakes. The view from the ruin they called home 'gives a queer sensation' and on a moonlight night 'it was too beautiful for words'.

On 7 January Mairi and Henri the orderly sat in Elsie and Mairi's bedroom and watched Elsie begin her conversion to Roman Catholicism, the first step in her marriage to Harry. The local priest, whom they knew well, instructed her in the basic tenets of her fiancé's religion. Mairi thought it seemed 'funny, but many things are funny in wartime'. The next day Elsie drove to La Panne for a spy briefing over lunch with Henry Maitland Maitland and looked for a villa where she and Harry could live. The weather was miserable, but the incessant rain meant that it was quiet on the front and Mairi only had one casualty to patch up. On Sunday, two days after her first lesson, Elsie was driven to her first Catholic mass.

Since the middle of December 1915, when they had made up 7,000 Christmas presents for Belgian soldiers, Elsie and Mairi had had a 'very slack time' as far as work was concerned; all the drama had been caused by Elsie's marriage papers not turning up and the wedding was now only days away. Elsie, Harry and Mairi planned to return to England the day after the wedding but that looked increasingly doubtful. The mood at the post swung from gloomy and damp to anxiety and anger that bureaucracy was making a tough time far worse. The sun came out for the first time in 1916 on 9 January, and the war kicked off again: the skies filled with aeroplanes on aerial reconnaissance and 'little puffs of shrapnel' as the guns on both sides roared into action, trying to bring them down. Elsie and Mairi, enjoying the sunshine, stood in the road watching as the Germans shelled the Belgian batteries behind them: 'the shells passed over our heads with a whirr'.

On 10 January Elsie learned of another reason for the delay. She and Mairi had invited two of his pilot friends, Baron Raoul de Cartier and the Comte Étienne de Robiano, based at Coxyde, to dinner. During the course of the evening they let slip that Elsie's fiancé had been 'very rude' to the priest attached to their squadron. To punish Harry the priest was holding back the marriage papers until he 'reformed and came to heel'. Elsie was 'most awfully disgusted' when she realised that her fiancé had caused the delay and was still behaving badly. Was Harry having cold feet or simply being a high-handed young Belgian aristocrat?

The next day Elsie was 'most awfully tired and worried about all the new trouble that had arisen'. She sent Mairi to do some errands in Steenkerke, and on her way home Mairi visited Harry at Coxyde and 'spoke very seriously' to him about Elsie's health, and how he had to make sure that things went smoothly. He promised to do so and said that he had been told they could marry the following week as the papers would be ready in three days. The next morning Elsie was still unwell and gave Mairi and the orderlies the orders for the day from her bed. Harry turned up briefly but could not stay long because of an appointment with his commandant. Mairi gave Elsie lunch in bed, and they were relieved when Harry Halahan called in offering to help them to get the Mercedes fixed. Mairi had also been suffering over the past few days: she was run down, had a 'vile stye' on one of her eyes and her mouth was 'horribly infected'. Her bottom lip was 'such an enormous size' that she could hardly open her mouth.

Harry Halahan was a good friend to them both, but Mairi especially liked him. He was thirty-two and from an army family. At home in Surrey he had a wife, Brenda, a vicar's daughter, and a five-year-old son, Humfrey. In November 1915 he had been awarded the Distinguished Service Order for his command of the naval heavy batteries and gunboats on the Belgian coast, and his work at the front. Halahan displayed 'gallantry and devotion to duty worthy of the best traditions of the navy'. *The Times* opined: 'it must be very seldom in an official document that such high praise came to have been bestowed on any officer'. A pipe smoker and all-round good egg, Elsie and Mairi nicknamed him 'the bloke'. A double photograph of him stood on Mairi's desk for the rest of her life, and he was remembered in her will with a bequest to a friend she was to know for sixty years.

Although the groom's paperwork was in order the bride's was still in a muddle, and on 14 January there was still 'no sign or sound' of the documents. Back in England Roderick Gooden-Chisholm was also feeling frustrated, complaining to his sister Lucy, 'the Perverse Women seem to change their minds every five minutes'. Elsie felt 'pretty sick' about the delays and decided to put the wedding off until February. Later, when she told a friend the palaver she and Harry had been through to get married, exasperation turned to sarcasm:

It seemed as if everyone had to give their permission . . . the man sends in his demand to get married, and with it his fiancée's birth certificate, and an account of her parents, stating whether they are of good family or not. Then the round begins. This goes to the Commandant; he considers it and signs it. He sends it on to the Commanding Officer of the Aviation, who does the same. From there it goes to General Headquarters. From there to the Ministry. From there to the War Minister. From there to the King. Then it reverses the route and crawls back again.

The next day, Saturday the 15th, Elsie drove to La Panne to collect food supplies, notepaper for the wedding invitations and the mailbags that contained the papers she needed to get married. The wedding could go ahead as planned on Wednesday 19 January, giving them four days to get everything done.

On Sunday 16 January Elsie drove to La Panne in a car that Harry Halahan had loaned her and booked the Hotel Terlinck for the wedding reception. When she returned Mairi helped her write the invitations. Mairi, who was to be Elsie's bridesmaid, was still feeling groggy with a swollen bandaged face. On Monday Harry Halahan collected them from Pervyse and drove them to Dunkerque to collect another bit of paper. The pain in Mairi's mouth was 'acute' and he handed over his car to Elsie so that she could take Mairi to see a doctor in La Panne. The doctor took her into an operating room and 'pulled my face about but could do no good' and then put the bandages back on. They raced back to Dunkerque to collect their letters and parcels and returned to Pervyse, where they learned from the orderlies that the Germans had bombarded the town but 'luckily there were no wounded'.

In her diary on Tuesday, 'the day before THE day', Mairi calls Elsie – who was older by a dozen years, and had a child of her own – 'the kid' and 'Winkles', and sounds more mature than the woman who was her boss. Mairi had recently seen more of Elsie's neediness. She did not respond well to disappointment, which sometimes ended in tears and tantrums:

How strange it seems to think that the dear kid is going to get married. We have so often talked about it and discussed it laughingly and now it is going to become fact. How things change. The last day I shall ever spend with Winkles. Pray God she may be happy. She deserves happiness if anyone does. Dear little Winkles, what a good friend you have been to me. You will never realise what it has meant to me to have you for these months – I shall miss you horribly.

In the morning Elsie dashed to La Panne to check on the arrangements while Mairi stayed at the post and packed for the trip to England. Her face was not quite as painful or swollen and she bathed it often. They spent their last evening together. Mairi confided to her diary that she felt an important part of her life was over: 'Goodbye Winkles darling – Good luck to you and all my very best wishes for your future life.' Although Elsie would still be working at Pervyse, Mairi believed that the marriage would necessarily change her relationship with Elsie – she felt 'the family was breaking up'.

'So dawns the day,' is Mairi's first sentence describing Wednesday 19 January. An old friend from the autumn of 1914, Captain Robert de Wilde, the best man, had an early 'brekkers' with them and packed their luggage into the ambulance. As they were leaving Pervyse, Elsie realised that she had left her shoes behind and they had to go back. They rushed on to Avecapelle, where they picked up another friend, the priest, Père de Groote. François, one of the orderlies at Steenkerke, was collected next, and they reached the Villa Chrysanthemum, which had been loaned to them, at La Panne by half past nine.

Elsie's wedding outfit was a simple navy-blue crêpe-de-Chine frock, a big black velvet hat trimmed at the front with an extravagant white plume and a musquash fur coat. Mairi removed the bandages from her face, and pulled on a woollen hat and warm coat over the best outfit she could assemble. There is no mention in Mairi's diary of any shopping trips, so presumably some of the clothes they wore had been taken from wardrobes in bombed-out houses. Elsie and Mairi walked to the Maison Communale for the civil ceremony. The bridegroom, Captain Vincotte of the 3DA, who was to give Elsie away in the religious ceremony, the Baron de Wahis commandant of aviation, Lieutenant Isserentant and Captain Robert de Wilde were waiting for them. Everything went smoothly, and the wedding party walked behind Elsie and Harry to the Villa Chrysanthemum. The marriage register described her as the widow of Leslie Duke Knocker, a lie which would cause trouble later on.

At eleven o'clock they all drove to the royal chapel for the religious ceremony, which Mairi found 'more beautiful than anything I have heard'. The military band of the 1st Chasseurs played through the service. Mairi followed Elsie up the aisle on the arm of a Belgian officer. The bride and groom walked out of the chapel into dazzling sunshine and were 'bombarded' by photographers capturing a special scene in the war-torn seaside town. Handsome in his uniform, Harry beams at the camera; Elsie clutches his arm, looking unusually frail she smiles nervously. She has got him and she is now the Baroness de T'Serclaes.

When they arrived at the reception the band of the 12th Regiment of the Line was playing outside the Villa Chrysanthemum while inside were King Albert and Queen Elisabeth of the Belgians, Prince Alexander of Teck and the Russian military attaché. Top brass of the Belgian army were present in full dress uniform: General Jacques, Colonel Joostens, Major du Kerchove and Major du Roy who was equerry to King Albert. From the Belgian air force were Commandant Dothey and Captain Dumont. Captain Vicary from the 1st Lancers and British officers and pilots from the Royal Naval Air Service also attended. Dr and Mrs Van der Ghinst were there, and Dot Feilding came with her mother and younger sister, Lady Claire, who had travelled by train, boat and car from Newnham Paddox. The glamorous American actress Maxine Elliott added stardust, while Elsie's sister Una Carey had come from Devon. None of the groom's family came to celebrate.

When the party was over the newly-weds and Mairi changed into their travelling clothes and drove to Calais in Harry Halahan's car but there were no boats going to England that night. They went by train to Boulogne to find a hotel. The next day, after going to six different offices for passes to cross the Channel, they caught a boat at lunchtime and arrived in Folkestone in the afternoon after a 'very bad' crossing. There was a very sick officer in their train carriage to Victoria and they asked the St John Ambulance Brigade to take care of him on arrival. Elsie may have taken Harry to Marlborough to meet her son Kenneth and her parents, and Mairi took a taxi to 20 Randolph Crescent in Maida Vale to stay with Aunt Lucy and Uncle Freddy, 'arriving unexpectedly looking very dirty but quite lively'.

While Elsie and Harry were in England they read *Tatler*'s report of their 'trench marriage'. The society magazine told its readers about a couple whose 'courtship took place under fire, and whose nuptials were celebrated within range of the enemy's guns'. There was so much detail in the *Marlborough Times* account that 'the new baroness' must have been the source. Elsie loved Harry's pedigree – he came from 'an ancient Belgian family' – his recklessness and gaiety. Years later she recalled eagerly embarking on her second marriage, happy to marry a man she hardly knew:

so much of me went into my work that I suppose I was easily swept along on a tide of glamour and frivolity. Perhaps I had a desire to drift for once, not to struggle. It was pleasant to imagine that all would turn out well, and after fifteen months' risking my life at the Front marriage seemed a comparatively small risk to take. I did want someone to take some of the burden off my shoulders and thought how good it would be for Kenneth to have a father.

It took Mairi two weeks to complete the paperwork for her father's post in Belgium. As soon as one hurdle was cleared another bulkier bit of bureaucracy reared up in front of them. Roderick Gooden-Chisholm was also staying at Maida Vale with his sister Lucy and her husband Freddy, a retired colonel of the Army Service Corps, who would have known all about orders and regulations. Although Mairi was 'fagged out' she raised money wherever she could. On her way back from a flying visit to Bournemouth to spend a night with her mother and sister Lucy, she stayed at her old school, St Katharine's in Woking, for two nights. Less than three years before Mairi had been a pupil, and now she stood in front of the girls, a war heroine with a medal from the King of the Belgians. As she regaled them with stories of her work at Pervyse, her teachers were proud to have such a role model for their pupils. Miss Jessie Wight, the headmistress who had sent such a loving letter to Mairi on her flying visit in November 1914, was impressed by her maturity and pluck and started the Chisholm Fund to raise money to support her work 'in the forefront of battle'. Miss Wight had leaflets printed showing Mairi in her uniform wearing her medal, and asked pupils and parents for contributions to ensure food supplies for the post at Pervyse for six months. By the end of the month almost two hundred pounds, equivalent to £13,000 today, had been paid into their bank account.

While she was at home, Mairi's brother Uailean, by now a temporary lieutenant in the British West India Regiment, was also in England completing his training at Seaford, and would sail from Devonport to Alexandria in Egypt, where he remained for much of the war.

Before Mairi left for Belgium she spent two nights at the Great Western Hotel at Paddington, where Elsie, Harry and Elsie's sister Una were also staying. The honeymooners were not due back at their posts for another week. On 2 February Mairi and her father travelled by train to Folkestone and caught a boat to Boulogne. Mairi collected a Mors lorry donated by the Belgian Red Cross and drove to Pervyse. When they arrived they were told a shell had badly damaged the garden at the back of the post but otherwise all was well except that Mairi and her father would have to share a room until his was ready.

Roderick Gooden-Chisholm had got his way and been sent to Pervyse, where he quickly settled into the rhythms of life at the post, putting up shelves where he kept his 'spare undies' and, having recently become a Catholic, hanging a crucifix and some religious postcards on the wall. He would have to accustom himself to taking orders from Elsie and, when she was absent, his twenty-year-old daughter. The cases they treated were mostly ailments such as cuts, coughs, constipation and burns, but they were preparing for the worst. Pervyse was filled with big guns, there was movement up and down the line, and they 'expected trouble quite soon'.

On 8 February Mairi and her father drove to Boulogne to collect Elsie and Harry, the 'Love Birds' as Roderick called them. They had had a bad crossing. Elsie looked 'pretty fagged-out' but Harry seemed 'very well'. While they waited for the boat her father had bought a bottle of gin and some vermouth to make himself feel a little more at home in his new life. Mairi took Elsie and Harry to their new home in La Panne and returned to Pervyse feeling 'it is good to have her back again'. On the evening of 11 February the big push they had been anticipating started: the Germans attacked Dixmude and Ramscapelle, and were repulsed. The sound of shelling and machine-gun fire could be heard for miles; the firepower on both sides was immense. Mairi thought it the noisiest night she had lived through since the fighting that preceded the opening of the sluice gates of the River Yser in the autumn of 1914. Mercifully there was little work for them to do at Pervyse and Steenkerke, and Mairi was able to take her weekly bath at the hut the following day.

Captain Vincotte, who had given Elsie away, visited them at Steenkerke on 12 February and collected comforts for his men – cigarettes, chocolate, mufflers, balaclavas and jumpers. When Vincotte left Elsie's mood dipped, and Mairi says she was 'rather a misery dog' and so they 'parted rather earlier than usual'. At half past five the next morning, Mairi, her father and their orderlies were woken by loud knocking. A soldier who had been shot in the face was bleeding heavily from his left cheek. Soon another man arrived, who had also been shot in the face and had his hand injured by a grenade. As soon as the men had been cleaned and bandaged, and given some refreshments and a rest, Henri drove them to the nearest hospital. Things quietened down. Mairi left the other orderly in charge and drove her father to La Panne, where they were to have dinner with General Jacques in the mess at Belgian army headquarters. As soon as they arrived Roderick installed himself in the dining room of the best hotel left standing, and Mairi visited Elsie at her villa, where they talked until Harry appeared. Dinner with the general was 'quite a bean feast': they had oyster patties, mutton, lobster salad, cakes, peach tart and cream, a delicious change from their usual diet of tinned beef and sardines. Thirty officers were present, and it was the first time that ladies had been admitted to the mess. The next day Elsie did not turn up at the post and Mairi wrote, 'owing to the bad weather I suppose'.

During the last two weeks of February, Elsie, Mairi and Roderick treated relatively few wounded soldiers, but dozens of men 'suffering terribly with colic', neuralgia, toothache, and colds that quickly turned to bronchitis in the freezing and very wet conditions in the trenches. The Germans were still bombarding Dixmude, which meant the nights were 'full of sound', but otherwise Pervyse was hardly shelled.

All the action was at Verdun 150 miles away, where the French were having a 'terrible time'. At the beginning of 1916 prospects for the Allies looked bleak: the attack on Gallipoli in 1915 had been a disaster and the Germans were firmly dug in on the Western Front. The French had launched the ten-month Battle of Verdun on 21 February but were taking enormous casualties.

In Pervyse and elsewhere the Belgian army doctors had little time or interest in treating the ailments their soldiers took to Elsie and Mairi, but the women looked after them, handing out such patent medicines as they had and mugs of soup and cheering hot chocolate, in the belief that if the troops were looked after properly 'one could save big illnesses'. In their spare time they wrote 'begging letters' asking for money to support their work in Belgium: carefully written letters to friends and relations, packed with detail, extracts from which often appeared in newspapers in Britain. Dorothy Jones, one of Mairi's school friends, a clergyman's daughter who lived at Kingstown near Dublin, had Mairi's letter published in the *Irish Times* a few weeks later.

Almost everything they needed had to be brought from England and collected from Dunkerque. Their petrol bill was eight pounds a month (£500 today); repair of the vehicles and spare parts were ten pounds (£600); coal and potatoes cost four pounds; meat for their homely soups cost two pounds, and bread, butter, eggs and the laundry bill came to six pounds a month. These basics cost thirty pounds, (£1,800), and this money had to be found every month of every year they were in Pervyse. The British Red Cross were still paying two pounds a month to Harrods to send them groceries, but Elsie and Mairi did not know how long this arrangement would last.

Another potential source of donations was the motorbiking sisterhood, and in February Elsie and Mairi entered a ladies' motorcycle-dress competition in *Motor Cycle* magazine. Writing as the Baroness de T'Serclaes, Elsie sent a photograph of herself and Mairi which showed them wearing their 'daily costume in the war zone', boots, breeches and woollen hats, their medals pinned close to their hearts and a covering letter entitled 'Skirt-less Dress in the Belgian Army'. They insisted their costume always looked 'nice and feminine'. Elsie reminded readers that she had been the only lady to try to climb Leith Hill in June 1914 on her big Chater Lea and sidecar. Learning that they had read *Motor Cycle* every week of the eighteen months they had been in Belgium must have pleased the editor.

Harry was then told that he would be posted to the artillery and Elsie planned to move out of their house and return to Pervyse. The news that Elsie was coming back to the post pleased Mairi, as she had missed her: 'I wish we had her for always – it is very different without her.'

As Mairi's twentieth birthday loomed on 26 February, she bemoaned the passing of her teens. The last eighteen months of her life had been action-packed and adult, at a time when young ladies' lives were generally much more circumscribed. 'It is rather alarming to feel that I am nearly twenty because I have always dreaded leaving my teens . . . there is something very attractive about one's teens, it's different to anything else.' Surrounded by such devastation and human misery she was in no mood to celebrate. Recently, a friend, a Belgian officer who was twenty-three, had been killed, and his younger brother with him was 'desperately wounded'. All the intelligence reports left her feeling low: 'It will be very terrible this year. So many good lives still being lost and absolutely nothing to be gained by it all. It makes one very sad to realise how unnecessary it all is . . . one wonders how it will all end.'

Mairi had her twentieth birthday, and Elsie and Robert de Wilde came for tea and some treats sent by Aunt Lucy, but there was no party like the previous year. Otherwise it was a working day like any other, except a thick blanket of snow lay on the ground. There were new furry faces at the post. Several cats moved in, one a kitten called Chink, given to Mairi by an English officer in the Royal Naval Air Service. When it was safe she would take Chink out on a lead, and she planned to take the cats home with her at the end of the war.

Mairi wondered what would happen to their part of the front line and doubted there would be any attack as long as the inundations remained. The two sides were bogged down, with a lake between them. Living in limbo there was time to speculate about when something might happen, and they made regular trips to the ruins of the town's priests' home, where the Belgian army had set up an observation tower in one of the two chimneys left standing. Elsie and Mairi would climb a ladder and look through binoculars for a bird's-eye view of the German trenches. Engineers of the 3DA covered their post and the dugout at the rear with sandbags, ahead of the anticipated bad weather and heavy bombardment.

At seven o'clock on the morning of 2 March Mairi was told that King Albert was inspecting the trenches at Pervyse and would visit them in an hour or two. Elsie arrived at half past eight and they rushed around madly trying to tidy up, but came to the conclusion it was pointless and that their post was 'not meant for a king'. Inside it was dark and sombre, 'a place used to muddy boots, rain and dust', and it was impossible in the time available 'to make it look like a drawing-room'. Elsie and Mairi decided that 'the best thing we could do was to leave it, and let the King see us as we really are'.

Shortly before nine o'clock Elsie and Mairi stood on their doorstep to greet the king. Escorted by two generals, he congratulated them for all they had done for his men, and told them they were 'very courageous to stay up here'. Surrounded by the blitzed landscape, Elsie and Mairi told the king how much they loved their work and being at Pervyse. Protocol demanded that the king be the first person to walk into the post, and as soon as he did Chink the cat dropped onto his head from the top of the door, a favourite trick. The king took it well because 'he was an awfully nice person'. The noise caused by Chink's performance brought their orderly, Henri, whom they had forgotten to warn about the visit, flying from the kitchen, yelling at them to shut the door in case Chink got out. He was flabbergasted to come face to face with his king. Elsie and Mairi showed their visitor round the post, which featured a portrait of him and his wife and children. They were overcome by the 'memorable moment' – which, oddly, Mairi's father missed, staying in his room throughout the visit.

Two weeks later news reached Pervyse of the slaughter at Verdun, and Mairi asked herself how the 'absolute butchery' could be brought to an end. She wondered if she would share the fate of the French at Verdun if the Germans crossed the inundations and overran their part of the front.

As March drew to a close the tension between her father and Elsie was troublesome enough for Mairi to tell Aunt Lucy about it. The Gooden-Chisholms had disliked Elsie from the outset, and now she was living at the post again Mairi's father had clearly been making unkind remarks about her. Letters from 'Mum' only made it worse. In a frank outpouring of affection, Mairi wrote to her aunt about how much she owed Elsie, and that she would never give her up:

Gypsy is too energetic for most people – as well as being outspoken – and can't stand slackness at any price. She has done me a world of good, knocked most of my laziness out of me, and is now trying to instil ambition into me. I suppose if I hadn't met her I should have lopped along in my old way, and been satisfied with lounging in an arm-chair in front of the fire – as I used to do . . . I value her friendship very highly because I know it to be sincere. For her I have a great affection which is only natural after all we have been through together. I don't think we'd ever see each other in a bad corner without giving everything we could in the way of help . . . I have no intention of falling out with Mum. She dislikes Gypsy intensely, and has told me so – and I think would like me to make a sort of choice between herself and G – of course that is ludicrous. I do not intend to fight with my family, nor do I intend to play the basest trick it would be possible for me to play – win a certain amount of reputation on another person's friendship and aid and then when it is all over calmly give her the cold shoulder.

Unfortunately my friends have never approved but that doesn't affect me – I have ceased to mind. At one time it hurt me terribly, but now I realise that I suffered quite unnecessarily . . . One would never get anywhere if one did not strike out on one's own . . . It is no use trying to make people understand the point, they simply won't see it. It is most unfortunate that things should be as they are – but as they are, so must they be. In the meantime we will have to continue with this job until the ghastly war is over and then we will see what happens.

As Mairi sat down to write this letter, her father was also penning a letter to Lucy. The letters, which travelled in the same mailbag to London, could not have been more different. His letter is an excited account of a shell that blew the window of the bedroom out as he sat reading, covering him with dirt and dust. A second shell blew in the window frames, 'narrowly missing Mairi's head as she was close to the window'. The so-called 'bomb-proof door' of the post was ripped by a piece of shrapnel, and a bottle of champagne was lost.

In the last week of April, the 3DA went *en repos* for a month, and another division took its place in the trenches at Pervyse. Elsie and Mairi took the opportunity to go on a fund-raising tour of England and Scotland, leaving the post in the hands of the orderlies and a Belgian doctor. Given their parlous finances, there was a degree of urgency. Roderick was left behind 'in his element in full charge' of repairing, cleaning and painting their five vehicles.

Starting in Scotland, they stayed at Whinnie Knowe in Nairn with Mairi's mother's cousin Janie and her husband Ronald Grant Fraser, a retired admiral of the Royal Navy. The Frasers were a childless couple in their fifties who had married the year Mairi was born. Elsie and Mairi's first lecture was on 27 April at the Public Hall in Nairn, and the local press, who had been kept well briefed by the family, ran articles that helped fill the room. They ran full-length photographs of THE HEROINES OF THE BELGIAN ARMY.

Provost Macrae presided over the meeting and warmed up the audience. The Baroness de T'Serclaes 'could tell a story to great advantage, was an eloquent speaker, a clear-headed far-seeing woman full of resource and initiative', and of Miss Gooden-Chisholm, 'whom they looked upon as one of themselves', they were proud 'for what she had done on the battlefields of Belgium'. Elsie launched into a gutsy description of the highlights of their eighteen months' work: the hand-to-hand fighting they had seen at Melle; how a bullet had whistled between them at Dixmude; the contamination of their water by a German mass grave and 'thrilling accounts of their motor experiences when conveying the wounded under rifle and shellfire'.

When Mairi got up she was loudly cheered. She explained how they budgeted for the running costs of the post, and what the money they raised would be spent on. There was a great round of applause when she said that one of their ambulances had taken 1,500 soldiers to hospital. Their vehicles did not last long due to the dreadful state of the roads and being hit by shrapnel and ricocheting bullets. During their visit they needed to purchase a new ambulance, which would cost £600; they also hoped to raise £2,000 on their tour to put their work on a sound financial footing. At the end of the evening, Mr Whitelaw, a local worthy, proposed the vote of thanks and told the audience that they were 'living in strange times'. He had not thought a year or two ago that he would be sitting in Nairn Public Hall 'having his admiration aroused by such a splendid record of women's work as they had heard that night'. He hoped the feelings of everyone in Nairn 'would be stirred', and he reminded listeners of the initiative Elsie and Mairi had shown. They were not 'merely clever nurses – told to go and do something, what to do and how to do it. They had done something far greater than that – they had found their work.' Mr Whitelaw went on to refer to Elsie's remark that sometimes she believed they were protected by angels, and he finished by saying he had 'a strong suspicion that the Belgian soldiers and others could tell who the real angels were'.

Back in Pervyse four more cats had moved into the post, driving Mairi's father mad by walking across a newly painted car bonnet. He admitted to his sister that his wife and daughter had had a sparky relationship for some time because they were 'so different and irritate one another'. His wife, Nonie, 'does not understand Mairi in the least, and Mairi like most modern girls wants an object in life'. Roderick told Lucy that Mairi and Elsie had seen Major Lumsden in Boulogne, and *'entre nous,* I rather hope she may marry him'. Mairi had told him, he said, that if she married it would be a man older than herself: 'someone she could look up to for advice!'

Two days later Elsie and Mairi went to Inverness, where they were given 'a most cordial reception' at the Queensgate Hotel, and 'a very substantial response was made in furtherance of their work'. They then left the Highlands and travelled south-east to Dundee, famous for jute, jam and journalism, where they stayed with the newspaper proprietor D. C. Thomson. Elsie and Mairi had been booked to speak at the Guild Hall at three o'clock on the afternoon of 1 May, but in the days leading up to their arrival, 'owing to the increasing interest in the visit of the ladies', it became clear that a bigger venue would be needed. Their host's newspapers, the *Post*, the *Dundee Advertiser*, the *Dundee Courier*, and the *People's Journal*, headlined them as HEROIC SCOTTISH LADIES and SCOTTISH HEROINES: 'It will perhaps prove to be the most interesting and unique war gathering held in the city since the great struggle began.' After all, the speakers' names 'are now known throughout the world'.

David Coupar Thomson escorted them to the new venue, the Victoria Art Galleries. Mairi's heart was in her mouth as she saw the crowds who had come. There was a huge cheer, and Mairi modestly thought they were greeting their host. Even the new place could not cope with the numbers, and an overflow meeting was addressed by Mairi in a smaller room in the same building.

The afternoon was 'an unqualified success', and the audience loudly applauded the 'pretty baroness', who was a 'splendid raconteur'. Elsie gave an insight into her maverick spirit when she anticipated the question of why the Belgian government did not pay for their work. They would do so, she said, but that would mean she would 'be under red tape, and if there was one thing she had always kept clear of it was that appalling red tape'. They laughed and clapped at the mention of the dreaded beast of bureaucracy. Elsie's narrative was 'so graphic and thrilling that one could scarcely credit it was all being unfolded from the lips of one who played a living part in the whole unforgettable drama'. She told them she could not speak highly enough of 'the plucky Belgians'; now that Elsie was a Belgian by marriage, she seems to have taken upon herself an ambassadorial role.

Elsie made a point of paying tribute to Mairi's devotion to her work, her calm and courageous spirit, and flattered her audience by saying they were quintessentially Scottish traits. She also told of the time when Mairi was left alone in Dixmude while under bombardment from the Germans. Elsie had to evacuate a wounded soldier and asked Mairi not to move until she came back. Hurrying back to Dixmude, Elsie ran into the retreating Belgian army and asked the soldiers if they had seen Miss Chisholm. They had urged her to leave, they said, but she had refused to move. When Elsie found Mairi she was 'calmly sitting behind a wall writing up her diary', thereby obeying orders with no thought for her own safety.

Lord Dean of Guild Dickie, who presided over the meeting, drew the afternoon to a close. Clearly under the impression they had two 'Scottish heroines' in their midst, he described Mairi's ancestry, and went on to polish the baroness's Scottish credentials by saying that 'all of the baroness's friends had been officers in the Black Watch'. We have to climb a long way up Elsie's family tree on her mother's side to find any Scots: her grandmother, Elizabeth Kerr, was the granddaughter of Lord Charles Beauchamp Kerr, the fifth Earl of Lothian. Elsie did not correct the false impression: if it helped their cause in Scotland to be Scottish, then so be it. At the end of the meeting eighty pounds (£5,000) was collected, and Mr Boswell Laird Nairn, a local ship-broker who was the Belgian vice-consul in Dundee, agreed to act as treasurer for the fund.

Before they left Dundee on the night train to north-west England Elsie and Mairi were taken to the War Dressings Depot at Hyndford House and the Broughty Ferry Canteen, where Elsie 'gave another proof of her versatility by playing draughts with a soldier'.

Between 2 and 4 May they spoke at Sale, Alderley Edge and Manchester. Billed as 'The Heroines of Pervyse', Elsie and Mairi presented a 'graphic description' of life in the trenches to a packed ticket-only, adults-only audience at Sale Public Hall on the night of 2 May. They stayed with the promoter of the meeting, Mrs Frederick Lucius, a member of the Belgian Funds Committee, at her home in Sale. The next day, their appearance at Alderley Edge inspired the formation of the Heroines of Pervyse Fund run by the Alderley Edge Committee, of whom Lady Sheffield was the president. Her husband, Sir Berkeley Digby Sheffield, the sixth Baronet of Normanby Park in Lincolnshire, was serving in France. Local ladies and tradesmen designed and produced a 'How You Can Help the Heroines of Pervyse' pamphlet. Listening to Elsie and Mairi's account they decided to focus their efforts on sending regular supplies of food as comforts for the heroes of Belgium, that 'gallant little country' suffering at the 'hard hand of a relentless foe'. On Gift Days, the first Saturday of every month, they took in donations of tea, cocoa, turtle-soup cubes, jelly squares, soap, chocolate, toffee, Bovril and biscuits or cakes in tin boxes.

John H. Billinge, a local solicitor and the honorary treasurer of the Manchester Belgian Funds Committee, arranged Elsie and Mairi's evening at the Albert Hall in Peter Street, Manchester. They were well into their stride by this stage in the tour. Standing on stage in their khaki 'costumes' and proudly wearing their medals, they told their story 'simply and modestly'. The Dean of Manchester, James E. C. Welldon, who presided, told the audience there was no hardship the heroines of Pervyse were not willing to bear and that they were 'conversant with all the terror and anguish of war'. The women revealed how the work affected them at times. Being under shellfire was 'not at all pleasant', Elsie told them, and 'you don't feel one bit brave, you are all taut, and if you are hit you suffer dreadful nerve shock.'

Thirty thousand soldiers were close by, and Elsie, Mairi and the orderlies kept the post open from midnight to midnight. There were no official opening times: anyone who was wounded or sick could knock on their door and get help at any hour of the day. John Billinge produced a pamphlet 'earnestly soliciting' money and gifts. The Belgian Funds Committee pledged to send money to Belgium every month, and asked for comforts for the soldiers such as 'woollen underclothing, scarves, socks, mufflers, chocolate, tobacco, cigarettes, pipes, shirts, soap, biscuits, sweets, paper and envelopes'.

Elsie and Mairi stayed on another week to complete the final leg of the tour, a trip to the West Country and a lecture in Exeter, Elsie's home town. Mairi's father had been expecting them back in Pervyse, and when he sat down to write to 'dear Loo', his sister Lucy, he sounded distinctly grumpy, complaining that he had heard 'nothing of the doings of the wild women . . . They really ought to be here but I don't know where to find them but as usual they have vouchsafed me no information of their movements and intentions.' On a trip to Boulogne to try and get spare parts for the vehicles, he had asked the advice of Mr Colby, an American who had become a naturalised Belgian so that he could take charge of the fleet of ambulances attached to the Ist Brigade of Cavalry. He was one of Mairi's admirers, but she 'couldn't stand his compliments'. Colby could not resist mentioning Roderick's 'charming daughter'.

Elsie and Mairi spoke at the Barnfield Hall in Exeter on 9 May. As she approached the venue Elsie passed the house where she had been born, where her mother had died in 1888 when she was four years old, and from which she and her brothers and sisters had been scattered when their father died in 1890. Her maiden name of Shapter guaranteed them a warm welcome and plenty of press interest. For such an important occasion the Sheriff of Devon, Sir Ernest Cable, chaired the meeting.

The *Devon and Exeter Gazette* noted that the baroness told the story of their work in a 'simple and lucid' manner. After her 'graphic narratives' of stretchers, shells and shock, she reminded the audience that she and Miss Chisholm were the only women allowed to nurse on the front line. At the War Conference in Paris in March 1915 all women had been banned from working anywhere near the trenches. Mairi contributed in a 'clear and lucid manner', and boosted by the fact that one of their own was doing something to the credit of the whole country, they raised more than two hundred pounds (£13,000 today).

Sir Ernest, whose only son George, a twenty-three-year-old second lieutenant, had been killed in action in France on 9 May 1915, a year to the day he chaired Elsie and Mairi's meeting, wrote them a cheque for a hundred pounds. Mr Trehawke Kekewich, the Recorder of Tiverton, proposed a vote of 'hearty thanks', saying 'no women had done more magnificently,' and made a donation of fifty pounds. The silver collection taken at the end of the afternoon yielded another twenty-five pounds.

By 14 May Roderick had still heard nothing from the 'wild women'. They were in London, getting the permits for the two Douglas motorbikes, one with sidecar, that they were taking back to Pervyse, stamped by the French ambassador. Harry was 'highly indignant' that they had not returned on 7 May as he had expected, and went looking for them in England. His log says that he did not fly between 6 and 17 May, and he was with them at least part of this time.

There are two photographs of Harry's time in England. In one he has folded himself in half to get into a motorcycle sidecar; his new bride is firmly in control, and Mairi is their outrider. In the other Harry is in control of the solo bike. Standing with them are Elsie's friends Gordon and Rosa Fletcher, a well-known motorcycling couple and members of the Gypsy Motor Cycle Club, who had loaned their motorbike and sidecar to Elsie and Harry.

When Mairi returned to Belgium a troublesome lump in her hand was operated on. It was thought to be a boil and she was not given anaesthetic, but when the doctor cut into the lump he found a tangle of muscle had grown on to the bone. In an exceedingly painful operation that took three quarters of an hour they 'had to force the good muscles back and to cut and scrape [the tangle] off' the bone.

There was a sense of drift and limbo in the weeks after their return to Belgium. Elsie and Mairi were uncertain where the men of the 3DA would be deployed and there was a possibility they would be sent to another part of the front, and the women would have to leave beloved Pervyse. While they waited Elsie came up with a new idea: to have tents sent out from England so that the wounded and the sick and men who had leave from the fighting, would have a place where they could play cards, dominoes and draughts, read and smoke. Mindful of the censor, Roderick was unable to tell his sister where they were, but in early June they had left Pervyse and were temporarily living on a farm at Rabelaar, eight miles away and close to the trenches. The nights were filled with noise: men marching on the cobbled road that abutted the farm buildings to relieve the troops in the trenches, the screaming of shells, and, closer to home, the sound of restless horses snuffling about and the scores of rats pattering about the dairy.

In the middle of June the recreation tents went up in the field behind the farmhouse. Mairi's father was not happy about them, calling them 'beastly', an odd remark considering they were there for the soldiers. But the adjective speaks volumes about his deteriorating relationship with Elsie. The forty-five letters he wrote to his sister during the war reveal his misgivings and increasingly intense dislike of her. Apparently, Elsie's only redeeming feature was that she was a 'genius' at dealing with the wounded. Negative remarks about her, which started soon after he arrived, when he called her a 'mad woman', became a regular feature of his letters to London. He said that she was tactless and would arrive at the post like a 'stormy petrel', that she loved the limelight and pounced on invitations like a 'bird of prey'. He and Mairi were methodical and tidy and 'got on quite swimmingly together', whereas Elsie's presence was 'disturbing and untidy'. After being at the post for a month he told his sister that 'Mairi was like her old self', suggesting that the problems he had had with his daughter, for which he blamed Elsie, had evaporated. He dreaded Elsie returning to the post when Harry was posted to the artillery: 'I do not know how I shall get on with her, it is very hard to be a Christian.' Waspishly, he told Lucy that Elsie's only other friend, except 'her little slave Mairi', had been Helen Gleason, who had 'only stuck with her to promote her own career'. As the day of Elsie's return loomed he said he hoped they would not fight, but there is a sense he was ready and waiting for a confrontation.

Although Roderick and Nonie had disagreed about Mairi going to London to do her bit – he had supported her plan – neither of them had been impressed with Mrs Knocker when they met. Motorcycling had brought Elsie and Mairi together and motorbikes had taken their daughter away from them. They saw a woman twelve years older than Mairi who was not of their social circle. Snobbery played its part in their first unfavourable impression of her: Elsie was a doctor's daughter and middle class, whereas the Gooden-Chisholms were wealthy clannish Scots and had moved in royal circles. Nonie may have been jealous of Mairi's admiration for Elsie and resented the influence she was gaining over her daughter, for whom the Gooden-Chisholms had had other plans. Might Mairi have married Jim Trinder if she had not met Elsie? Undoubtedly the Gooden-Chisholms felt they were losing their daughter to the war and a more worldly woman. Years later, when Mairi spoke about her time in Belgium, she mentioned her parents' attitude to Elsie, which was influenced by their belief that she was half-Jewish, though there is no evidence in the Shapter and Bayly family trees that she had any Jewish ancestry. Casual anti-Semitism was rife in British society at the time, and if the Gooden-Chisholms thought her dark eyes and dark hair suggested Jewishness that could have been another black mark.

During his time at the post Roderick had to take orders for the first time in his adult life from women, and this clearly rankled. As a captain in the Seaforth Highlanders, he had been the one to give orders. Roderick may also have been resentful of Elsie's elevation to the Belgian aristocracy through her marriage. There was in addition the unavoidable truth that if it had not been for Elsie writing to Mairi and suggesting they go to London to help in the war effort, he would not have had the opportunity to do *his* bit, in the thick of the action. So committed was he to the work they were all doing at Pervyse that he asked his contacts in Trinidad to raise money to help support their efforts. The Langes, his son's prospective in-laws, also raised money for them, and Roderick himself donated regular sums to help pay for the upkeep of the vehicles, his special interest and expertise.

The tents were extremely popular (one had boxing, another sold beer) and the post buzzed with officers and visitors keen to meet the two most famous women on the Western Front. Mairi's father was grumpy that Mairi was typing Elsie's letters and resented the fact that there were so many people around a lot of the time. Other matters may have been worrying him at this time: his son was fighting in Egypt; his estate in Trinidad, and the forthcoming sale of their home in Dorset and the inevitable disruption that would cause. Roderick had been away from his family and friends for six months and he may have been homesick and bored. With regard to Elsie, he found it best to avoid her as much as possible, by staying in the garage, fixing the ambulances and cars, but sometimes Mairi's patience with her father wore thin. He wrote, 'I was sent for the other day and fished out of the garage. "Come along Gypsy thinks you are avoiding us", "So I am," I said, but was fired questions at before I could explain that when I am in the room they either whisper together or Mairi slobbers over Gypsy so naturally I don't think I am wanted.'

*   *   *

It was a quiet time in June and the first week of July, with little action on either side as they hung around waiting for 'the advance', hoping they would be in Brussels by Christmas. Elsie and Mairi acquired a new title, the 'Madonnas of Pervyse', partly because the khaki scarves they wore resembled nuns' wimples, and also because there was a Catholic shrine opposite the entrance to their first-aid post.

Queues of men waited for treatment for venereal diseases, for which the only medication was mercury. Boils were attended to by Mairi, the 'boil expert'. The most 'ghastly' ones were those between the buttocks, and she could never understand how the men coped with the pain of marching or merely standing up in the trenches for hours. Of the many she treated, this one belonged to a French soldier: 'It must have been the most terrible pain, and to treat them they nearly stood on their heads with their bottoms in the air and I was poking around between their legs . . . trying to get these things out . . . My entire viewpoint of this poor fellow was his bottom-end.' On 12 July 1916, the grateful Frenchman wrote Mairi an 'utterly beautiful and absolutely enchanting poem' which she kept in her scrapbook for years. Translated, it declared:

> Vainly does one admire you, vainly does one love you,
> Alas! There are flowers one dares not touch
> And these are the most beautiful.
> If, however, you knew what my heart feels,
> Horribly smitten with your sweet person,
> One would finally see,
> Lingering on your tender lips,
> Mocking and winning,
> 'The Sunshine of your Smile'

A week later, on 23 July, Elsie and Mairi re-created an English school sports day and fete for the men who visited the recreation tents, organising a hundred-metre race, a sack race (for the soldiers, too undignified for the officers), a three-legged race, a tug of war and musical chairs. André Lynen of the 107th Battery illustrated the publicity leaflet with a pen-and-ink drawing of Mairi on her motorbike kicking up a tremendous cloud of dust. Before recently joining the artillery, twenty-eight-year-old Lynen had been one of Belgium's war artists.

A few days after the fete Elsie and Mairi had sad news about Sarah Macnaughtan. After leaving Belgium in October 1915 she had joined the Red Cross and gone to Russia, but after months of frustration caused by red tape, she left to work in Persia in February 1916, but was taken ill shortly after her arrival. She returned to London and on 24 July died of coeliac disease complicated by pernicious anaemia.

After nearly nine months in Belgium, Mairi's father was itching to get back to Trinidad, particularly the warmer weather. He was happy to be at the post while the 'Perverse Ladies' had plenty for him to do – he was happiest when he was busiest – but there is boredom in some of his letters. Apart from hearing mass in a tent, he dreaded Sundays, when the tents were full and the band played all day. The cats drove him mad, and a fox had moved in, although he minded it less as it did not smell as 'high' as the cats.

Before Elsie and Mairi set off for a fund-raising trip to England, there was news of another of Mairi's Trinder cousins, who had been killed on the Somme on 15 September. Roderick's nephew Major John Robert Trinder of the 18th Battalion of the London Regiment (London Irish Rifles) died at Festubert, aged twenty-six. This was the second of Aunt Annie and Uncle Arnold's three sons to be killed. Mairi's cousins Jim and John were two of the 699 Wellington old boys who would be in killed in the war.

More than three-quarters of a million British and French and an unknown number of German soldiers were killed on the Somme, from 1 July until 18 November, when the first snow of winter fell. On 10 August, while the battle was still raging, the first-ever war documentary, *The Battle of the Somme*, was screened to shocked audiences in cinemas all over Britain. The film showed the British public what the men had endured and were enduring. Accompanied by a pianist or orchestra, the eighty-minute film (part of which was staged) showed the Western Front in an unforgiving light. Twenty million tickets were sold to the British population of forty-three million. Public opinion was dazed and apprehensive about the future.

While they were in England in September and early October Elsie and Mairi sent accounts to the newspapers that had run stories, showing how the money raised had been spent, and posed for photographs, their faces and medals beaming out of the *Daily Mirror*, the *Daily Sketch*, *Ladies' Field*, and the *Tatler*. Elsie went to Marlborough to see her son before he went back to school.

As soon as they got back to the post, Mairi's father left to catch a boat to England and Trinidad. He had been with them for nine months. His pride had been badly dented – 'I could sit down and weep' – when he was rejected for active service by the War Office, but had been restored by the work he had done in Belgium. Elsie had been a thorn in his side but when he returned to Trinidad he had tales to tell about *his* war work.

Earlier in 1916, when Elsie and Mairi were trying to reach the widest possible audience, an admirer of theirs, Major A. A. Gordon, suggested that a book describing their experiences would be a good fund-raising tool, and their cherished diaries, 'little fat, mud-stained books' that had been 'kept entirely for their own interest', were handed over to Geraldine Edith Mitton, who turned them into a book with a bulky title: *The Cellar-House of Pervyse: A Tale of Uncommon Things from the Journals and Letters of the Baroness T'Serclaes and Mairi Chisholm.* Coyly, and surely with tongue in cheek, Mitton wrote: 'The Two had always hated publicity, but owing to the unique character of their work and the approval of the King of the Belgians, they had not altogether been able to hide their light under a bushel, as they would have preferred to do . . . and handed over the journals to see what could be made of them.' All the royalties went to buy a new motorbike ambulance and help pay for the work at Pervyse.

Geraldine Mitton was well known. She was a vicar's daughter who, in her twenties, had come to London in 1896 to be a writer. Her first novel, the jauntily titled *A Bachelor Girl in London*, was published in 1898, and before she wrote *The Cellar-House*, there had been a string of history and travel books and novels. She had edited Sir Walter Besant's *Survey of London. The English Woman's Year Book* and *Who's Who.* Her trip to Ceylon and Burma in 1906 had inspired the racy-sounding *Bachelor Girl in Burma*, published the following year.

Elsie and Mairi were back in Belgium by the time the book was in the shops in November, timed for the Christmas market. *The Cellar-House* attracted dozens of reviews, mostly glowing. Almost all of the Scottish and West Country press praised the book, loyal to women they were proud to call their own: 'it has all the interest of a romantic novel, and a much more serious intent and purpose,' said the *Scotsman.* The *Nairnshire Telegraph* thought the book was written in 'excellent taste' but the reviewer was labouring under the illusion that Geraldine Mitton was a man. The *Glasgow Herald* took against the book, its frosty reviewer seizing the opportunity to take a swipe at the

Red Cross: 'it is an interesting comment on the orgy of Red Cross motoring, which at one time seemed in a fair way to bring our aeroplanes to a standstill for lack of petrol,' and he wondered 'a little whether these two brave young women were really serving any useful purpose in maintaining their little post'. The *Guardian* described it as 'a record of a harebrained but astonishingly heroic adventure of two English girls . . . and few individual achievements in this war can outshine that which is herein recorded'. The *Evening Standard* said it was 'an incredible tale' and that 'no women can have faced death such hundreds of times'. One other sourpuss was the pompous *Times Literary Supplement*: 'We are bound to say that the tone of the narrative does not altogether please. It is too kittenish . . . one seems to hear the writer going off into a giggle whenever a handsome man comes into the story. That is a jarring note and it is a great pity that it should have been struck, for the adventure itself is a very fine one, and moves on a plane in which giggling is really quite out of place.'

During the autumn of 1916 several wooden huts were built next to the recreation tents, and on 20 November Elsie and Mairi invited about twenty of their Belgian officer friends, including Harry and his pals, to a dinner in the Rabelaar Hut to celebrate the publication of the book. The courses had local names – potage aux tomatoes à l'eau de l'Yser, Filet de sole au Canal de Loos, poulet au Rabelaar, petits pois aux mitrailleuses, truffles à la Pervyse – and were followed by cakes, fruit and dessert, washed down with liqueurs and champagne.

On 9 December Mairi left for England for a nine-day holiday, and then returned to Pervyse. Elsie also spent Christmas in Belgium – with her new husband, whose last flight of the year was on Christmas Eve. At the end of 1916 Harry's flying log reveals a busy and dangerous year; from his first day back from their honeymoon on 12 February, until 24 December, he had been up as an observer on ninety-four missions. On twenty-four occasions Harry flew on reconnaissance flights to look at enemy positions, railway traffic and troop movements; the forty-two artillery missions he flew were to locate and attack the Germans' heavy artillery with machine-gun fire, and five times he released bombs by hand from the plane. In September Harry was decorated with the Croix de Guerre.

Every minute they were in the air was fraught with danger. Planes were relatively easy targets for an expert gunner, and these were the early days of aviation with mechanical problems causing frequent crashes. Bad weather including the sudden appearance of cloud could also spell disaster. Many of the missions that Harry and his fellow airmen flew were necessarily short, sometimes only thirty minutes. No one wanted to stay in the air any longer than necessary, many pilots and observers suffering so horribly with air-sickness that they had to abandon missions.

VI

Sandbags Instead of Handbags

E lsie and Mairi are hard to find for the first three months
of 1917. Apart from reviews of *The Cellar-House,* they
were not in the newspapers until March, when they
appeared at the Alhambra Theatre in Leicester Square. There is
a sighting when Mairi applied for a pass to travel to England
for a few days at the end of 1916. The diaries had gone by the
board. There were other priorities: new ideas to keep their profile
high and the fund-raising show on the road. The war smothered and sucked the life out of everything. The start of 1917 in
Flanders was bleak and grey: the biting wind gouged its way
across the clay fields and seeped into the bones of everyone in
its path. They were too cold and weary to pick up their pens
and tell us about it.

We do know about Harry in those leaden Flanders skies in
the early weeks of 1917. On 23 January he was flying an artillery
mission with Sergeant Ferreol Gustave Jenatzy, known as 'The
Pit'. Famous for his daring and iron nerves, Jenatzy had been
a racing driver before the war. The engine of their aircraft failed
and they crash-landed, but although their machine was destroyed,
they escaped unhurt. Two weeks later, on Valentine's Day, Harry
and Jenatzy were nearly shot down by a German plane while

they were on a reconnaissance trip over enemy lines at Beerst, a mile or so from Pervyse. Elsie knew how often the engines of the planes failed, and she would have been constantly worried.

By February the airfield at Coxyde was too vulnerable to German artillery and Harry's squadron moved a few miles west to Les Moeren, a hamlet between Adinkerke and Ghyvelde. Elsie was living with Mairi at Pervyse, and Harry was billeted not far away with his squadron.

There is a clue of a romantic entanglement for Mairi. In an interview in 1976 she talked about the 'jolly brave' Royal Naval Air Service officers, 'who were the greatest possible fun', who used to visit her and Elsie at night: 'I think we were one of their entertainments.' She was particularly fond of a 'lad' called Jack Petre, a squadron commander. Born at Ingatestone in Essex, John Joseph Petre was the same age as her brother and the youngest son in a family mad about flying. His elder brother Edward was killed in a flying accident on Christmas Eve 1912 while trying to fly non-stop from Brooklands racetrack to Edinburgh. Jack was a hero from the pages of a Boys' Own adventure book: a 'thoroughly upright, straight-forward boy', a corporal in the Officer Training Corps at Stonyhurst College who had won the Public School Race at Brooklands for solo motorbicycles in 1914. Mairi's new friend was also a good dancer and had been the best skater in his school. When Mairi met Jack, he had already won the Distinguished Service Cross and the Croix de Guerre for his gallantry and skill in operations over Dunkerque and Ostend. Mentioned in dispatches several times, his service record glows with remarks like 'an exceptionally brilliant pilot' and 'considerable experience in air fighting'.

So flimsy were the warplanes of the time that they were known as 'kites'. Unlike German and French pilots, British and Belgian airmen were not given parachutes until the last few months of the war on the grounds that they were supposedly too bulky (and only after persistent lobbying, with some pilots letting it be known they had bought their own). The real reasons were that the Air Board had decided that they 'might impair the fighting spirit of the pilots and cause them to abandon machines which might otherwise be capable of returning to base for repair' and that parachutes would lead to a loss of 'moral fibre'. Mairi remembered Jack doing a lot of low flying – extremely dangerous as low-flying planes were easy targets for higher German aircraft and machine-gunners on the ground. Earnestly he told her, 'I'm most interested in testing out forms of small parachutes and I'm going to parachute things down to you and you must let me know afterwards exactly where they fall.' He chucked boxes of chocolates and other gifts out of his plane, including a valuable brooch she chided him about in case she had not been able to find it.

As the war on the ground took to the skies overhead, the scope of Elsie and Mairi's work grew: they found themselves retrieving pilots' and observers' bodies from the inundations and no-man's-land. They sent their identity discs to their commanding officers and any personal effects to their families back in Britain. Until bodies were found many airmen were posted in the newspapers as missing in action, and their families hoped that they were still alive, perhaps prisoners of war. Elsie and Mairi felt strongly that the families should not live in false hope that their sons, husbands or fiancés were still alive, so they offered a bounty of a hundred francs to Belgian soldiers and civilians for every British airman's body brought to them.

One day they saw an English plane, engine spluttering, flying so low over the trenches they could see the pilot's face. He pancaked in to the water. They ran to him across the duckboarded walkways to see if he was still alive, arriving just before the Germans, who were expecting to take him prisoner and capture the plane. The Germans called out to Elsie, asking if he was injured. She snapped back in German (Mairi's translation), 'Well what the Dickens do you think after thumping down like that, of course he's wounded and we're going to take him.' The Germans agreed but said they would have the plane. The (unharmed) pilot was taken back to the post, and his CO and two other officers called in to see him. When the officers told Elsie and Mairi they were going to inspect the plane to see if it could be removed, the Angels of Pervyse begged them not to go as it would be 'absolutely madness because the Germans have a machine-gun trained on it . . . it's a suicidal job'. They would not listen and the sound of machine-gun fire soon told Elsie and Mairi what had happened. Two hours later the CO's body was brought in to them; the second officer was badly wounded and the third in shock.

Living so close to the Germans, their trenches often only a hundred feet away, Elsie's ability to speak the language meant that she and Mairi had many informal contacts with the enemy. When Bavarian soldiers took over in the German trenches relations were relaxed: the Queen of the Belgians was a Bavarian, and many of them were fonder of her than of the Kaiser. The Germans did not want to kill Elsie and Mairi and told them to wear woollen hats rather than tin helmets, which could lead to being mistaken for soldiers. When the women wanted to retrieve bodies from no-man's-land they sent Shot, their little black-and-white dog, over to the Germans with a note telling them what they wanted to do. Mairi had fond memories of how well the Germans behaved when she and Elsie were in no-man's-land: 'they looked upon us, I suppose, as being thoroughly daft . . . but they were always nice to us'.

At Christmas and Easter things got very jolly when Elsie and Mairi visited the Belgian soldiers in the trenches:

> We would shout across greetings and friendly, facetious insults to the Germans, and they would reply in kind. To add to the fun, the Germans would sometimes hoist placards on long poles with such phrases as THE BELGIANS (or it might be THE BRITISH or THE FRENCH or all three) ARE BLOODY FOOLS. This would be riddled with bullets. Next might appear ALL GERMANS ARE IDIOTS, and of course this would be heartily applauded. Next it would be LET'S ALL GO HOME, and this would cause great applause and laughter, and a feeling of mateyness. After such incidents the men would be restless and depressed.

On Sunday 11 March 1917 Elsie and Mairi swept into the Alhambra Theatre in Leicester Square, one of the biggest venues in Britain, to a rapturous welcome. Eva Moore had organised a special concert for the 'Heroines of Pervyse', to raise money for comforts for the soldiers. Miss Moore warned in the programme that they would only be able to attend if there was a lull in the fighting, so their arrival was keenly anticipated. Twenty leading actors and actresses, singers and musicians from the London stage sang and performed, including Ella Shields and Violet Loraine. Shields, an American male-impersonator in the style of Vesta Tilley, became famous with 'Burlington Bertie from Bow'. Audiences loved her cheeky working-class lad putting on the airs and graces of a toff. Violet Loraine, who recorded her big hit 'If You Were the Only Girl in the World' with heart-throb George Robey, had started her career as a chorus girl and would marry well.

In one of Mairi's scrapbooks there is a sliver of a newspaper cutting announcing that Jack Petre, the lad who had dropped parachutes of love in the form of boxes of chocolates and other gifts out of his plane, had been killed. At 11.50 a.m., on 13 April 1917 Petre died while practising firing at ground targets when his aeroplane's wings snapped off. He plummeted 300 feet to the ground at Dernacourt, near Albert, in France. A letter of condolence sent to his parents told what happened:

> By curious coincidence I came across a man the other day who was actually on the aerodrome when he was killed. Apparently what happened was, your boy was flying a Nieuport Scout, and was practising firing at a target on the ground. It seems that the more skilful pilots do this by diving vertically at the target, firing while in a vertical position, and then pull their machine up into their proper flying position when some hundreds of feet above the target. Your boy had made several dives in this way with his engine full on, and consequently attaining terrific speeds downwards. In the last of these dives it appears that he pulled his machine out of the dive quickly and something broke, so that the machine went straight to the ground.

Jack had a number of raw young pilots in his squadron and to give them confidence had been doing a lot of flying and also demonstrating spiral nosedives. A week after his death, two nurses, members of the Voluntary Aid Detachment, who knew Jack and his squadron, wrote to Mr and Mrs Petre:

> We have known your son and his friends now for more than a year . . . and we felt we must write to say how terribly upset we are about it all, and how deeply we feel for you.
>
> Out here he was thought so very much of, for his work was splendid, and he was a splendid fellow. One of his best friends passed through yesterday and said that the blank in the Squadron was awful, everyone loved him, and would have done anything for him. We have both lost brothers and friends in this war, and though letters cannot help much, yet one is so proud to hear

about them ... We have seen wonderful and very sad things too ... we have simply written because we have felt it so much.

Officers and men of the bombing school and the Royal Naval Air Service attended the requiem mass with naval honours in the family chapel at Ingatestone Hall, Essex on 27 April 1917. Jack's sword, cap and Distinguished Service Cross were placed on the catafalque, covered with the Union Jack, and a bugler from the Royal Naval Air Service at Chingford sounded the last post. Bodies were repatriated to Britain only in exceptional circumstances; he was actually buried in the village of Derna-court, where his friends put up a cross made out of a propeller. When the war was over he was re-interred at Cerisy Gailly Military Cemetery, ten kilometres south-west of Albert.

Jack had signed Elsie's album with the bold flourish that you might expect of an ace pilot, and had drawn a sketch of his aeroplane. There are some tiny photographs of his beaming smile in Mairi's photograph album. She reminisced about their wartime courtship but not about his death when she was interviewed sixty years later, although she did tell her family that they would have married if he had not been killed.

In May Mairi went back to England for two weeks. On the 16th, the night before she left, the officers of the 3DA gave a dinner for her. Elsie, Harry and Captain Vincotte, who had given Elsie away at her wedding, were there too. A sketch of her on the menu suggests they might have been trying to cheer her up for a difficult trip. She may have borrowed a motorcycle and paid a visit to Jack's parents at Ingatestone: fellow officers and friends of men killed in the war would often visit the parents of the bereaved to comfort and perhaps to receive some support in return.

While Mairi was away Elsie was given a marrow plant by

'Chips', a British officer who had returned from leave, which she planted in the 'muck-heap' at the back of the trenches. To everyone's excitement it grew to an enormous size during the summer. Elsie got Chips and his pals, their orderlies and the Belgian orderlies involved in her 'Marrow Scheme': 'The plan was to let it grow until it was really vast, and meanwhile we would go down to base and scrounge sugar to make marrow jam. Anyone going down to Calais or Boulogne was told to bring back sugar, ginger, or jars. Gradually the marrow became quite a legend. The soldiers used to salute it as they passed, everyone talked about it and noted its progress and looked forward to the Great Jam-making Day.'

On 11 June 1917 *The Times* announced the engagement of Lady Dorothie Feilding to Captain Charles Joseph Henry O'Hara Moore, of the Irish Guards, of Mooresfort, Tipperary. The marriage took place 'very quietly' at Newnham Paddox, on 5 July, partly because of the generally sombre mood but also because the family was still grieving for the death of Hugh, the youngest of Dorothie's three brothers, who was killed at the Battle of Jutland on 31 May 1915 on HMS *Defence*. Dorothie, whom the *Daily Sketch* had recently called 'our Joan of Arc in Khaki', wore a gown of cream georgette and Brussels lace; her veil was held in place with a wreath of silver leaves. There were no bridesmaids, but two of her nephews were pages. The Feildings and the Moores were joined by the wounded soldiers being cared for in the house, tenants and estate workers. Dorothie's work with Munro's ambulance corps ended with her marriage.

Except for occasional bombardments the Yser front had been quite quiet for much of the time since early 1915. Both sides knew that nothing could change unless and until the Germans could overcome the inundations, and a way of life developed in the watery landscape. Miles of duckboarded walkways criss-crossed the flooded farmland. These had to be heavily defended to prevent the Germans using them in an advance. Millions of sandbags were brought in and laid down; embankments were built to serve as above-ground trenches; and concrete and wooden shelters were dotted along the front line to offer the men some shelter from whatever the Germans and the Flanders weather threw at them. Once the building work was completed, the Yser sector settled down to a time of wait-and-see, and boredom crept in. Some soldiers posted to this part of the Western Front treated it as a holiday, a time of rest and recuperation. There was time to sketch, to study, to play cards, to grow vegetables in the gardens immediately behind the dugouts.

But in Whitehall major decisions were being made in the spring of 1917 to try to end the stalemate that had developed along the Ypres salient. Elsie and Mairi in Pervyse were at the mid point of a more or less straight line from the town of Ypres to the coast at Nieuport-les-Bains. While the inundations prevented them from being directly involved in the proposed new offensive, they were aware of rumours concerning the front a few miles to the north and south. General Douglas Haig's plan for 1917 was for the British to take back the ports of Ostend and Zeebrugge, where much of the German submarine fleet was based. This would be followed by a major assault on the German lines near Ypres and an amphibious landing near Nieuport. The British took over the coastal sector at Nieuport from the French and a number of villages along the line from the coast to Ypres were evacuated of their last remaining inhabitants. Although Pervyse always remained within the Belgian sector, a British officer did try to evacuate Elsie and Mairi from their post. From Elsie's account years later we learn that the poor man had blundered in where only the Angels of Pervyse trod. She remembered:

> When the heavy artillery started coming up I had a sharp clash with the Major in command. It was a lovely warm day for a change, and I was sitting at the end of a trench sunning myself and sewing, when this Major Christian came on to the scene. He strode over to me and stood there, his legs apart, hands on hips. I took no notice of him. 'And just what the hell do you think you're doing here ?' he roared. 'The sooner you get out of this the better.' He informed me he was setting up his big guns, and couldn't possibly be expected to fire them across trenches with women in them. He'd never known such a damned ridiculous lot of nonsense in his life.

Elsie told him that she and Mairi had been in Pervyse for three years and had no intention of leaving unless at the end of a bayonet. He spluttered and returned the next day with General Sir Henry Rawlinson, commander of the 4th Army. Elsie had to leave them to deal with some wounded men, but made her position clear as soon as she returned, by which time they had been joined by her allies the Earl of Athlone and Sir Bertrand Dawson, 'who were thoroughly enjoying the scene'. They backed her up and Major Christian had to accept defeat.

In the event the amphibious assault at Nieuport and the attacks on Ostend and Zeebrugge were postponed until the spring of 1918, and the big push happened at Ypres, now known as the Battle of Passchendaele.

A stream of Belgian and British officers and men and assorted worthies visited Elsie and Mairi; their signatures and brief messages appear in Elsie's war album. At the end of June Thomas Frederick Dawkins called in. A dashing barrister in pre-war days, he was also an official handicapper at Brooklands racetrack and the Jockey Club. In 1914 he volunteered as a driver with the British and French Red Cross. Lieutenant Anwyl Seldon of the 1st Gloucester Regiment came to Pervyse on 2 July with his second lieutenant, William Gilbert Tunnicliffe. Twenty-two-year-old Seldon won the Military Cross in September 1918 'for conspicuous gallantry and devotion to duty'. In command of an isolated position attacked from three sides, Seldon 'put up a most gallant defence . . . inflicting considerable losses'. Tunnicliffe survived the war but his left arm did not. He was badly wounded in France, and his arm amputated on 4 November 1918, in the last week of the war.

During July 1917 there was a reminder of Jack Petre, when news filtered through that Cyril Askew Eyre, who had visited Pervyse with Jack and other members of their squadron in December 1916, had been killed on the 7th. Blond and fresh-faced, he looked younger than his nineteen years. Cyril was a flight commander with the Royal Naval Air Service based at Bailleul when he was shot down over Dadizeele, a few miles east of Ypres, while escorting a photographic patrol. His younger brother Edward, also in the RNAS, was killed a few weeks later.

So newsworthy were Elsie and Mairi that Ernest Brooks, one of the two official British war photographers, visited them at Pervyse in July and early September, and took pictures that appeared in the British, French and Belgian press. The youthful-looking 'Baby Brooks' had worked as a photographer on the *Daily Mirror* following the royal family before the war. In 1914 Brooks joined the Royal Naval Volunteer Reserve Anti-Aircraft Corps and in April 1915 the Admiralty sent him to Gallipoli to record the British campaign in the Dardanelles. In 1916 he was transferred to the War Office which appointed him and John Warwick Brooke its official photographers. They were given the honorary rank of second lieutenant and sent to the Western

Front. Brooks was at the first day of the Battle of the Somme on 1 July 1916. When he returned to London at the end of July he told the *Daily Mirror* he was having an 'exciting and arduous time' and had been working 'right in the firing-line under great difficulties . . . with shells and shrapnel bursting all around'.

When Brooks arrived in Pervyse he was on his way to the Battle of Passchendaele, which started on 31 July and went on until 10 November. When he returned to see Elsie and Mairi on 7 September, his pictures of them had been published and he had witnessed the earliest days of a massive battle whose fearsome casualties would make the name of the little village in Belgium infamous.

The public were fascinated by the heroines of Pervyse, and Ernest Brooks's shots gave an intimate glimpse of their lives. In some of the pictures they shade their eyes with their hands or look into the distance through binoculars, serious about their business. There is a silhouette of Elsie rolling bandages. Others show Elsie and Mairi out and about: clambering over mounds of rubble, in the trenches joshing with Belgian soldiers, looking on admiringly as a machine-gunner fires at a 'Boche plane'. In the *Daily Graphic* they were headlined as WOMEN WHO WORK IN THE DANGER ZONE and are seen in the ambulance presented by the people of Sutton Coldfield.

They were shown treating a man on a stretcher, and preparing to get him back to the post. At times Brooks posed Elsie and Mairi like models, poking their faces through holes in brick walls and getting them to loll against doors. A shot of Mairi leaning against a sandbagged wall was captioned by the *Tatler*: 'Sandbags Instead of Handbags'. The interiors reveal cosy domesticity in shabby rooms in a war zone. The caption to a photo of them feeding a 'maimed soldier' whose head is swathed in bandages calls them 'Ministering Angels' and 'The New Ladies of the Lamp', referring back to the work of Florence Nightingale in the Crimea sixty years earlier. Gabriel, their current orderly, obliged Brooks by wearing a sling and pretending to have something taken out of his eye to illustrate the variety of injuries they dealt with. They also modelled bulky gas masks, to remind readers that they faced the threat of poison gas. And there is a nice picture of Elsie and Mairi with Gabriel, Shot the terrier and three of their cats, Chink, Dunky and Bogie. Mairi wrote on the back of her copy of the photograph, 'Family Group'.

Ernest Brooks' pictures could only present a carefully stage-managed slice of their lives. Images of Elsie and Mairi dealing with shell-shocked soldiers would not have played well to a public uncomfortable with the reality of traumatised men. Elsie's skill had been needed when a young British officer was brought to the post in a terrible state:

> The British put a field battery plumb opposite our post near the side of the road . . . and the Germans made a big show . . . and the shelling was very severe . . . When the fire died down for a bit, the gun crew brought over a young subaltern who had only been 48 hours in active service . . . and he was an absolute wreck. He was crying his eyes out and calling for his mother . . . he wasn't a soldier and it wasn't his place to be in the lines . . . She got this boy onto the camp bed and put her arms around him and he cried and cried . . . and was with him two solid hours and she wouldn't give him morphia until she fed into his subconscious that he was not a failure.

By this stage of the war Elsie and Mairi had to deal with the problem of soldiers who may or may not have been malingering. Mairi remembered trench life being 'a terrible grind for the men who got themselves tied up in knots'. They had to treat cases where men had shot their fingers off with their own rifles. Soldiers would give themselves violent stomach upsets by eating cigarettes soaked in vinegar, hoping to be sent to hospital. If the women believed injuries were self-inflicted they were expected to report the men, who would be court-martialled.

One night an eighteen-year-old Belgian sentry shot dead one of his officers, and the boy and the body were brought to the post. The lad had challenged his superior officer for the pass-word but the officer had ignored him and walked on, and acting on instructions the sentry had fired. He was 'frightfully upset and felt sure he would face a firing squad or something ghastly' when the military police arrived soon afterwards to arrest him. Elsie would not let them take the boy away, insisting that he stay the night with her and Mairi, as he 'is severely wounded in his mind and that I have to see to. I am not letting this boy go, he needs urgent attention.' The MPs left reluctantly, and returned the next morning with news that the sentry had acted correctly and would not face a court martial.

On 4 and 5 August 1917 Captain Lindsay Willett Batten of the Royal Army Medical Corps, a young doctor in his twenties who had trained at St Bartholomew's Hospital in London; Eden Wilberforce Paget, director of transport of the British Red Cross and the Order of St John, a fifty-year-old gentleman who lived on his own means; and nineteen-year-old Second Lieutenant Victor Margetts Ruston of the Royal Garrison Artillery visited the post. When they signed their names in Elsie's book the Battle of Passchendaele was in its sixth day, and the rain would not stop for many weeks in the wettest summer and autumn in living memory. Flanders mud was glutinous slime whose adhe-sive qualities were legendary: wounded soldiers could drown in it. One of the most famous images of the war is of seven stretcher bearers up to their knees in mud, struggling to evacuate a wounded soldier, taken on the second day at Passchendaele by Ernest Brooks's colleague John Warwick Brooke.

On 7 September Frank Bassill arrived in Pervyse with Brooks after several weeks in Ypres. Before 1914 Bassill had been a projectionist at the Leicester Square Empire and had worked as a cameraman for the Warwick and Pathé film companies. At the outbreak of war Pathé had sent him to the front and in 1917 he was an official kinematographer assigned to the great silent-film director, D. W Griffith. Bassill, who was in his thirties, was from Lambeth and had a wife and two children at home in Brixton. He survived the war and was a prominent newsreel cameraman in the 1920s.

Bassill and Brooks spent several days in Pervyse shooting film and taking pictures of Elsie and Mairi going about their business. A few precious feet of this silver nitrate film survives. Scenes of Elsie and Mairi riding through the ruins of Pervyse on a motorbike and sidecar were edited into films extolling women's war work and screened all over the country. For the first time British cinema audiences saw the Pervyse heroines in action: Mairi wheels their machine out of a sandbagged building and kick-starts it; Elsie climbs into the sidecar and Mairi slings her leg over the petrol tank and they go whizzing about in a grey, grainy and crackly landscape of rubble and ruins.

Brigadier General Clennell William Collingwood, who commanded the heavy artillery of the British 15th Corps, bristled into Elsie and Mairi's post the day after Brooks and Bassill. The corps had been involved in operations on the Belgian coast from the middle of June until mid-November, and had been involved in intense fighting to defend their Allied position at Nieuport, where the front line ran into the sea and was bitterly contested by the Germans. In the third week of August General Haig and Admiral Bacon had abandoned the idea of an amphibious assault on the Belgian coast, especially the submarine pens that caused such havoc to Allied shipping. Collingwood's visit to Pervyse was part of a roving mission to inspect all the artillery pieces under his command, and there was also a public-relations aspect – to jolly up the Belgian artillerymen and to spend time with the most famous women on the Western Front.

Around this time several young pilots from the Royal Flying Corps and the Royal Naval Air Service at Dunkerque inscribed their names in Elsie's visitors' book. Nineteen-year-old Flight Sub Lieutenant Alan Colin Campbell Orde was lucky to survive the war. Shortly after he visited Pervyse his Sopwith Camel was completely destroyed but he walked away unscathed, while a month later he broke his right leg in another incident. Captain Robert Willan Paylor Hall of the Royal Flying Corps was from Lancaster. A dentist's son, he survived the war and married his fiancée, Nannie Wakelin, in 1920. Eighteen-year-old Flight Sub Lieutenant Oliver William Redgate was from Nottingham. Within six weeks of meeting Elsie and Mairi he had shot down two German aircraft above Pervyse, one of which he chased down to a hundred feet above the ground and forced to crash three miles behind the German lines. He survived the war but was only thirty when he died in 1929.

Owen Johann Scholte and John Chevallier Boughton, both from the Royal Flying Corps, also visited. Scholte, twenty-one, was the son of an Amsterdam-born Savile Row military tailor and had recently been decorated with the Military Cross for 'gallantry and devotion to duty'. On 2 July 1917, while flying a patrol over Ostend, he spotted five Gotha planes returning from a raid on England. He dived to the attack, and 'as a result of his vigilance and promptitude one of the enemy planes was destroyed'. Two weeks later he was flying over Flanders and attacked seven hostile planes, which were driven off. He did not survive the war, but died of his wounds in France on 30 July, 1918. Scholte's friend Second Lieutenant Boughton was ten years older than him and the son of an Ipswich publican.

At the beginning of October Mairi pasted a poignant news cutting into her scrapbook reporting the death of Flight Commander Theophilus Chater Vernon, an airman in his twenties from the RNAS who had visited Pervyse. In 1915 he had had a serious accident while learning to fly, suffering severe shock and facial injuries. On 15 September 1917 he was shot down in his Sopwith Camel while making a 'gallant attempt to save a machine of his squadron', and was buried at Malo-les-Bains. Tiny pieces of newsprint about men who died are scattered all over Elsie and Mairi's albums.

A senior government minister, Ian Macpherson, under-secretary for war, visited Elsie and Mairi's post in early October on one of his regular visits to the front. Before the war Macpherson, a Gaelic-speaking barrister, was the Liberal member of parliament for Ross and Cromarty. He had defended two suffragettes, Kitty Marion, a well-known music-hall artiste whose career had been halted by her activities, and Clara Giveen, a 'lady of independent means'. They were found guilty of setting fire to buildings at Hurst Park racecourse on 8 June 1913, the day that Emily Wilding Davison died of the injuries she sustained making her protest at the Derby four days earlier.

In Elsie's war album a page of autographs conjures up a scene of fun and high jinks, of men dressing up as women and putting on make-up. On the night of 6 October the Crumps, a troupe of entertainers named after the sound of an exploding shell, gave a concert party in Elsie and Mairi's hut at Steenkerke. Like the other concert parties the Pedlars, the Cads, the Irresponsibles and the Iddy Umpties, they toured the front to boost morale. There were twelve Crumps that evening: a captain, a gunner, a couple of corporals and lance corporals; the rest were privates serving with various units in the British 41st Division. They did card tricks, performed sketches, came on as winsome, white-faced, heavily pompommed pierrots, sang and danced – bringing gaiety and greasepaint to Elsie and Mairi's chilly hut. Private Purkiss, who signed himself 'the girl' in Elsie's album, had a bobbed wig, Cupid's-bow lips, and showed his stockinged legs, teasing his audience by playing with the hem of his flowery frock. It was a rare night of fun in that dank landscape.

At home Elsie and Mairi's work in Pervyse was being generously supported by Scottish mine owners and miners, who donated money to the British Red Cross Society for the two ambulances they received in September. Robert Smillie, president of the Scottish Miners' Federation, and William Anderson of the Scottish branch of the Red Cross, wrote to Mairi expressing their gratitude for 'doing such excellent work for the benefit of those who are fighting so nobly and suffering so sorely . . . in this cruel war'. Mairi promised to send them photographs Ernest Brooks had taken.

From the middle of October to the spring of 1918 Brooks's photographs of Elsie and Mairi appeared regularly in the English, French and Belgian newspapers, to coincide with news that they were to be awarded the Military Medal. King George V had recognized the women's long-standing 'gallantry in the field'. Their friend Dorothie Feilding, who got hers in September 1916, was the first English woman to be awarded the Military Medal. Elsie and Mairi were two of four nurses decorated that autumn for their courage, and were praised for having 'carried on' for more than three years.

Elsie's husband Harry spent much of 1917 as observer with Second Lieutenant Robert Marie Théodore Émile Bonnevie, who was four years younger than him. Harry and Robert would take off from Les Moeren, reconnoitre the area and fire on the Germans below. When Harry was off duty he would take his pals from the squadron to visit Elsie and Mairi, where they signed the visitors' book with the sort of flourishes one might expect from men banking and wheeling over enemy lines avoiding machine-gun fire. Bonnevie had been posted to Harry's squadron 2 May 1917, and a week later he and Harry went on an hour-long reconnaissance mission, the first of fifty sorties they flew together. Their artillery flights on 25 May, 3 June and 12 August were successful – 'the target was dealt with' their log reveals. They encountered enemy aircraft several times but managed to get back to base safely. On one occasion their engine failed, forcing them to land, safely, at their old airfield at Coxyde. On 17 October they were attacked by three German planes in the skies over Dixmude but thanks to Bonnevie's skill got back in one piece.

On the 28 October Elsie and Mairi travelled to England, and Mairi stayed at Brown's Hotel in Dover Street rather than in Maida Vale. Perhaps her uncle was unwell: letters from Pervyse to Maida Vale and back had been full of concern about 'dear Uncle Freddy's' health. Mairi had her portrait taken by Abdey, a husband-and-wife team of society photographers (Herbert and Winifred), wearing her khaki coat and scarf tied nurse's style. They posed her facing the camera with her arms folded, drawing attention to the two rows of medal ribbons sewn to her coat.

During their two-week visit the publisher Adam Black presented Elsie and Mairi with the specially designed ambulance motorcycle and sidecar paid for by the royalties from Geraldine Mitton's book *The Cellar-House of Pervyse*. Elsie was photographed astride the eight-horsepower Douglas Matchless, her hands firmly on the handlebars, itching to be gone. Immediately behind her stands Adam Black, a veiled Miss Mitton and John Billinge, their loyal supporter from Manchester, in front of Black's office in Soho Square. Mairi looks unhappy or perhaps bored. Elsie was always more of a lover of the lime-light, Mairi uncomfortable at being the centre of attention. Inside the sidecar a young man lies down to demonstrate the capabil-ities of the special machine. The Empire Sidecar Company had thought of everything: it was long enough to lie down in, uphol-stered and fitted with 'luxurious cushions', a hood, side curtains and a tarpaulin to 'protect against the elements'.

Elsie and Mairi got back into their routine of talking about their work and making sure their faces were in the newspapers; for this Ernest Brooks's pictures were invaluable. They wanted to enlarge the post to treat more men and wrote a new pamphlet, 'Our Red Cross Work in Flanders', which was launched during their visit. The pamphlet began:

> We wonder how many people realise what it means to be going through a fourth winter in Flanders? Our work is endless, day and night; the sick and wounded in the front line cannot choose the time of their arrival. They come at any time and our door must ever be open. It is almost impossible for those at home to realise what the work is, or the tremendous area that it covers. They do not know that *never* can we honestly say 'Now we are off duty.' They do not realise that even if we are sick and ill, we *must* exert ourselves almost to breaking point, in order to see the work carried through.

The tone was personal and emotional, describing bluntly their gritty daily lives, the hopeless cases they collected in their ambu-lance and those they brought to the post, some of whom were too bad to be evacuated to hospital. One young boy was brought in with a ghastly head wound, and all Elsie and Mairi could do was to make him comfortable and watch him die: 'For one hour and a half he lay there gasping – chest heaving, mercifully unconscious – dying the soldier's death. For one hour and a half we stood by him and watched, praying agonised prayers that the thin, frail thread might be snapped, and that Death might wrap him in her arms, and lull him to sleep. At last it came.'

Because Elsie and Mairi were so close to the front line, many of the men they watched die were friends: 'It is heart-rending work, because we *know* so many of our patients. In a hospital, strangers come and go, but we live amongst the officers and men.' Elsie and Mairi knew about their mothers, wives and girl-friends, had discussed their future plans. The pamphlet also explained the routine they followed when a man died: they called for a doctor to give a cause of death, then they would empty the man's pockets, tying his letters and postcards from home, cigarettes and money into a bag, and sending it to his commanding officer to be returned to his next of kin. Elsie and Mairi admitted it was difficult to convey all the horrors they had seen. They worried that people 'would shake their heads and say that it was impossible' and 'it is for that reason that we slur over the reality, and only touch on it here and there, leaving it to the imagination of those who cannot imagine, because they have not seen'. They hoped to start 1918 without having to worry about a lack of funds.

On 6 December Elsie and Mairi were presented with the Queen Elisabeth Medal by the Queen of the Belgians, an honour given to 'Belgians and foreign individuals who have devoted themselves to war work'. On 14 December Elsie returned to England alone as Mairi could not be spared from the post. Elsie was guest of honour at a dinner given by the Pervyse Committee of Friends at the Midlands Hotel in Manchester. She then gave 'lantern lectures' and a 'thrilling account' of their work in Altrincham and Sale, and collected a hundred and fifty pounds (now £18,000) to take back to Pervyse. Ernest Brooks's photographs were used to make a Christmas card featuring 'Greetings and Thanks from Ourselves and from the British and Belgian soldiers'.

Elsie and Mairi were both in Pervyse for the fourth Christmas of the war. They were still living a dugout life; the war was as bogged down as it had ever been. Some friends had been killed, and also a loved one, Jack Petre. Harry and Elsie celebrated their second Christmas as the Baron and Baroness de T'Serclaes. We do not know where the rest of Harry's family were: they may have been living in exile in England or Switzerland. Perhaps Elsie's ten-year-old, Kenneth, in Marlborough with the Upcotts, wondered when his famous and brave mother would be coming home, with a father for the first time.

VII

Gas!

In January 1918 Elsie and Mairi entered into a lively correspondence about handlebars with 'Boadicea', *Motor Cycling*'s lady columnist. Motorbikes had taken them on the first stage of their journey to war and it was these beloved machines they chose to read and write about during those bone-chillingly cold days. Reminiscing about tyres, ruts and hairpin bends would have been a welcome distraction from the gnawing fear that the prospects for an Allied victory seemed bleak. The Germans were dug in on the Western Front and could not be budged. The Russians had withdrawn from the war and were making peace with Germany, freeing hundreds of German soldiers from the Eastern Front. The Allies' naval blockade was starving German civilians and hurting their production of munitions, but the U-boats were also causing havoc to British food supplies. Feeling optimistic about the prospect of success the German high command was planning to break the deadlock with a new offensive in the spring.

In the middle of February Elsie and Mairi returned to London to receive another award, the Honorary Associate's Cross of the Order of St John of Jerusalem. Eva Moore was present in the medieval oak hall at St John's Gate, Clerkenwell, and said it

Elsie and Mairi with Prince Alexander August Frederick William of Teck (the one with the stick), 1917. Because of anti-German feeling he anglicised his name and became Alexander Cambridge. Elsie remembered 'we were all so sorry when "Tecky" became the Earl of Athlone. It seemed such a fearful comedown.'

Mairi in a punt with 'Tecky' (top). Elsie in a punt with 'Tecky', Commander Halahan and Captain Laurie (bottom). 'Nobody enjoyed a prank more than Prince Alexander of Teck … who was a frequent visitor of ours. We found an old punt in the ruins which gave us much amusement. It was put into a waterlogged shell crater and distinguished guests were taken there for a picnic. It was known as 'Henley' for we would sit there and pretend we were at the Regatta.'

Six of The Crumps who performed for Elsie and Mairi and their patients at Steenkerke on 6 October 1917. Named after the sound of a shell exploding, they were one of dozen theatrical troupes who toured the Western Front to raise morale and enliven the long winter evenings. Private Purkiss was 'the girl'.

Elsie and Mairi were the most photographed women of the First World War. Mobbed by their admiring public when they made flying visits to England, pavement artists would advertise their appearances in halls all over the country. (Those are camouflage screens beside the road.)

Their terrier Shot, an important member of the team who took messages to the Belgian trenches, accompanied Elsie and Mairi on their photo-shoot with Ernest Brooks, the official war photographer, in the summer of 1917. Shot was also a frequent visitor to the German trenches, vital when the enemy wanted to send a message to the women about avoiding a forthcoming bombardment.

This photograph of Elsie and Mairi's third first-aid post was taken in the late summer of 1917. They treated wounded soldiers in this battered building until March 1918 when they were gassed. Elsie kept the Red Cross flag, which she called 'The Pervyse Flag', as a relic from her time in Belgium, and would bring it out for photographs in the decades to come.

The *Daily Mirror* captioned this 'The New Ladies of the Lamp'. Elsie and Mairi were put on the same pedestal as Florence Nightingale.

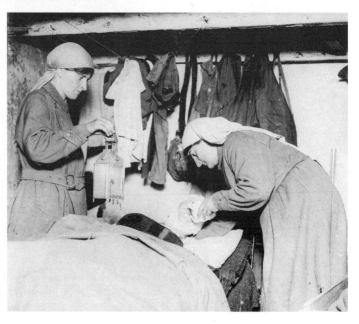

Elsie and Mairi had to take cover when they were visiting the trenches with Ernest Brooks. Their orderly has been knocked to the ground by the explosion.

Mairi wrote 'Family group' on the back of this photograph taken in 1917. Elsie holds their terrier, Shot; Mairi has her hands full with Chink and Dunky; and Gabriel holds Bogie. Everyone survived the gas attack in 1918 except Shot, whose barking had woken them up, but who died soon afterwards.

In pain and unable to stand, Elsie recovering from the gas attack in a nursing home in Chelsea. 'We were accustomed to bombardment. I suppose our dug-out must have been hit a hundred times. But in this last attack the shelling was more dreadful than anything we have ever known.'

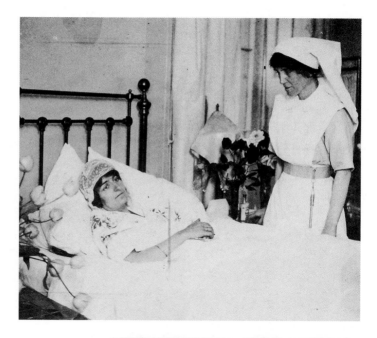

Mairi stayed with the theatrical couple Eva Moore and Henry V. Esmond at their home in Chelsea while she recovered from being gassed in March 1918. She went back to Pervyse but was gassed again. It was through Eva and Henry that Mairi met Noel Coward and was lionised by his set.

The engagement photograph of Mairi to Captain William Thomas 'Bob' Hall of the Royal Flying Corps, taken in August 1918. They met in June when she joined the Women's Royal Air Force. Jack Petre, the man whom it is said she would have married, had been killed in France in April 1917. For reasons that are not known the marriage did not go ahead, although his picture remains in her photograph album.

Mairi's life-long friend, May Davidson lived at Cantray House near Nairn. May's mother invited Mairi to stay for a rest after her hectic war work and later she helped the Davidsons run their Highland estate. The house burned down in October 1921.

Mairi's brother Uailean was in his thirties when this photograph was taken in Scotland in about 1928. During the war he served with the British West India Regiment in Egypt and Palestine.

Mairi and May relocated their poultry-breeding business to Maisonette, near St Helier in Jersey, in the 1930s. May took this photograph. Back row, left to right: Miss Davis, the governess; 'John's' sister; Mairi and 'Bird'. Front row, left to right: 'John' and Mairi's nephews Alastair and Ruari.

Every inch the Baroness, Elsie in her pearls and fur, with her dog in the 1960s. Photographed in front of her handsome son's portrait at 'Pervyse Cottage' in Ashtead, Surrey. Wing Commander Kenneth Duke Knocker was killed in July 1942 in a raid on Bremen, leaving a widow and two small sons.

From the early 1950s to the 1970s Mairi would spend the morning corresponding with the Clan Chisholm Society and then take the dogs for a walk. Memories of the war were never far away, a favourite chair was a pilot's seat from an aeroplane and she used a walking-stick made from a propeller.

was one of the most impressive occasions she had ever attended. Two days later, on 17 February, Elsie and Mairi were again on stage at the Alhambra Theatre in Leicester Square, among a star-studded cast performing at 'Eva Moore's Matinee for the Women of Pervyse'. Wearing their bemedalled khaki coats, khaki headscarves and big boots, Elsie and Mairi reprised their routine. It was a full house – 4,000 – and many more were turned away. In the wings the leading ladies and men of the London stage waited. Frank Bassill's recent film of Elsie and Mairi at work was screened, and lantern slides were shown of the post. There was a plan to open more dressing stations on the front line, each needing concrete walls five feet thick and thirty-six layers of sandbags. Mairi's aunt Lucy, there that afternoon, noticed that her niece 'looked very slight and pale, her face so sad'. At the end of the afternoon Joe Coyne, an American musical comedy actor, auctioned the relics that Elsie and Mairi had brought back from Flanders. The hands of the church clock at Pervyse went for sixty pounds; fragments of the church bell raised twenty pounds and a silver medal Elsie had taken from a dead German officer realised a hundred and twenty-five pounds.

Elsie and Mairi returned to Flanders on 19 February, taking with them cash and pledges of money worth £1,500, (£60,000 today). A full-page photograph of the 'brave and devoted ladies' appeared in the *Tatler*. In March they also appeared in the British Official War Photographs Exhibition at Grafton Galleries in New Bond Street, where they were shown in their uniforms and medals and looking after a patient in their dugout. Tribute was paid to the photographers, who had plodded 'painfully through the mud often at the rate of a few hundred yards in many hours, while the ground about them is being swept with shell-fire'.

On 6 March, capitalising on the dry weather that had reduced the inundations on the Yser front, the Germans launched an 'exceptionally heavy' bombardment of shells and poison gas before their storm troops assaulted the Belgian lines between Nieuport on the coast and Pervyse. Elsie and Mairi's friends beat off the Germans with rifles and machine guns and retook the line. During the next two weeks the Germans launched attacks along the Belgian line that were eventually repulsed in bloody hand-to-hand fighting. Starting on 15 March Pervyse was bombarded for several days ahead of the offensive launched on 21 March to try to seize British-held Dunkerque.

For two days Elsie and Mairi were caught in the thick of it, the shelling so intense 'you couldn't hear yourself think'. Mairi remembered, 'the whole place went up, the whole line was one long roar and it went on non-stop'. The women hid in their dug out with their orderlies, the wounded and their pets, every sense assaulted by the continuous bombardment. 'We slept in tiny bunks, you could touch the walls all round, and the passageway from where we received the wounded had been entirely blown in with shellfire . . . There were slanting cuts for air, which we stuffed with our Aquascutums as there were shell splinters coming in from all directions.' In the early hours of the morning of the 17 March 1918 Elsie and Mairi were nearly killed in a gas attack. Since poison gas had been used for the first time, on 22 April 1915, at Ypres, they had been equipped with gas masks, but until now they had had no need for them. In the days leading up to the 17th they had worn their masks as a precaution, but 'we were nearly dead with it because they pinched your nose hard, and you breathed through a tube which dribbled down your chest'. They had taken the masks off just before the Germans lobbed a salvo of arsenic gas shells into the broken-down passageway which led straight back into their position. Even though no one was wearing their masks, Elsie, Mairi, the doctor, Gabriel the orderly and the current patients survived, but one of their drivers was killed. The gas made their heads swim, they vomited and coughed and gasped for air. Their terrier Shot, who had been so efficient at dealing with the growing rat population and who had wandered into so many of Ernest Brooks's photographs, died. A month later Elsie, who was frail and almost unable to stand, described the scene to a journalist from the *Daily Express* from a nursing home in Chelsea:

> The firing was so heavy that I got out of my bunk and said to Miss Chisholm, 'We had better dress, there are sure to be wounded.' While dressing I heard a shell burst outside our dug-out, and a moment later I found Gabriel, our soldier orderly, lying on the floor. I rushed up to him to see if he were wounded, and suddenly I felt as if a rope had been fastened round my neck. I could not breathe and was utterly helpless. Miss Chisholm was rolling on the floor. My little dog, Shot, who had been with us for three years, came up and looked at me with wondering eyes. He licked my hands and then died. I don't think that ever before I had felt I hated the enemy, but ever since my dog was gassed I've wanted, I've longed to kill a German.

The three cats survived by crawling under a pile of blankets, and their chickens were unharmed. Elsie and Mairi were taken for medical treatment to La Panne in a lorry as their ambulance had been destroyed, and Elsie remembered gulping for air, surrounded by dozens of soldiers, thinking her lungs would burst or be 'torn from my body'. A nurse gave her a sedative injection in her thigh, and she thought how funny she must have looked with her breeches pulled down in the midst of all the men.

Elsie and Mairi's clothes were destroyed as they were saturated with gas. Two days later they were moved to Lady

Hatfield's Hospital at Boulogne, where a Swiss specialist was 'frightfully intrigued with us because of the arsenic'. Opinion had it that if it had been pure mustard gas they would have been killed. Elsie, who was more badly affected, had to be evacuated to a London hospital and then a nursing home. Her return to Pervyse was forbidden.

> I was in no condition to be able to put up much of a fight when I was firmly told that this time the post at Pervyse would have to close down – for good. Surrounded by comforts and expert nursing, I was more desolate and wretched than I had ever been in my life. Not even the flowers that filled my room or the kind phone-calls that came from Queen Mary and Queen Alexandra could rally me. My life seemed to be in pieces, and I had not the heart to try and put it back together again.

On the 26 March Mairi received a letter from the commanding officer of the 3DA, who was sorry to hear that 'an intoxication arising out of the gas emitted by enemy shells has necessitated your admission to hospital'. He continued:

> The entire Belgian army and especially the many soldiers on whom you have unfailingly bestowed your care and kindness, will, upon learning of this news, have been greatly moved . . . In spite of the warnings that were given you on various occasions about the dangers to which you were exposed, you have, like any <u>soldier</u> aware of his duty, sought to remain at your post. Alas, a perfidious and inhuman means used by the enemy has obliged you to abandon it against your will . . . It is nevertheless essential that, from this time forth, you should no longer be exposed to all the dangers of war.

But Mairi had no intention of abandoning her work, and after convalescing in London she returned to Pervyse. Three weeks later she was gassed again and the Belgian army closed the post for good, thanking the women for all the work they had done. On 7 April, as soon as she was fit to travel, Mairi packed up their things and returned to England with the cats and chickens (one of whom would be auctioned in a charity bazaar). She was spotted at Waterloo by someone who told the *Sunday Pictorial* that she looked 'lovely but very frail' as she waited to catch the train to Bournemouth for a holiday with friends. She then returned to London to stay with Eva Moore and her husband at their home in Chelsea.

News of this latest ordeal of the 'dauntless' women did not appear in the British press for a week, but a flood of stories and photographs of Mairi and Elsie filled the pages of newspapers and magazines during April. Wearing a Belgian lace nightcap and surrounded by bouquets of flowers, a nurse hovering by her bedside, Elsie looked delicate and fed up when she was photographed by the *Daily Mirror*. She told journalists she had been in 'great pain' and melted the heart of a *Daily Express* reporter, who depicted her as 'a frail and beautiful figure' as she lay back on the pillows describing the bombardment and pointing out that she and Mairi had been used to it, but 'in this last attack the shelling was more dreadful than anything we have ever known'. Elsie made an appeal for a dog to replace Shot, a black-and-white rough-haired terrier: 'I want so much to get another dog [as much] like him in appearance and character as possible. Perhaps someone could help me find one.'

VIII

Back to Blighty

O n 12 April the *Daily Mirror* filled its front page with
TWO HEROINES AND THEIR PETS. Mairi, wearing her khaki
uniform was being helped by Eva Moore to feed the
chickens she had brought back from Pervyse; there was a picture
of their orderly Gabriel, and a close-up of Mairi cuddling Chink.
Readers were also reminded that Elsie and Mairi used to drive
their motorbikes 'through London traffic in a way that brought
one's heart into one's mouth'. And in *Motor Cycling* 'Boadicea'
paid tribute to Elsie, for whom 'all women riders are grateful
as one of the pioneers of feminine motor cycling, and whose
example during her absence, had borne fruit in the hundreds of
women now riding motorcycles on national service'.

As they were recovering from their injuries Elsie and Mairi
read the sad news in *The Times* on 26 April that their dear
friend Captain Harry Halahan had been killed three days earlier,
on St George's Day. He had led a naval storming party of 200
men of HMS *Vindictive* in a daring and complicated attack
involving dozens of ships on the German sea defences at
Zeebrugge, which harboured enemy torpedo craft and
submarines. Halahan had written to Admiral Keyes, in command
of the operation, 'I would very much like to take part in it. I

would willingly accept the condition that I should not expect to come back.'

The Royal Navy planned to sink three old cruisers to block Zeebrugge's access to the North Sea, but before they could do that the *Vindictive* and two Mersey ferries had to land assault parties on the mile-long pier and two submarines filled with explosives were to be detonated under the viaduct that linked the pier to the shore. The viaduct was blown up but one of the blocking ships was damaged before she could reach her position. Star shells lit up the night sky, exposing the *Vindictive* to German gunners as she tried to manoeuvre into position. Many men had been killed or wounded before Harry and his men set off. He was the first of his party to be mown down by machine-gun fire. His body was brought back to Dover, but 'as he had always expressed a desire for burial at sea his wish was complied with'. Over 200 'gallant souls' were killed and 400 men were wounded in the partly successful raid on Zeebrugge. A year later Harry's widow Brenda was presented with a gun captured on the day her husband had been killed by the man who had been in charge of the operation. It is hard to understand how receiving a German trophy could ease the pain of losing one's husband or father, but such ceremonies were frequently conducted at the time.

Elsie was an impatient patient. She had time to 'brood' and worry about getting back to work. One of her visitors was Major General Sir Godfrey Paine, master-general of personnel of the Royal Air Force, who asked her if she would like to join the brand new Women's Royal Air Force, founded on 1 April. Mairi was also invited to join as an officer. Paine warned her it would be a tough job. Elsie immediately accepted but told him she needed a rest before she took up her new post.

In May Elsie went to stay with 'Daisy' Greville, Lady Warwick, a mistress of the late King Edward VII, at Easton Lodge, her country house at Dunmow in Essex. After nearly four years of roughing it Elsie enjoyed the luxury of a four-poster bed and being able to have as many hot baths as she liked. One day riding on the estate she was shocked to find herself face to face with a man in a German army uniform, one of six prisoners of war employed by her hostess.

The war was still raging and Elsie and Mairi kept in touch with Pervyse, sticking news cuttings in their scrapbooks about what was happening. Elsie was dazzled by Daisy, 'who had been a great friend of King Edward VII, and I could quite understand why, for not only was she very beautiful, but had a rich and fascinating personality'. There was a menagerie in the grounds, and four pet monkeys ran riot through the house: 'They ran up and down the corridors, and in and out of rooms, doing just what they liked. They would swarm all over the table during meals and snatch anything they fancied – it might be a nice little lamb chop or a piece of toast . . . One breakfast-time one of them scooped up a handful of butter and sloshed it on my hair.'

Lady Warwick was a society hostess who had founded a needlework school for girls at Easton and Studley Agricultural College for Women in Warwickshire. An extravagant ball she hosted in Warwick Castle in 1895 was criticised in the pages of the socialist newspaper the *Clarion* by its editor Robert Blatchford. She asked to meet him and as a result was converted to socialism. Elsie enjoyed her holiday at Easton, the gossipy evenings when Lady Warwick regaled her guests with indiscreet stories of the high life before the war had come along and spoiled everything. H. G. Wells rented a cottage on the estate and was a frequent dinner guest. Elsie, who liked to talk, faced serious competition from Wells: 'he hardly ever stopped talking, fortunately quite enthrallingly, in his funny high-pitched voice'. But she felt intimidated by his knowledge: 'he was full of theories of the past, present and future, and the play of his intellect was in itself the highest possible kind of entertainment'.

Elsie and Mairi were interviewed for the Women's Royal Air Force by its newly appointed commandant, the Honourable Violet Douglas-Pennant. The heroines of Pervyse were regarded as inspirational figures likely to attract the large numbers of women needed as officers, drivers, cooks, clerks and mechanics for the fledgling organisation. They were pictured in the newspapers being trained in motor mechanics at Woolwich, peering at the engine of a motorcycle, about which they probably knew more than their moustachioed instructor from the British School of Motoring.

However, even administratively experienced, capable ladies like Lady Gertrude Crawford, who had preceded Violet Douglas-Pennant, had struggled to cope with the many problems that quickly emerged: a shortage of uniforms, anger over pay, dismal living conditions in some camps and the new recruits going on strike. Created at the same time as the RAF, the WRAF was something of an afterthought, and it muddled through its first year. Lady Crawford, wife of a lieutenant colonel in the Indian Army and well known for her woodturning before the war, resigned after a month, frustrated by the logistical and personnel problems of the new organisation.

In May, Violet Douglas-Pennant, in her forties with several years' experience as a national health commissioner for South Wales, got to grips with the job. During her first month she toured the country, visiting many of the WRAF's 500 camps, and was dismayed to find that there were only seventy-five officers to supervise sixteen thousand women. She was concerned by inappropriate behaviour, having to admonish three clerks for 'hysterical horseplay in déshabillée' after office hours. There were persistent rumours about immorality among members of the RAF and the WRAF at Hurst Park Motor Transport Depot, near Hampton Court Palace. Perhaps relying on hearsay evidence, she became convinced that the colonel in charge 'was giving night leave to the girls and that they were in the habit of returning at four o'clock in the morning sometimes drunk in Government motor-cars'.

On 5 June Elsie and Mairi were snapped selling flags outside the Berkeley Hotel in aid of the War Hospital Supply Depot in Kensington. The IRREPRESSIBLES OF DEVOTED WAR SERVICE were in their Pervyse khaki, and their friend Eva Moore was wearing a nurse's uniform. Two weeks later Elsie ran a stall at a flower fair in Trafalgar Square in aid of the British Ambulance Committee, which had supplied 300 ambulances and brought home 300,000 wounded men from France. The square had been transformed into a 'fragrant garden' for the six days of the fair. Huge water lilies jostled for space in the fountains and there was an exhibition of 'enticing vegetables displayed on black velvet with orchids in front of them and roses and carnations on either side'. To remind everyone why they were there, 'an ambulance shattered by shell-fire from the Front' stood close by.

June 22 1918 was the last time Elsie and Mairi appeared in public together. They were invited by Eva Moore to the Children's Salon held at the Connaught Hotel in Great Queen Street, where prizes were awarded to upper-class children for painting, singing and dancing. A scheme founded by the *Gentlewoman* magazine in 1890 for 'the children of the rich to work for the children of the poor', by 1915 there were over four hundred 'fairy godmothers', 'rich little girls who each took a poor little girl under their care' and sent them gifts and 'cheery letters'. The money they raised had provided eleven cots in London hospitals. Surrounded by beautifully dressed children and their nannies, Elsie and Mairi looked soldierly in their khaki uniforms and big boots watching Princess Mary awarding the prizes. Elsie then told the children about the work she and Mairi had done in Pervyse, reminding them that there were many wounded children in Flanders.

In July Elsie and Mairi were appointed hostel administrator and deputy hostel administrator in charge of catering and welfare at a WRAF officer-training centre at Roper Hall in New Eltham in Kent. Under Elsie's influence it was a happy place where the trainee officers had 'a right jolly time', with plenty of hard work and regular sing-songs. On 29 August she celebrated her thirty-fourth birthday by throwing a party for 200 wounded soldiers from local hospitals in the grounds of the college. The probationary officers laid on the tea and refreshments, while Elsie and her staff of fellow officers played games with the men. In the evening Commandant Violet Douglas-Pennant visited the party and gave out prizes, putting on a brave face the day after she had been dismissed from the WRAF.

Mairi was not at the party; at the end of August she had become engaged to Second Lieutenant William Thomas James Hall, known as 'Bob', of the Royal Air Force, who like Elsie's husband was an observer. Pictures of the couple in uniform appeared in many newspapers, the captions announcing they had met while they were both training officers. Mairi has a tight shy smile on her face. Her fiancé was five feet nine inches tall, a Londoner a couple of years younger than her, and had been to Westminster City School. He lived in Portland Place and his father was a caterer. He had joined the Royal Flying Corps in August 1917, but his less than perfect eyesight had prevented

him from training as a pilot. Second Lieutenant Hall was somewhat accident-prone, and was concussed four times in his short
flying career. Several weeks after his engagement to Mairi, on
15 October 1918, Hall and his pilot were returning to their airfield
in France when they overshot the runway and crashed. Both
men managed to scramble out of the wreckage and ten days
later William Hall was admitted to a hospital in Bryanston
Square. His war was effectively over with this final accident,
for early in 1919 he became ill with shell shock attributed to the
crashes, and was sent to Hastings to convalesce. Mairi's aunt
Lucy, who could be critical, liked him, calling him a 'nice honest
natural boy'.

On 7 September the WRAF announced in *The Times* that
Mrs Gwynne-Vaughan, chief controller of Queen Mary's Army
Auxiliary Corps (QMAAC), had been appointed commandant,
its third in six months. Before the war she had been a professor
of botany at Birkbeck College in London, and only reluctantly
took over from Violet Douglas-Pennant. Her predecessor had
criticised the way Hurst Park was run to her superior officer, a
close friend of the colonel in charge: 'He [Sir Sefton Brancker]
seemed very angry and told me that though he understood I
was very efficient, I was grossly unpopular with everyone who
had ever seen me. He spoke in a bullying, blistering and
contemptible manner.' There was public sympathy for her, and
a select committee of the House of Lords heard evidence from
witnesses in 1919. Their lordships concluded there had been no
impropriety at Hurst Park, and Douglas-Pennant was sued for
libel and lost. She never fully recovered from her dismissal and
its aftermath.

Elsie and Mairi arrived at Hurst Park at the beginning of
September, where Elsie was put in charge of the motor transport
section. They trained women to drive Crossley tenders, large

lorries that were the armed forces' workhorse. They were big beasts that needed to be hand-cranked with a starting handle. Elsie and Mairi did not turn a hair when they saw their accommodation in the mews of Hampton Court Palace; they were used to far worse in Flanders. Elsie was impressed with the trainees at Hurst Park: 'the speed at which the women got off the mark at a moment's notice to all parts of the country made me quite proud of them. We were getting some excellent officers through.'

On 20 September Elsie was in Liverpool for a WRAF day and rally, to try to recruit women for the new organisation. There was an exhibition including the aeroplane of a 'famous Hun airman', machine guns, bombs and photographs of the work and social life the new recruits could expect. Elsie led a procession round the city in the afternoon, and in the evening spoke at the rally in St George's Hall: 'I know the men are looking to the women of England to help them. Shall we appeal in vain for twenty thousand women? I look to Liverpool to give us a good send-off.'

On the platform with Elsie was Dr Letitia Fairfield, medical director of the WRAF and sister of the writer Rebecca West. Dr Fairfield had the honorary rank of lieutenant colonel and enjoyed noting how the top brass reacted when they met her for the first time:

> I have been round dozens of camps and am getting used to lunching with Generals . . . One never knows whether one is going to be received as a sort of head cook by a junior subaltern (very rarely) or whether as happened the other day one will be treated as a member of the Higher Command and find the Colonel and the next six officers in the camp waiting to receive one. I regret to say in the latter instance the Adjutant gave the show away by bursting into giggles and saying to the Colonel, 'We didn't expect a lady, did we, sir?'

Letitia Fairfield was upbeat about her new role. She visited the aerodromes which were 'springing up like mushrooms' all over the country, she liked her 'lovely uniform' and enjoyed her work despite having only a handful of doctors on her team six months into the job. Finding women doctors and assistants was difficult as they were thin on the ground, and one time she chose 'one girl of whom I knew nothing because I liked her long black eyelashes'. The men she worked with were 'delightful', especially General Munday, who got permission for her to be flown to many of her inspection visits. 'To proceed by aircraft' was a unique privilege, and she told a friend, 'You won't realise the significance of this for I believe America even trains women pilots but in England it is a court-martial offence for a woman to get into an aeroplane.'

On 11 November 1918 the Armistice was signed and the war was over. The country erupted into joy mixed with a numbing sadness at the thought of all the men and boys who would never return, of the nurses and munition workers who had been killed doing their bit and of the men who had come back but would never fully recover from their injuries and experiences. Every town, village and hamlet had cause to celebrate and grieve. Elsie was apprehensive about the future. She had mixed feelings about the end of the war and 'could not join in the fun without reservations'. It was a 'bitter blow' not to have been in Flanders to see the Germans swept out of the country: 'after being with King Albert's Army for three and a half years in its time of trial it was hard to be denied a part in its moment of triumph'. Elsie had enjoyed leading the recruiting rallies all over the country but rightly guessed that the 25,000-strong WRAF would be demobilised and the organisation disbanded (as happened at the end of 1919). With 'the dew of my Pervyse fame' on her she had been somebody, but years later she remembered worrying that the dew would not get her a job, and she wondered what she was to do next. There had been no visit from her husband while she was recovering from the gas attack or in the months leading up to the end of the war. Perhaps her anxiety about the end of the war was fuelled by fears for her future and that of eleven-year-old Kenneth.

Mairi was engaged to be married and yet she surely had mixed feelings about the most fulfilling time of her life coming to an end. While the war was on she could overlook the fact that she had no home to go to in England as her parents had settled permanently on their plantation in Trinidad. Relations with them were still strained because of her friendship with Elsie. Her brother Uailean was to return to Trinidad as soon as he was demobilised from his regiment. Mairi's relationship with Bob Hall may have ended at this time; for reasons which are not known the engagement was called off, although his photograph remained in her album.

Forty-eight of the boys and men who had joined up from Mairi's village, Ferndown in Dorset, would never see their homes again. They had been killed in action or had died of wounds, pneumonia or dysentery, sometimes as prisoners of war, on the Western Front, at Gallipoli, in Palestine and Mesopotamia. Ferndown's war memorial records their names lest we forget. Most of them were Mairi's contemporaries, lads in their late teens and early twenties who would have seen Captain Chisholm's motorbike-mad daughter and son clattering round the lanes. There were Freds, Harrys, a Percy, Berties, Jims, a Sid and an Alf – sons of farm labourers, brick makers, carpenters and railwaymen. Some were married with children. Neat black armbands were seen on the streets of the village where the Gooden-Chisholms had come to live. As the survivors returned from the various theatres of war, painful gaps in many families became obvious, like missing teeth in a mouth.

IX

After-Lives

After Elsie and Mairi were demobilised from the Women's Royal Air Force they never saw each other again. A deep friendship started on motorbikes and in the heat of battle fell apart never to be repaired.

The end of the war brought the end of Elsie's second marriage and her plans for the future. The handsome baron was conspicuous by his absence, and we have to rely on Elsie's memoirs, *Flanders and Other Fields*, written almost fifty years after the end of the war. Curiously Harry is never mentioned in the book after their wedding. The last reference to him is: 'After a lightning honeymoon we hardly saw one another again. I was too busy at Pervyse, and my husband had to return to his squadron.' This is not true. Harry visited her at the post several times over the two and a half years that remained until the end of the war, as his signature in her visitors' book attests.

Elsie spent several frantic months in 1919 searching for work and a direction in her life. On 16 March the 'Famous Baroness of Pervyse' spoke to a meeting of the British Empire Union at the Criterion Theatre in London about her experiences in the trenches and announced she was launching a movement

to help wounded soldiers to return to civilian life. She and
Kenneth were staying temporarily in Croydon with friends,
Brigadier General Andrew Laurie Macfie and his wife, who
keenly supported her project. Born in Scotland in 1859, Macfie
had had an army career before becoming a sugar refiner in
Liverpool. Elsie toured the country drumming up interest in
her work: in Harrogate local RAF pilots dropped leaflets
advertising her appearance in the town and so many people
turned up she had to hold three overflow meetings. Elsie was
in her element. It was just like the old days when she had
been on the road with Mairi raising money for the post at
Pervyse.

Then in May came the announcement that Elsie was embarking
on another venture, a 'colony' outside London where her British
Warrior Film Company would employ wounded demobilised
officers, men and nurses as actors and extras and technicians
to make films about the war.

> There will be no stars, as there were no stars in the trenches.
> Every man, even if only one of the crowd in a film, will receive
> a minimum of £3 a week, and the scheme, like the trenches, will
> be cooperative . . . Everyone will share in the profits. When the
> villain in one is not needed . . . in the next film he will not be
> out of work. Carpenters, scene-shifters, photographers, printers,
> developers, mechanics, farmers, gardeners are needed to make
> this colony self-supporting . . . Soon we shall establish a rest
> house where the men can go into hospital for a day or two to
> rest if the wound troubles them. Qualified VADs will attend to
> them. The men we were told about in war time as being wonderful
> are the same men now. We must realise that and make use of
> their wonderful lives.

Brimming with enthusiasm and impassioned idealism but

lacking any expertise or experience in film-making, Elsie's ambitious plan seemed unlikely to succeed. Perhaps she got the idea from Frank Bassill when he filmed her and Mairi in 1917, and she must have seen *The Battle of the Somme*. Elsie's desire to help wounded soldiers to earn a wage was coupled with her own need to earn a living. She admitted feeling 'a little sorry' for herself and worrying about her future, and hare-brained though her idea might seem to the modern reader, she tried desperately hard to make it work. It tells us about Elsie's 'can-do' mentality, her love for the war wounded and her supreme confidence in her own ability to make things happen. In keeping with her new public profile, Elsie had a makeover: a photograph of her in 1919 shows her every inch the flapper, with her hair in a bob, a satin headband and a rope of pearls. She looks ready to charleston across the dance floor and shimmy the night away.

Elsie's ambitious plans were sabotaged by Horatio 'Botty' Bottomley, journalist and con man, the self-styled 'Soldiers' Friend', who wrote THE BRAVE BARONESS AND HER BUSINESS, A FILM COMPANY AND A COLONY A LA LOS ANGELES, an insinuating editorial in his *John Bull* magazine, the forerunner of the worst of tabloid journalism. He was member of parliament for South Hackney, and some of the headlines that preceded his attack on Elsie's film company are a clue to his motivation: THE MAYORESS AND HER SHIRKER BROTHER, SMILLIES SMELLY SENTIMENTS, A SCOUNDREL IN A SURPLICE: THE POLICE AND THE BESTIAL BEHAVIOUR OF A SUFFOLK RECTOR and the WOMEN'S ROYAL AIR FORCE SCANDAL. In reality, *he* was the scoundrel who should have been denounced.

Telling his readers that he had been making enquiries into her film company, he slyly undermined the contents of one of her leaflets to devastating effect. She promised her potential backers that many of the men who wanted to take up 'cinema-acting . . . find it helps them to forget the horrors of the war, and moreover provides an opportunity for earning a good living.' Elsie needed £5,000 (now £200,000) and promised that she would guarantee its repayment with 5 per cent interest after six months. Bottomley quoted from a covering letter he said she had written to him: 'I have always wanted to meet you because I know you understand the British Tommy and feel for him at this present moment . . . It makes my heart ache when I realise how soon we are forgetting what these men have done for us.' But by the time Bottomley visited the British Warrior Film Company's offices the organisation had 'ceased to exist' – its name had been taken off the brass plate at 5 Bloomsbury Square, which aroused Bottomley's worst suspicions. He then launched into her lack of business acumen: 'One of the "Women of Pervyse" evidently has her own Way of combining charity – she proceeds backwards. The Company disappears, but in its place comes "My Scheme, And Why Your Cooperation is Needed – Now."'

Bottomley said that 'certain persons who put money into the British Warrior Film Company are most anxious as to its present whereabouts' and had apparently recently been asked to invest more money in her scheme. He 'unhesitatingly' advised 'the charitably inclined and those who wanted to make a small profit not to confide their capital to Elsie.'

> The Baroness may be a wonderful nurse, although 'four years in the front-line trenches' might be allowed to speak for themselves. She is clearly no business-woman. And only harm is done by making appeals to the public for ill-considered schemes doomed to failure, particularly when those appeals are made to the very people who during the war opened their purses wide for the succour of the sick and suffering. 'I always knew my work would never end with the war,' writes Baroness de T'Ser-

claes. But nursing is nothing like film acting, nor does attending the wounded furnish experience for running companies.

Faced with the widely circulated article, Elsie abandoned the idea of a film company. She caved in to the first salvo of bullying from Bottomley: 'suddenly out of the blue my dream was shattered . . . What Mr Bottomley's source was for these accusations I do not know, but certainly he never bothered to send a reporter to interview me or any member of the Committee.' Despite suffering from fatigue the importance of the work had kept her going, but 'I simply collapsed, and despite the urgings of the General [Macfie] and many other loyal friends, decided I must withdraw.' She disbanded the organisation and the funds were handed over to charities, 'but at least I had tried to blaze the trail for others'. Elsie was ill for two months but she had to pull herself together for her son and consider his future. Aged twelve, he was keen to join the navy and Elsie arranged for him to join the training ship HMS *Conway*. She had to 'earn money to make life possible for us on the most modest scale'. In October General Macfie wrote her a reference for a job: 'I have much pleasure in recommending the Baroness de T'Serclaes as a motor driver. She has driven me long distances, as much as two hundred miles in one day, and while fully alive to the chances afforded by a straight piece of road, takes no risks in traffic.'

But where was her husband? If their marriage had been intact she would surely have been living in Belgium with her new family. But she was not. Why is Harry the absent presence in *Flanders and Other Fields*? He *was* living in London from the beginning of May to August 1919, during the period when the beastly Bottomley was busy stirring up trouble for Elsie, working as the Belgian military attaché, but at the end of the summer he asked to return to Belgium and his place was take by Lieutenant Willy Coppens, one of the pilots he had flown with during the war. Willy survived the war but without his left leg, which was amputated after he was shot down in the last month of the conflict. The fact that Harry wanted to return home suggests that his marriage to Elsie had unravelled irrevocably. In 1920 he would rejoin the army regiment he had entered in 1909, but he was demobilised in 1921. In September 1923 he joined the Aéronautique Militaire but was invalided out on 24 August 1924.

Harold's departure from London suggests that he may have discovered that Elsie was not a widow, but a divorcée whose husband was still alive, which would have made him a bigamist in the eyes of the Roman Catholic Church. The baron's family would have been concerned when they heard that their only son had married someone they did not know and had never met. Their new daughter-in-law was older than their son and had a child by a previous marriage. Elsie told everyone that she was a widow. Such a lie could not have been a worse sin for anyone marrying into the deeply Catholic world of the Belgian aristocracy. Harry had relations in the Vatican; there were not many Belgian families more influential in Rome than his. To us the stigma of divorce is a relic of the past but in Elsie's world 'widowhood' was the best way for divorcées to give themselves the fresh start they needed.

Mairi also found out that Elsie had lied to her, telling her that her husband had died in Java, leaving her with a baby son, and that she had gone to Australia, where she broke in horses, before coming to England to train to be a nurse. Mairi discovered that Elsie had produced paperwork showing that Leslie Knocker was dead when he was actually alive, and that the Roman Catholic Church had found out about Elsie before the war was over. It is likely the Church told Harold and his family about his wife's past and the implications this had for their

marriage. His signatures appear in her visitors' book so we know
he continued to visit, the last time in the autumn of 1917. Twice
Mairi saw Elsie being passed over for communion by the local
priest when mass was said at their post. They had been told
they were being awarded the Ordre de la Couronne by the
Belgians but it was suddenly withdrawn with no explanation.
Having nursed on the Yser front, Mairi had often wondered
why she and Elsie were not presented with the Yser Medal, and
if it had anything to do with Elsie's dodgy marriage, but in fact
the medal was only given to Belgian soldiers and officers who
had fought on the Yser in the first months of the war. Mairi
was no trophy hunter but came to feel that she had been tarred
with the same brush as Elsie by the Belgians, and this bothered
her. Mairi's family say she was strait-laced and unforgiving
where divorce was concerned and would never have been party
to Elsie deceiving Harry. Elsie's deception about her widowhood
was surely what ended their extraordinary friendship.

Mairi was also casting around for a new life. Apart from
waspish Aunt Lucy and ailing Uncle Freddy, Mairi was on her
own in London as her parents had settled permanently in
Trinidad. Mairi running away to the war still rankled with her
mother, who was also unhappy at the amount of attention her
daughter attracted to herself, with which Uailean could not
compete. Mairi's beloved brother, who had spent a few weeks
in London before leaving to rejoin the Trinidad Constabulary,
was to marry his fiancée, Claire Lange, in the summer. Mairi
was hard up, the allowance her father gave her meagre, and
she needed somewhere to live and a job. She stayed with Eva
Moore and her husband for several months but in May 1919
placed a classified advertisement in *The Times*: 'Miss Mairi
Chisholm, one of the Women of Pervyse and lady friend require

temporary employment; must be remunerative and within twenty miles of London, motoring preferred.'

The lady friend was Miss Evelyn Bertha Hope, and replies were to be sent not to Aunt Lucy but to Evelyn's home, The Chalet at Old Hunstanton in Norfolk. Mairi had no obvious links with this part of East Anglia: perhaps she met the Hopes through knowing their son Lieutenant Humphrey Bryan Thomasson Hope of the Royal Flying Corps, who may have visited Pervyse. He was killed in action, shot down by six enemy aircraft in April 1917, the same month that Jack Petre died. Mairi took her friend Evelyn Hope to tea at Aunt Lucy's several times in 1919 and 1920.

On 16 July 1919 the Gooden-Chisholms and the Langes gathered in Trinidad for the wedding of Uailean and Claire. Uailean's thirteen-year-old sister Lucy was one of the three bridesmaids, who wore cool, pale dresses, pretty hats with brims to shade the sun from their eyes and carried vast bouquets of flowers and ferny foliage. Claire's long veil was arranged to curl at her feet and flowers were placed below her bouquet as if they had fallen from it. Uailean wore his dress uniform and held his bride with one hand and his pith helmet in the other. The groom's father folds his arms against the world and looks away to the left at a sharp angle, avoiding the camera's lens. His wife Nonie also looks away from the photographer, and it seems as if she is being gobbled up by the plants on the verandah of the building. Mairi did not go to her brother's wedding, perhaps because she was too unwell to make the long journey. Being gassed twice affected her health for the rest of her life.

Mairi used to suffer from 'very bad faints'. A heart specialist in Wimpole Street insisted on treating her free of charge 'for months and months, which was terribly nice of him. He said: "I haven't had the privilege of serving myself but I am jolly well going to do everything I can for you.'" She was told that in addition to the damage done to her lungs by the gas, she had a twisted cardiac artery and a bent heart valve from too much heavy lifting, and this was the cause of her fainting spells. Though Mairi would sometimes lose consciousness for a few moments no one ever thought to prohibit her from getting behind the wheel of a motor vehicle.

Around this time Mairi became a good friend of the marmalade millionaire Alexander Keiller, who was born in Dundee in 1889. He was nine when his father died, leaving him the heir to a business and a fortune that today would be worth forty million pounds. He left Eton in 1907, when his mother died, and went to live abroad. Returning to Britain in 1911 he joined the 7th Battalion of the Gordon Highlanders. Keiller resigned his commission in 1913, married for the first time and bought the Sizaire-Berwick Motor Company, whose range included a Rolls-Royce lookalike model and which had offices in Piccadilly. When he joined the Royal Naval Air Reserve at the end of 1914 he gave motor engineer as his profession, and was sent to work in the armoured cars division. He gained his pilot's certificate at Chingford in 1915. But in January 1916 was invalided out of the sky and joined air intelligence. He and Mairi had plenty in common – a love of cars and driving, service in the war and being a similar age and Scottish. He had a 10,000-acre estate at Morven, near Ballater in Aberdeenshire. In 1919 Keiller hired her as his chauffeuse, and she would also deliver cars from the Sizaire-Berwick showroom in Berkeley Street to their wealthy new owners. He was a rich, interesting and good-looking man with a reputation; in July 1919 his wife divorced him for adultery. On 26 September 1920 there is a tantalising remark in Aunt Lucy's diary that her niece Mairi had been to supper and 'seems likely to marry her Marmaduke'. This may have been Aunt

Lucy's nickname for Keiller, the marmalade millionaire. It is possible that Mairi was smitten enough for her aunt to make that comment in her diary, but his divorce was too big an obstacle to overcome. Mairi was independent and this would have been her decision. She did not marry her 'Marmaduke', and Alexander Keiller remarried in 1924 and divorced again ten years later.

On 5 October 1920 Mairi became an aunt when her brother and his wife had a son, Alastair Andrew Fraser, in Trinidad. But at nine o'clock on the morning of 18 October Mairi's 'beloved seadog daddy Horatio Barnacles', Admiral Robert Grant Fraser, an uncle by marriage, shot himself in the head 'while of unsound mind'. He was sixty-two years old and had been 'melancholic' for ten days.

Mairi and Elsie had stayed with Nonie's cousin Janie and her husband the admiral during their fund-raising tour in 1916. The couple had no children and he had often told her that 'if he'd had a daughter it would have been me'. Mairi travelled to Scotland to be with his widow. The day after she arrived she sent a postcard to the late Jack Petre's mother at Ingatestone: 'Am <u>so</u> sorry about your letter . . . but it was sent up here. Have just arrived and am answering your letter tomorrow. This is just to explain why I have been seemingly rude. I hope you forgive me, yours affectionately.' The Petre family photograph albums show how important Mairi had been in Jack's life. She was memorialised in the story of his life by his mother and younger sister Sybil. There are news cuttings of Mairi at Pervyse and of Jack visiting her with his chums, and there is a page of photographs arranged in a triptych. Two pictures of Jack nonchalantly leaning against his plane, hand on hip, flank four smaller pictures of Mairi cuddling her cat and of Jack and his fellow airmen.

During Mairi's stay Cousin Janie introduced her to Mrs

Davidson of Cantray House and her daughter May. This meeting would change the course of Mairi's life. May was four years older than Mairi and they soon became good friends, discovering that their fathers had known each other in 1892, when they were in the 3rd Battalion of the Seaforth Highlanders based at nearby Fort George. Mrs Davidson was concerned by Mairi's frailty and invited her to stay at Cantray House. A few miles east of Inverness and south-west of Nairn, the Cantray estate at Gollanfield was 3,500 acres and included fine grouse shooting. It was bisected by the River Nairn, and the London Midland and Scottish Railway line to Inverness ran along the southern boundary of the estate; guests of the Davidsons who travelled to Cantray by train were allowed to make a special stop to alight there. Mairi, who had been warned by her doctor, 'My good child, you're going to be dead in a very short time if you go on like you're going on, you must have a country life and really resuscitate your lungs,' came for a rest and eventually stayed for the rest of her life.

Edith May Davidson, only child of Captain Hugh Davidson and Harriette King Hugonin, was born at Rhysnant Hall near Oswestry on 2 June 1892. Her father had fought in the Afghan campaign of 1886 as adjutant of the 3rd Battalion of the Manchester Regiment before joining the Seaforth Highlanders, where he met Mairi's father shortly before May was born. A handsome and eligible bachelor, and heir to thousands of Scottish acres, he had married Harriette, whose father was also a landowner and whose mother was from Nova Scotia.

In April 1910, when May was eighteen, her father died suddenly at home in his early fifties of kidney disease, leaving her two estates amounting to 8,000 acres, heiress to a substantial fortune when she became twenty-one. In the years leading up to the outbreak of the war Mrs Davidson was busy gathering intelligence on a suitable husband for her daughter. Mother and daughter were spotted in Nairn in August 1912 for the amateur golf tournament, at the Ross County Ball at the Ben Wyvis Hotel in Strathpeffer in October and at the Second Ball of the Argyllshire Gathering. When war broke out May collected money for the Official Committee for the Relief of the Belgians.

In 1920 Elsie was still casting around for suitable employment, exploiting her title and using the initials MM (Military Medal) after her name. Living in cheap lodgings in London and eking out her small private income, she found herself facing up to the possibility of having to go into domestic service, perhaps as a housekeeper, previously unthinkable for a doctor's daughter and a national heroine. Hundreds of thousands of women were trying to adjust to a new social order and Elsie sounded bewildered when she described these events fifty years later. It was a topsy-turvy world when a 'brave baroness' was reduced to earning a living as a housekeeper, even if it was for a millionaire.

In 1920 Elsie went to work for the textile industrialist Henry Greenwood Tetley as 'supervisor' of his new weekend house at Alderbrook, near Cranleigh in Surrey. He was a self-made Yorkshireman born in the year of the Great Exhibition, the son of a Bradford 'stuff merchant'. In 1917 he became chairman of Courtaulds Limited, which under his aggressive leadership became the world's largest producer of rayon. He had a reputation for trampling on people and any other obstacles in his way. His bad temper was legendary, and like everyone else who worked for him, Elsie would soon discover what an exacting employer he could be. The Tetleys' private life was very much so, and while little is known about his first wife Gertrude, who died in 1899, even less is known about his second wife Charlotte, whom he married in 1916, or any of his children. Elsie says nothing about Charlotte at all.

Tetley was surely pleased to have a national treasure working for him. He was impressed with what she had done in Flanders, and her reputation for hard work and self-sacrifice went before her. Elsie was to run the Tetleys' weekend home and farm at Alderbrook, hire all the staff, keep the accounts and send fresh produce up to their London house in St John's Wood. She was given the use of a 'magnificent Daimler', which she loaded up with her luggage and headed off to Surrey. At last a bit of luxury after the penny-pinching of the past months: 'The scene there could not have been more different from the digs I had just left. I felt very small and rather bewildered in the great, empty, luxuriously furnished house, wandering from one reception-room to another, down long, deserted corridors . . . I sank down into a cushiony armchair and relaxed.'

Elsie was warned that her new employer was punctilious about timekeeping and detested inefficiency and extravagance. She had a month to get the house ready and knew that 'if Mr Tetley said a month, he meant a month, and not a day or a fraction of a day longer'. She saw him dismisss a chauffeur because he was five minutes late bringing the car round, and he always maintained 'there was no such thing as a mistake'. She was happy at Alderbrook, where Kenneth was allowed to stay with her during the holidays. Life was looking up: '[Tetley] believed in a reign of modified terror, which did not suit everyone, but I found I throve on it. I had a horse and a pony and trap, and a car, and Kenneth had the time of his life. Mr Tetley called me "Madam", and often sent for me to ask advice about this and that. I got quite used to making out cheques for thousands of pounds at a moment's notice for his signature, but I made it a rule never to become familiar with the family.'

In August 1921 Elsie would have received news from the Knocker family solicitor that her first husband, Kenneth's father, had died in a nursing home in Croydon on the 2nd of the month. Leslie Duke Knocker was forty-six and had been working as a bank cashier before becoming ill with the liver disease that killed him. Knocker had not remarried and his will, which he drew up in August 1911 while he and Elsie were in the throes of their divorce proceedings, left everything he owned in the world, £534.16s (now £26,000), to Kenneth to inherit on his twenty-first birthday. Kenneth's uncle Anthony was the executor and trustee.

On 19 August Elsie was in trouble with the police, charged at Guildford Magistrates' Court with breaking the Aliens Order of 1920. Being married to a Belgian meant that in England she was regarded as an alien and was required by law to register with her local police. She had told the police in 1919 she would register in Marlborough but forgot to tell them she had moved to Cranleigh. They did not trace her until June 1921. It was a simple oversight but despite her reputation she was fined five shillings and five shillings in costs. It was not a vast sum of money but a flourish of red tape would have hurt and infuriated her. Considering her widely reported war record, Elsie might reasonably have expected discretion, a warning and the case being dropped.

Two days after her appearance in court disaster struck when Henry Tetley had a heart attack as he walked up the stairs at Cranleigh and died. The house was sold and after eighteen months Elsie was again looking for a job.

Around this time Elsie read *Women Who Dared: Heroines of the Great War,* a new book that devoted two chapters to her and Mairi's work with Dr Munro's corps. Written by Kent Carr, whom most people assumed to be a man, it was in fact by Mrs Gertrude Kent Oliver. Although not a children's book, the gushy tone sits happily with the books Mrs Oliver had been writing for the last ten years (*Rivals and Chums, The Reign of Lady Betty* (1908); *Timfy Sykes, Gentleman* (1910); *Love Stories of Royal Girlhood* (1913); *Queens Who Were Famous* (1915). Mairi would have been surprised to read that 'Whenever men speak of it [Munro's corps], it is with a little quickening of the breath. You see, the deeds they have to record are of a daring so great that is it difficult to find the right words to describe them. Some of its field-women, like eighteen-year-old Mairi Chisholm, were little more than children.'

When Mrs Oliver interviewed Elsie for the book she seems to have been mesmerised by her; when it came to Mairi's role she relied on photographs and other people's accounts. Her comments about the two women are perhaps perceptive. She describes Elsie as 'beautiful and ardent' and having 'oddly fascinating manners and when her subject interests her she becomes all afire'. She could 'hold her audience by the spell of her looks and talk', and Carr was sure that 'the only person who would ever be able to tame Mrs Knocker would be Mrs Knocker herself'. Mairi seemed the exact opposite: 'her young Scotch face is placid and strong and sweet. She has fair hair, blue eyes and a wholesome smile. She does not look as if she could be easily, if ever, perturbed. There is something beautiful and healing about her serene tranquillity.'

It was only a matter of time before Mairi was whizzing round the track competing at Brooklands. In 1921 she entered a speed trial there, driving an AV Monocar whose 'steering was a couple of pulleys on the dash, crosswise cables that went to each of the front wheels . . . you can't imagine the whiplash that started up'. Things could go horribly wrong if the steel wires frayed on the bobbins on which they ran. The night before Mairi was billed to drive she had 'one of these very bad faints and I was actually prohibited from taking this thing out'. The enthusiastic amateur driver Major Reginald Calvert Empson took her place, but his AV Monocar, affectionately known as 'Whizz-bang', careered off the road: 'the cable went and he got most horribly smashed-up'. Empson was nearly killed when the car overturned in a culvert full of water. Pinned down by Whizz-bang, 'several people rushed to prevent him from being drowned', and he was taken to Weybridge Cottage Hospital, where he was treated for a badly fractured leg, broken ribs and shock.

By autumn 1921 Mairi had relocated to Scotland and was living with the Davidsons in the dower house of the estate at Rose Valley, as Cantray House had been let for shooting to Mr Stewart Barney, a New Yorker. Uailean and Claire had another son, named Ruari, on 21 September. During the evening of 3 October one of the kitchen chimneys at Cantray caught fire and soon the whole house was ablaze. Within three hours the place was gutted. Mairi and May stood by helplessly as the place burnt down, watching the flames consume the dining room, which was laid for dinner. Nothing could be done as Cantray was miles from the nearest fire brigade in Inverness, but Mairi had the presence of mind to remember that they had not renewed the insurance policy. She wrote out a cheque and sent a local boy on a motorbike to Inverness to post the cheque through the letter box of the insurers before the office opened in the morning. Everything was lost, including valuable paintings and a library of eighteenth-century books.

Meanwhile, Elsie had managed to get herself another job. At the end of 1921 she went to work for Mrs Hocker, a successful businesswoman with twenty years' experience as a hotelier and a colourful past. She owned a string of grand hotels, including both Palmeira Towers and Westward Ho! at Westcliffe-on Sea in Essex, and half a dozen in Mayfair, unusual at a time when men were the owners and managers, and women did the cooking, cleaning and waitressing. During the war she had proudly advertised in *The Times* that her hotels were under 'English proprietorship', that 'no alien enemies' were employed and that since they had concrete roofs they were bomb- and fire-proof. Before Elsie went to work for her, Mrs Hocker had been in court several times, prosecuting guests whose cheques had bounced or who had damaged their accommodation. Given the smart location of her London hotels she had plenty of experience of dealing with troublesome toffs and the 'slim young things' who helped wayward young men spend their generous allowances. In 1917 she took a deranged couple to court 'for damages for injuries' to the flat they rented at the Grosvenor Court Hotel in Mayfair. (They had been thrown out of the Hotel Cecil in 1915 for bad behaviour.) The couple had turned the flat into a menagerie, keeping lizards and guinea pigs in the bathroom. They also had cats and dogs, including a huge hound, ferrets, doves and other birds.

Attracted by Elsie's can-do personality and war record, Mrs Hocker was also shrewd enough to know that a baroness with a chest full of medals would be good for business, and hired her to manage her new hotel, Addington Manor in Winslow, Buckinghamshire, which she rented from Lord Addington. It was to be a luxury country house hotel for wealthy Americans, and Elsie was involved with the project from the outset. She ran it the way she had run the Tetleys' house at Cranleigh. It was such a success that sometimes she had to give up her quarters to extra guests. 'I spent many a week-end on a camp-bed in a box-room, and took my baths in the early hours of the morning when everyone else was sleeping.' Elsie loved being in a tight spot and fighting her way out of it, but most importantly, being needed.

Relishing her role as the chatelaine of Addington Manor, Elsie could ignore the fact that she was at the mercy of her employer for a roof over her head. Sometimes she may have forgotten that it was not her home:

> Before every meal I spent about half an hour inspecting the dining-room, to see that the silver was gleaming, and the plates too, and the flowers on the table beautifully arranged. I took care that I did not mix with the guests, though there is little doubt that my title and war record was an added draw. I would be just charming, and mingle with them for short spells, though any guests could come and see me in my office at any time.

Elsie arranged car tours, riding and fishing trips, and tennis matches; there was a billiards room and endless games of cards. In 1923, after two years, Elsie left to work for another hotelier, Mrs Stevenson, as her general manager and factotum. She loved driving her boss around and advising on different aspects of the business. Elsie was happy working for Mrs Stevenson because 'she was full of fun, extremely amusing as well as being a keen businesswoman'.

In 1922 Mrs Davidson, May and Mairi moved into a new house built in the grounds of Cantray, close to the burned-out ruin of their old home. Around this time Mairi and May took up poultry farming and breeding, then a respectable way for young women to earn a living and one of the few rural activities in which they could excel. At the International Show of 1923 in London, Mairi and May won the Championship Cup and the Pullet Cup for the best white silkies, and took second place with their elegant white Indian runner ducks. In 1924 the Misses Davidson and Chisholm and their highly successful Cantray Duck and Poultry Farm were written about in glowing terms by 'Red Feather' and 'Rajah' in *Poultry News*, *Feathered World* and the *Scottish Poultry News*. The ladies were well known as 'enthusiastic duckers' and had 'laid down their plant with great care and foresight . . . they have given the poultry industry their very careful consideration, and no haphazard measures are tolerated on this farm'. The 'fair owners' of the farm planned on making Cantray 'a big fattening centre' for Scotland, 'their object being to relieve poultry farmers of all their surplus birds and do the fattening for them'.

The idea had been Mairi's and she was the heart and soul of the business. On May's twenty-first birthday in 1913 she had come into her inheritance and had assumed the role of laird, but she did not concern herself with financial matters. When she met Mairi she was happy to let her friend run the estate and poultry farm and balance the books. Two young 'poultry-girls', Catherine Bridget Partridge, known as 'Bird', and Grace Barbara Johnstone, known as 'John', were hired to do most of the work. Bird, who was from Suffolk, was fourteen when she started at Cantray in 1922, and John was fifteen and from Norfolk. For both of them it was their first job. Bird eventually inherited a small private income and could afford to run a car. By the middle of the 1920s the reputation of the 'Two Lady Fanciers' had grown; they had won dozens of cups and had represented Great Britain at the World Poultry Congresses in Barcelona in 1924 and Ottawa in 1927.

In December 1923 Arthur Gleason, who had been such a good pal to Elsie and Mairi but with whom they had fallen out over his book *Young Hilda At The Wars*, died of pneumonia in Washington, aged forty-five. He never wavered from his interest in left-wing causes and was working on an article about John Brophy of the United Mineworkers of America at the time of his death. After the war he and Helen lived in Connecticut but had recently moved to the literary colony in San Diego, California.

Mairi and Dr Hector Munro stayed in touch after the war. Away from the drama and danger of the war zone they were firm friends until he died in London in 1949. He used to stay at Cantray and tried to encourage her to sunbathe like him. All year round he would sit on the top floor of his clinic in Portman Place, open all the windows and have his breakfast stark naked. He advised her: 'When there is this fine rain there are wonderful ultra-violet rays in the Highlands, you ought go up to the top of a mound and strip all your clothes off and dance naked . . . It's marvellous for the skin and hair and will keep you young forever.'

Munro had tried to open a nudist camp at Cawdor near where his father had gone to live. Accordingly to Mairi, 'he did it very politely away in the backwoods' but was 'seen off by the police . . . it simply wasn't done in those days'. Not in chilly Scotland at any rate. Munro was eighty when he died, a good advertisement for his long-held views.

In June 1922 Uailean's father had brought him to England to specialists in Harley Street, who diagnosed incipient diabetes. The trip was the first of several he and his parents made backwards and forwards across the Atlantic during the rest of the decade. His health had suffered during and after the war and would blight his remaining years. They stayed with Aunt Lucy and Uncle Freddy, and Uailean visited Mairi at her new home in Scotland.

Two years later it was decided that Uailean's sons should be educated in England and plans were made for the family to relocate. Uailean's love of practical jokes and lack of reverence for authority had caused the abrupt end of his career in the police. To make a point about the lack of security at his police station, he burgled the place, removing all the records and paperwork. He was moved sideways into the fire brigade but then that career also came to an end. He was drinking too much, perhaps as a result of his war service in Egypt. Whatever the reason, it was ill-advised for someone with incipient diabetes who loved driving his Buick fast and roaring around on a motorbike to drink. Insulin was first produced in 1922 but management of the condition remained difficult.

Uailean and Claire left Trinidad and arrived in London in early 1925. They stayed with Chisholm relations and travelled north to stay with Mairi and May at Cantray. A house was rented at Great Missenden in Buckinghamshire, and their sons, aged five and four, were brought to England by friends of the Langes. Their daughter Lilias, who was eighteen months old, remained in Trinidad to be looked after by her Lange grandparents. Uailean bought a motorbike and sidecar and looked for a job but with little success. Unable to afford the rent on their house they had to move into a small cottage that looked onto the railway line. For the first time in her life Claire was without servants; after the warmth, sunshine and dazzling colours of Trinidad, life seemed cold, bleak and grey.

In July Uailean was admitted to hospital in Edinburgh. His parents crossed the Atlantic to visit him and Claire at Great Missenden, leaving for Trinidad on 2 January 1926. They were back again in the late spring, and steamed home again, always travelling first class, on 25 September. During their stay in England they saw the country grind to a halt for nine days in May during the General Strike. Uailean had rolled his sleeves up and driven a lorry: strike-breaking was the only work he had done that year. In April the government had ended a subsidy to the coal-mining industry and on 2 May Prime Minister Stanley Baldwin broke off negotiations with the Trade Union Congress, who then called a general strike the next day. Nine days later, the TUC ended the strike, but in some mining communities the struggle continued for months.

In 1920 Elsie's adoptive parents, Lewis and Emily Upcott, had sold their house in Marlborough, and were living in Torquay when Elsie left Mrs Stevenson and went to live with them in 1924. Lewis was seventy-four and Emily almost seventy. The town's directories boasted that it was 'one of the [country's] foremost watering-places' so, thinking it would be a good place for Kenneth to return to in the holidays, have-a-go Elsie went to Torquay and turned her hand to something completely different. She bought a knitting machine, opened a shop called Elizabeth and stocked it with the skirts, jumpers and cardigans she made. It was a success: 'I started with a tiny capital, but the business flourished – so much so that someone made me a good offer to take it over, and I accepted.'

Then in 1925 Elsie went to work for Harold Kinder Griffith, a local surgeon: 'he knew that I was a first-class nurse, and had several times asked me what I was doing in a shop'. He was a couple of years younger than Elsie and came from a medical family; his father was a distinguished obstetrician. Growing up in Harley Street, in 1914 he married the girl next door, whose father was also an eminent doctor. During the war he was a captain in the Royal Army Medical Corps. Elsie enjoyed working for him: 'I attended many interesting cases.' It was work she enjoyed and was good at, but two years of everything that Torquay had to offer were enough for Elsie. Her feet were itching for another challenge and in 1926 she headed back to London. 'I had seen Kenneth though his education, and he had gone to sea. The worst of the struggle seemed to be over, and I began to wonder what next I could turn my hand to – if there was not some adventure I could get mixed up in.'

The records of Baron Harold de T'Serclaes in the Belgian Military Archives throw some light on the state of his and Elsie's marriage in 1925. He had retired from the army in 1924 and was living near Brussels when he made his final attempt to have it annulled, and also wrote to the army pay office asking about the money he had saved during the war. Although they may not have seen each other since he left London in 1919, while they were married Elsie was entitled to money from the Aide et Protection, a fund for officers' families, but there is no record of her ever drawing on it. Harry had probably started proceedings as soon as he returned to Belgium but getting an annulment was a slow business. His case, which was rejected several times, was finally rebuffed in 1925 by the Cour de Cassation, the highest court of justice in Belgium, whose verdict could not be appealed against, which accepted that although Elsie had lied to him about being a widow, this *tromperie* and the fact that she was a divorcée were not sufficient grounds to nullify the marriage. Therefore, Elsie remained a baroness, but in name only. She did not include a photograph of him in her autobiography and revealed nothing about the end of what had been a great wartime romance.

Elsie devoted a whole chapter to her work during the General Strike in *Flanders and Other Fields,* the autobiography she published in 1964. It is the story of a woman reprising her war work with relish; at forty-two this might be her last big adventure and she was not going to let it pass. Her description of what peacetime had come to mean for so many people – 'a nightmare of worry, unemployment and near starvation' – sounds personal. She was not a person to stand by and not get involved when the country was faced with 'an unprecedented emergency'.

> It sounds selfish, maybe, but I was in my element, and excited at the challenge. I went to Downing Street, where Mrs Baldwin had opened an office for the enrolment and organization of volunteers, but found all was confusion and timidity. However, I did overhear a telephone conversation to the effect that 'on no account were any cars to be sent to Poplar, it was far too dangerous'. It appeared that an ambulance had been overturned and burned there.

If there were two things that Elsie detested they were confusion and timidity, and the words 'on no account' would have driven her to be at the heart of things in Poplar. She volunteered to go but was refused permission and 'flew round' to Rochester Row police station, where Commandant Mary Allen of the Women's Auxiliary Service, an organisation previously known as the Women's Police Volunteers (funded by subscriptions and private donations), had opened a centre. Before the war Allen had been to prison three times for her suffragette activities and had gone on hunger strike and been force-fed. She joined the Women's Police Volunteers during the war as a constable, and since 1920 she had been in charge, striding around in riding breeches, skirted coat, flat cap and military boots. She did not try to stop Elsie but warned her, 'anything I undertook at Poplar would have to be off my own bat and at my own expense'.

Next stop was Grosvenor Crescent and the headquarters of the British Red Cross, where she asked Major Eden Paget (who had visited Pervyse) for a car, a driver and medical supplies. Because of the shortage of electricity, the hospitals were only admitting emergency cases. Elsie knew a first-aid post would be needed, 'and by all accounts it would be right up in the front line'. War zones and high drama were oxygen to Elsie and military terms were embedded in her vocabulary. Paget told her to choose a vehicle and a driver from the car park, which was full of volunteers and their machines, from Rolls-Royces to Austin Sevens. Elsie knew exactly what she wanted: 'a tough, strong, reliable man'.

In the car park she saw 'such a man standing by a large sports car; he was tall and dressed in a sports coat and riding-breeches'. She walked over and offered him a job. He was a Scotsman, an ex-RAF officer whom she called Scottie, and she warned him it 'might be rather risky'. Two other young men joined Elsie and Scottie in the bright-red sports car as they drove to Poplar, where they 'ran the gauntlet of some distinctly hostile stares and gestures . . . it was a strange sensation to be going gingerly into enemy territory – in your own country'. Elsie reported to the local police station, explaining that she wanted to open up a first-aid post, pointing out that she had 'no politics and wanted only to help my fellow human beings'. They allocated her a disused butcher's shop next door to the Green Man, an eighteenth-century public house at 68 Poplar High Street, and gave her a few rough woollen blankets. The place stank; it was infested with vermin and there was a squalid privy in the backyard. One of the first things she did was to hang the Red Cross flag they had flown at Pervyse out of the top window of the premises. She 'hoped that people would understand its universal message of help with no strings attached'. But Elsie and her helpers were not welcome and were soon made to feel they were part of 'the army of occupation'. When she walked into the pub for water to make tea the place went quiet and the landlord, James Britton, refused to help; and as soon as she walked out, there was 'a roar of excitement' and she could feel 'the whole district twanging with tension'.

During their first evening the local superintendent of police warned Elsie that the district strike committee wanted them out of Poplar immediately, telling her, 'they mean to burn this house down tonight, with you in it. This will mean rioting, people wounded, and deaths. I would be powerless to help you.' Anyone else would have found this alarming but Elsie was having none of it. The officer told her that the flag had made things worse: the locals thought she had been sent in by the army because they were planning to attack, and that Elsie was there to look after wounded troops. But she refused to leave. The two young men asked to go. Scottie drove them back and was told by Elsie to collect Walter 'Dicky' Hudd and Bobby Haslam, two actors Elsie had met when they were fighting in Flanders, who were out of work because the theatres were shut. When Scottie left the superintendent pleaded with her again to leave: 'Of course I had heard all this before, from a French Admiral in Furnes in 1914, as well as from many British Army and Navy officers throughout the War. I was used to ignoring male solicitude.'

Worryingly for the police, the crowd outside was getting louder and more hostile but Elsie guessed 'the Poplarites were splitting into the pro- and anti-me factions'. She thought 'there might even be a fight on our hands which would produce a casualty or two, and give me an opportunity to prove that I was there to look after civilians'. She told the superintendent she was not afraid and was not expecting thanks but, 'I *am* going to do my duty.'

A young man appeared and handed her an invitation to attend a meeting at Poplar Town Hall at ten o'clock the next morning, and the crowd melted away. She prepared the room where she, Scottie, Dicky and Bobby were to spend the night, laying down blankets and sprinkling a fairy circle of rat and mouse poison around them. More than thirty years later Elsie's memories were of the sound and the drama of the moment, the glamorous looks of her two newly arrived friends and the intense excitement she felt that night.

It was nine o'clock when I heard Scottie's car zoom up at great speed, and the tyres squealing with urgency as he clapped on the brakes. What a relief to see Walter Hudd . . . and Bobby Haslam step out, looking very smart and sophisti- cated, carrying some parcels of food! I was dying for a cup of tea. Dicky put the kettle on and we settled down to a good chat. Both he and Bobby had known me in Belgium and were prepared to rough it. They were delighted to be in such an unconventional outpost, and it was a tremendous comfort to know that I had three helpers who would never desert me.

Dicky Hudd had toured the country in repertory before making his London debut in 1923 and became a well-known actor, producer and writer of one-act plays. Bobby Haslam's career did not take off until the year after the events in Poplar.

At Poplar Town Hall she was interrogated by the strike committee, who agreed to let her run her first-aid post and gave her a pass to carry with her at all times and a picket in case there was any trouble. Scottie offered to do all the driving and buy the food, while Dicky wanted to be head cook and bottle- washer even though he disliked both jobs. He was a 'good trouper and his sense of fun was so unquenchable' that he kept their spirits high. Bobby looked like a doctor in the white coat Elsie gave him to wear, and despite being squeamish was a useful assistant. As well as dealing with any cases that came to the first-aid post, every day Elsie and Scottie would drive round Poplar treating people who could not come to them. This was the kind of district nursing she had cut her teeth on when she had trained in London fifteen years before. Elsie enjoyed being in the middle of things again but she knew it would come to an end: 'Everyone was so kind and helpful that it was hard – and to me, despite that hard floor, almost sad – to believe that we were only temporary neighbours.'

Poplar High Street quickly got into a party mood when the strike was called off: 'The Green Man was gay with fairy lights and music and the gramophone shop down the road had all its machines playing at once . . . Children skipped about the streets . . . and the armoured cars vanished.' Elsie packed up the Pervyse flag and drove back to the West End with Scottie, Dicky and Bobby. 'Despite the hard boards, the hard work, and the cold water, we were all in a way sorry to say good-bye. It is always such a pleasure and a privilege when one is shoved through or under or over the class barrier. It's so miserable and anti-climactic when one has to creep back to one's own "station" in life. At least, that's how I felt, and feel.'

Even though their poultry business was flourishing, Mairi had to tell May the news she dreaded: that the estate finances were not good. In July 1926 May authorised the sale of her estates at Cantray and Clava by auction in Inverness.

Since the war she had had to sell land to her tenant farmers to make ends meet but the thousands of acres left included some of the best farms in the district, salmon and trout fishing in the River Nairn and some of the finest moors in Scotland for grouse and other game. However, May could not bear the thought of selling and the auction was called off. In England things were not getting any easier for Uailean and his family, early in 1927 Mairi received a worrying letter from Claire. She visited Great Missenden and suggested that the family come to live with her and May at Cantray. In March they moved to Scotland, Uailean riding the motorbike and Claire having an uncomfortable ride in the sidecar; the boys were sent on by train in the care of the guard. Uailean and Claire moved into the gardener's cottage and the boys lived in the new Cantray with Mairi and May. It was a heavenly place for two little boys of seven and six; May owned all the land as far as the eye could see, and there were the ruins of the old house to explore.

In the summer of 1928 the Gooden-Chisholms arrived from Trinidad and visited Mairi and Uailean in Scotland, returning home on 24 September. Three weeks later Claire sailed from Dover to collect her five-year-old daughter Lilias from Trinidad. Uailean explored the Highlands on his motorbike, and Alastair and Ruari were sent to a preparatory school, but when Mairi visited and saw how dirty it was she removed the boys and hired a governess for them. In 1929 the Gooden-Chisholms were back again, visiting their son and daughters (Lucy had come to London to be an artist) and grandsons, perhaps concerned at the impact Uailean's drinking was having on his health and finances. However, his father refused to pay for him to be treated by a specialist in Edinburgh. They sailed back to Trinidad on 25 July, and twenty-seven days later Uailean was dead.

In the days leading up to his death in the early hours of the morning of 21 August Uailean had been admitted to a nursing home at Ness Bank, Inverness. His health already compromised by his diabetes, Mairi's brother was a sick man. His wife was in Trinidad; he was dependent on his sister and her friend's generosity for a home, and he was out of work. His parents' visit may not have helped his fluctuating moods, and we might recall the note his father wrote twenty years earlier on his son's registration form for Cheltenham College: 'I have left in my will that he inherits only a small sum sufficient to keep him from starvation until he can show that he has been capable of earning £150 per annum for five years.' The record of death describes Uailean as a retired police captain and states that he died at a quarter to four in the morning. The death was reported by a 'law agent'. The column giving the cause of death was initially left blank. On 23 August the *Inverness Courier* reported that Uailean had died suddenly at home in the Garden Cottage at Cantray of heart failure: 'his death, which occurring as it did when he was only thirty-five years of age, came as a severe blow to his friends.' Ten days later the procurator fiscal authorised the cause of death to be stated as 'poisoning' and that it had taken 'about one hour'.

On the day he died Uailean had been allowed to visit Cantray on his motorbike and had returned to the nursing home that evening. Apparently when he returned the nurse who gave him his usual nightly sleeping draught left the bottle on his bedside table instead of removing it. Uailean took the bottle and finished it off. At some point he called for help, but they could not save him. There was no post-mortem because Mairi did not want one. Upset at the possibility of a verdict of suicide, she persuaded the procurator fiscal and registrar not to insist. There should also have been an inquest, as there had been when Admiral Fraser died, but Mairi's personality and her reputation – even after ten years – meant that she was able to spare the family a stigmatising verdict of suicide, and Uailean was buried in consecrated ground. Having spent time with Cousin Janie, she would have remembered the shock of the local community when the details of the admiral's death emerged. Uailean's wife and parents were thousands of miles

away in Trinidad and could not come to the funeral. Aunt
Mairi and Aunt May would be stand-in parents for Uailean's
sons for at least another year.

Elsie returned from Poplar to her tiny flat at 74 Queen's Road
in Bayswater with some trepidation, wondering what she would
turn her hand to next. She heard from her son Kenneth that he
wanted to leave the Navy and perhaps join the Royal Air Force,
but wanted to spend some time with her before he made up his
mind. Elsie and Kenneth would share a home for the first time;
his Upcott grandparents had been hitherto the rock in his life.
For the rest of 1926 Elsie earned her living as a driver, chauffeuring people about in her car, and in 1927 spent 'perhaps the
most miserable year of my adult life – working in a nursing
home'. It was the worst job she ever had: 'the conditions of
work and the attitude of the matron were enough to make
anyone want to strike'. The patients were charged plenty but
the nurses only earned a pound a week and had to pay for their
own laundry. Elsie felt like a servant: 'it was one of those huge
Victorian houses: there was no lift and we had to carry trays
up and down endless flights of stairs'. She was depressed: 'I was
bitter, frustrated and humiliated. It was hard to stay polite, let
alone cheerful. My experience counted for nothing. In fact I had
to keep quiet about it.'

On his twenty-first birthday, Kenneth came into the inheritance his father had left him when he died in 1921. Perhaps still
smarting from her unhappy marriage to Leslie Duke Knocker,
Elsie does not mention that he was the source of the money
that in 1928 enabled Kenneth to rent and furnish a comfortable
flat for both of them at 26 Russell Road in Kensington. She left
the nursing home and returned to chauffeuring people around
in her own car, enjoying earning her own keep rather than doing

nothing, which she had 'never been able to stick'. Determined not to be forgotten, an 'Armistice Message' Elsie sent to the *Daily Mirror* on the tenth anniversary of the end of the fighting shows she was still haunted by her years in Flanders.

> Armistice Day – peace from war.
> That can never be for those who served in the front line trenches.
> To obliterate the nights of death and terror, the endless days of wounds, noise and weary toil is impossible.
> Miss Chisholm and I served in this atmosphere for four years.
> Those who came back are torn in body and mind. My sorrow goes to all who knew these horrors and still live to suffer them.
> We are living for our real Armistice, the peace of the Last Post.

Elsie drove herself so hard that after a year she had a physical breakdown: 'my reserves of energy were just not there anymore . . . and I was in a state of collapse'. Luckily she had recently met two important women in the British Red Cross Society who knew about her work in Pervyse and Poplar. They arranged for her to spend three months in the Red Cross Nursing Home at Weybridge: 'Slowly I recovered, though when I first went into the grounds I had to be wheeled around the paths, I was so weak . . . I had quite simply conked out. However, after three precious months of care and good food and no worry, I slowly crept out of my hole and was ready once more to do battle with my funny world.'

In the spring of 1930, six months after the death of Uailean, May Davidson did sell her Cantray and Clava estates by auction. Money was tight and she could no longer turn a deaf ear and a blind eye to the gloomy financial news Mairi had been reporting for some time. To create the right impression for prospective bidders they needed a smart car in the driveway and Alexander

Keiller loaned them the money to buy the latest Lancia. For tax reasons, May, her mother and Mairi moved to Jersey, taking Alastair, Ruari and their governess, Miss Davis, and the poultry girls Bird and John, to open a poultry business there.

Roderick Gooden-Chisholm paid for a bungalow to be built at Maisonette near St Helier, for Claire and her children, not far from the poultry farm, where the others lived. He was also persuaded by a cross and grieving Mairi to pay for Alastair and Ruari's education at Ampleforth School and settle £300 a year on Claire, who arrived with Lilias during the first year in Jersey. As well as looking after the poultry, John was also the housekeeper. Bird, who did not settle down well in Jersey, left the island for a while to time do poultry work at Loseley Park in Surrey. In 1932 Mairi, Bird and John travelled to England to take part in the Poultry Show at Crystal Palace, where they won prizes for their silkie pullets.

May and Mairi missed Scotland too much, and in 1934 packed their lives up again and took Bird and John back, not to Nairn, to which May could not bear to return, but a hundred miles away to the west coast of Scotland. May was forty-three, Mairi thirty-nine, John was twenty-eight and Bird twenty-seven. May's mother went to live in Bournemouth. They moved into two adjoining crofts at Cnoc-an-Fhurain, in Barcaldine, not far from Oban, overlooking a shallow fjord called Loch Creran, and established their third poultry farm. To the west was the Isle of Mull. Mairi would live here for the rest of her life.

When Elsie left the nursing home in Weybridge her influential friends in the Red Cross lobbied for her to be given a home on the Earl Haig estate for ex-servicemen and women at Ashtead in Surrey. She moved into the two-up, two-down newly built house some time in 1930: 'it meant a real, secure home for me and my son'.

We know what Elsie thought of herself, how she summarised her life. Her entry in the telephone directory for 1931 remained the same for over forty years: 'Baroness de T' Serclaes, M.M., Pervyse Cottage'. Her title, her decoration and naming her house after the place that had been her home during the war were charged with emotion and fulfilment. Elsie had been at the height of her looks and powers during the war and she was not going to let anyone forget it.

By now Kenneth was in the RAF. In 1931 he was awarded his pilot's certificate at the Central Flying School at Wittering. He would fly over Pervyse Cottage, 'shoot her up' and loop the loop. As he waved at his mother from the cockpit, Elsie would have been reminded of the time she had been up with Gustav Hamel at Meyrick Park in Bournemouth in the spring of 1914. How she must have itched to be up there with him. It was a happy time in her life: she had her own home and was having fun with her son. 'We had some hilarious times in the cottage, treasure-hunts by car, and gay parties. I loved to be part of it all and to be able to join in the fun without killing it. I was in my forties then, and perhaps should have been more sedate.'

In the 1930s Elsie took a variety of jobs to help make ends meet. She did private nursing for local doctors, but her love of the open road and working for herself prevailed. She bought a big saloon car and started a private car-hire business, driving clients all over the country. One night, waiting outside a house in the cold and feeling grumpy at not being invited into the kitchen for a hot drink, a tramp got into the car and told her the story of his life.

Elsie next became a commercial traveller. She persuaded a London ladies' clothing firm to hire her as their representative for Surrey and would drive around with a suitcase of clothes, making 'raids' on the biggest houses in the poshest parts of that well-heeled county. Things were going well until one day she was conned. She called at a house and asked to see 'Madam' but was told by a 'very snooty-looking butler' that his mistress was unwell. He asked if he could take some things up to show her and Elsie handed over a suitcase of smart frocks. Ten minutes later he reappeared saying that Madam had not liked any of the colours, escorted her to the car and 'held the door open for me most courteously'. When Elsie got home she found that the suitcase was full of paper and rags and the frocks had been stolen. The firm did not want to involve the police but made her pay for what had been stolen.

Elsie gave up commercial travelling after a suitcase of expensive knitwear was stolen from her car. A general's wife who lived near Aldershot agreed to hold a party where Elsie could sell her jumpers and cardigans. When Elsie arrived she thought that the manservant who had answered the door would bring the suitcase in from the car. He did not appear, and when she went to get the case it had gone, and the servant was nowhere in sight. 'I felt I had to keep quiet. It was an awkward situation which demanded tact and a great sense of humour, but for me it was jolly bad luck. After paying for that lot I decided I had had enough . . . it was ruining me.'

Perhaps being on the road so much prompted Elsie to write to *The Times* about the best way to treat shock when there was a road accident. Her war work permeates the language of the letter, like damp through a sandbagged building. Injuries are 'wounds' and the stretcher sidecar she and Mairi drove in Flanders is remembered with affection:

May I boldly state that I believe 50 per cent of the time lives could be saved if a serious thought were given to the patient at the accident? . . . If the patient is kept quiet and warm, the heart adjusts itself sufficiently to enable a journey to be undertaken, and the doctor has a chance to attend to wounds and save a life . . .

A useful mode of transport in outlying districts would be a stretcher sidecar. I had one in Flanders and found it invaluable. I do not speak from inexperience: I have studied shock for four years in the trenches, and have a record of most interesting cases.

On 25 October 1935 *The Times* announced the death of Lady Dorothie Moore, Elsie and Mairi's friend from their Pervyse days. She died at Mooresfort, County Tipperary, after a long illness aged forty-six. During her eighteen-year marriage to Charles Moore she had a son and four daughters. Dorothie, the only one of the four women in Munro's Flying Ambulance Corps subsequently to have children, was the first to die.

During the 1930s Elsie gave talks and showed lantern slides about her war work, sometimes for the Lest We Forget Association. She would polish up her medals, gather up bits of memorabilia, get 'ridiculously nervous and emotional' and talk about her good old days. Musical interludes were performed by the St Dunstan's Band of war-blinded musicians. A photograph appeared in the *Daily Express* of her in her back garden wearing her wartime khaki coat, her tin helmet worn at a jaunty angle and swathed in the Red Cross flag they had flown at Pervyse. A ladylike dancing shoe peeps out from under the flag.

At this time she made friends with the jockey Steve Donoghue, thinking him 'perhaps the greatest, and certainly the most wonderful jockey the turf has ever seen'. He was born in 1884, the same year as Elsie, but they came from very different backgrounds. The six-times Derby winner, who had been born poor in Warrington, had a colourful private life. His marriage was dissolved during the war because of his adultery, and he was then romantically linked with Lady Torrington, the actress Eleanor Souray, who was married to the ninth Viscount Torrington, whose horses he helped her to train. Elsie remembered Donoghue as 'very soft-hearted' and 'an easy touch for a sob-story'. Consequently money slipped through his fingers.

In the 1930s Kenneth was chief instructor of the Bengal Flying Club at Dum Dum in Calcutta, where he married Miss Susie Pauline Bennett in 1934, whom he had met in England, the first woman in New Zealand to be awarded a full commercial pilot's licence. When Elsie remembered the late 1930s, she recalled being exasperated by the ineffectiveness of the League of Nations and 'the way Hitler and Mussolini were allowed to throw their weight around Europe', and was appalled when Neville Chamberlain returned from Munich in 1938 'with that idiotic piece of paper'. She took a course in air raid precautions and qualified as an anti-gas instructor for the Ashtead area. In 1939 she was asked to supervise the training of women ambulance drivers. Eventually she was given a car and an office – coincidentally, in Poplar Town Hall – and the task of selecting buildings that would make suitable dressing stations if war broke out. She had a happy time catching up with old pals from 1926. When war began on 3 September 1939 Elsie was quick to join the Women's Auxiliary Air Force, for her next big adventure.

Throughout the 1930s Mairi and May would go on motoring holidays in their Austin Siddeley car to France and Germany. In 1939 they were so unsettled by the mood in Germany they cut their holiday short. In the early years of the decade, like many people from all kinds of backgrounds, Mairi had been attracted to the apparent leadership skills and strength of Oswald Mosley. For people who dreaded another war and craved a strong leader, Mosley looked and sounded impressive. To the modern reader, with the benefit of knowledge of Hitler's extermination programmes, the idea of supporting him for any reason is repulsive. But thousands of people bought Mosley's pamphlets and books. Eventually Mairi was persuaded by May, and also Bird and John – who by now had crossed the line from being employees to almost members of the family – to abandon her support for him.

X

The Second World War

During the war Mairi did her bit in Scotland. She and May took in two female evacuees from Glasgow with whom they kept in touch for many years. Mairi was appointed by the Ministry of Transport to run the volunteer car pool for Argyllshire, organising drivers to take government officials and other bigwigs all over Scotland at very short notice. John drove for the Red Cross and was awarded an OBE for her work, and Bird joined the Land Army. Mairi and May's parents died during the war: Mrs Davidson in Bournemouth in 1942 and both Gooden-Chisholms in Trinidad in 1943.

Elsie could not wait to go to war again and joined the (WAAF) in September 1939. She was fifty-five years old and horrified to learn that despite her time in Flanders she could not enlist as an officer but had to begin in the ranks just like everyone else. Her title, foreign surname and Military Medal annoyed and confused the sergeant who took down her details at West Drayton Reception Centre. Elsie found it 'trying' to share a dormitory with thirty other women much younger than her. She considered their personal hygiene and table manners not up to scratch; the vision of a girl who sat opposite Elsie one mealtime and spat fat and anything else she took exception to onto her plate remained etched on Elsie's memory twenty-five years later. What an incongruous presence Elsie must have been in that wooden hut among excitable girls, many of them away from home for the first time, who found themselves living alongside a veteran of the Great War. Her cut-glass accent may have been mocked. It was not what Elsie expected when she joined up.

> It was as cold as charity – the winter of 1939 . . . and the marching and drilling really took it out of me . . . The constant square-and-road-bashing had a disastrous effect on my feet. I arrived at West Drayton wearing a size 5 shoe, but the swelling was such that I had to visit the store three times for replacements, and ended up with a size 8 . . . After a route march in full kit I was glad to flop out on my bed and listen to the girls giggling as they tried on their berets . . . I was gathering strength simply to sit upright again . . . and totter to the noise and plain fare of the dining-hall.

After a few months she took examinations, which she passed, and was ordered to report to Balloon Command to serve under Lady Welsh. Balloons were positioned over strategic locations, such as docks and along the Thames, to force low-flying enemy aeroplanes higher and into concentrated anti-aircraft fire. Elsie was an assistant section officer based in London but visited balloon stations all over the country. In 1940 she was transferred to the hush-hush world of 60 Group (Signals), 'the heart and soul' of the chain of radar stations around the British coastline, calling this chapter in her book 'Radar Queen'.

Elsie quickly became a senior WAAF officer within 60 Group, although she had to work hard and was worried she would be seen as an 'old fogey who lived in a First World War past'. Before long she was known as the 'Queen Bee', and was travelling to aerodromes and radar stations around the country supervising the welfare of airwomen. Elsie found the women 'as keen as mustard', and was in her element making sure 'her girls' were properly looked after and kept as safe as possible from air raids. Driven about and flown up to the remotest parts of the west coast of Scotland, she learned to play the mouth organ during one visit and practised on her driver. In the middle of August 1940 Elsie was at Rye in Sussex and watched a dogfight in the Battle of Britain take place 'thousands of feet over our heads, surrounded by the lovely, abstract doodles of violence left by the vapour-trails'. The sight of men parachuting from burning planes reminded her of the 'plummeting bodies' she had helped drag from the mud of Flanders.

In 1941 Elsie was moved from 60 Group to continue her welfare work with the women attached to Bomber Command at Heslington Hall in York. She was disappointed to leave her girls in the radar stations, whom she had loved looking after – they were 'like a big family to me', she knew the names and movements of everyone under her care. Before she joined Bomber Command she had two weeks of lectures, drilling and 'physical jerks' for more examinations and promotion to squadron officer. Because of petrol shortages Elsie sold her car and bought a powerful motorbike, which gave her greater mobility. It was a reminder of her new-found freedom in the summers before 1914.

People did not realize that I had been a pioneer of motor-cycling, and were at first shocked at what they regarded as my reckless-ness. But they got used to it when I kept coming back in one piece, and even showed that I knew how to strip the engine and carry out my own repairs.

As a concession to convention, I would stop my machine about half a mile from the station I was visiting, take off my overall, helmet and goggles, powder my face and apply a touch of lip-stick, put on my WAAF cap and drive slowly and solemnly up to the gate where my pass was checked. It always amused me when my tour finished, I walked back to my machine and made ready to depart. It was surprising the number of groups that suddenly gathered and the faces that appeared in windows as I mounted. I am quite sure that the men were just waiting for me to fail to get the engine started and run to them for help. They never had the pleasure and about a mile down the road I would stop again, change into my overall, helmet and goggles, and really turn on the speed.

Kenneth, his wife and sons Christopher and Paul had returned to England by 1935. In 1942 Wing Commander Knocker was CO of 3 Group Bomber Command, stationed at Stradishall in Suffolk. Elsie saw him from time to time, and although he rarely talked about the 'ops' he went on she knew he was unhappy about having to bomb civilian targets in Germany: 'it made him sick to set out to kill women and children in crowded cities and industrial areas'. In July 1942, three months after their last lunch together, Elsie was going through some paperwork in her office at Heslington Hall gathering information about the movement of WAAFs around the country, when she came across a message that read, 'WE REGRET TO INFORM YOU THAT YOUR SON IS MISSING BELIEVED KILLED.'

I began to think, 'It isn't true. It just isn't true.' I looked out of the window. The sun was shining and the ducks on the lake were quacking, the trees stood there solid and shady . . . I knew that it was true. Kenneth was dead. I felt miserable, and wondered where I could find the strength to bear the knowledge . . . I felt drenched with sadness, and the knowledge of a new and utter loneliness, but I did feel calmer; I steadied up.

*   *   *

Elsie threw herself into her work, refusing to take any time off. For several weeks she pretended that he might come back: 'it was a sort of luxury to toy with . . . and it gave some comfort to my would-be comforters, and saved them from racking their brains for soothing things to say'. But slowly the truth emerged. Between eleven o'clock and midnight of 2 July Kenneth and his crew of seven men from 214 Squadron had taken off from Stradishall in one of over 300 bombers taking part in a raid on Bremen in Germany. Visibility was good, but on the way back, at ten minutes to one on the morning of 3 July, Kenneth Knocker's plane was hit by machine-gun fire from a night-fighter over the Dutch city of Groningen. The plane caught fire, exploded and crashed into the mudflats near Westernieland, the wreckage scattered over several kilometres. Kenneth's was the only aircraft from 214 Squadron that failed to return.

Three days later a German soldier took eight Dutchmen to recover the bodies of the pilot, Wing Commander Kenneth Knocker; second pilot, Sergeant Tristram Palmer; Petty Officer Daniel Malofoie, the observer; Sergeant Peter Inman, the wireless operator; Flight Engineer Sergeant John Underwood; and the three gunners, Sergeant Richard Fairhurst, and Flight Sergeants Ernest Wilson and Robert Ritchie. The bodies were put in coffins screened by black curtains and kept in a barn for a couple of days then buried by the Germans with military honours at Westernieland. Local people came to the farm bringing flowers.

That night in Bremen five civilians had been killed and four injured, a thousand houses and four small industrial firms were damaged and seven ships hit in the port.

In the spring of 1942 Elsie heard that Emily Upcott, her adoptive mother, had died at Clevedon in Somerset, where she and her husband had been living for some years. Lewis Upcott wrote to her asking for help. He was ninety years old and alone in a large, gloomy house. 'We had had our differences, Uncle and I, but after all, he and Aunty had been very good to Kenneth; had made it possible for me to bring him up and to be with him in the calmer intervals of my disturbed life. I had a lot to thank them for.'

Elsie, who was almost sixty, left Bomber Command and went to the rescue, cooking, cleaning and nursing the increasingly frail old man. Eventually it all got too much for her and she took him to live with her at Pervyse Cottage. But she missed her service life desperately, where she had known 'friendship, respect and real security'. She resented not being 'as near the front line' as she could get. Instead of 'a family of hundreds of WAAF's, I had one very old man to care for'. When time permitted, Elsie did welfare work and private nursing and bashed out ideas for a league of women on her typewriter. She argued that because women were playing such a crucial role in helping to win the war, when it was over they should have a voice 'in coping with the aftermath of it'. Never interested in party politics, Elsie wanted a women's organisation to advise on domestic and foreign policy and work closely with parliament, and hoped such a scheme could be replicated round the world as an international league, a kind of 'International Sisterhood'.

After the war was over Elsie was appointed welfare officer of the Epsom Branch of the Royal Air Forces Association. It was unpaid work which she enjoyed, helping to 'bring some sort of order and perspective into the muddled lives' of the wives and widows of airmen who needed help: 'I was no wealthy Lady Bountiful straining to understand how others could be so poor . . . I knew from personal experience.' Her league of women was put to one side while she coped with 'Uncle' and the pressing concerns of the families under her care. To raise money for the RAFA, Elsie ran jumble sales and organised dances and parties in the Peace Memorial Hall in Ashtead, which had been built after the First World War. On 10 March 1947 Lewis Upcott died, aged ninety-five, at a nursing home in Banstead in Surrey. He left £9,000 (worth over £250,000 today), of which £2,000 was to be invested by his trustees to provide an income for Elsie until she died. She also shared the remainder of his estate, which was held in trust for his nephews and nieces.

A piece of the jigsaw of Harold de T'Serclaes' life reveals that on 31 August 1944 he went on the run with Suzanne Marteau, his twenty-five-year-old 'secretary' and accomplice. In 1947 they would be tried *in absentia* by the War Council of Brussels and found guilty of betraying Belgium and her allies, spying for the enemy, infiltrating the Antwerp resistance movement and denouncing its members. Some of his victims were executed or imprisoned by the Germans. He betrayed those who hid Jewish families. Both de T'Serclaes and Marteau were condemned to death by firing squad.

A book published in 2003 about the role of the Belgian nobility in the resistance during the Second World War also mentions aristocrats who collaborated with the Germans. For reasons of 'privacy' the author does not give the surname of a certain 'Harold' but it is clear the person being written about is Elsie's estranged husband. After he retired from the army in the 1920s Harold started a business dealing in wild animals and opened a zoo on his estate in Gronendaal with his 'wife', who was known as the baroness, Marguerite Anciaux. Through his business contacts he met the man who eventually became responsible for the Bremen *Abwehr*, the German military intelligence organisation. Even before the Second World War Harold was known to be pro-German, and may actually have taken German nationality; as soon as Belgium was occupied he contacted the German authorities and was made head of the *Abwehr* in Belgium. As an aristocrat and highly decorated veteran of the First World War with eight 'front-stripes', indicating he had served on the front during the entire war, he was a great catch for the Germans. His role was to spy for his new masters and infiltrate the Antwerp resistance movement. He lived under a number of aliases, his favourite being Lambert, Mairi's middle name perhaps unconsciously embedded in his memory from Pervyse. Members of the resistance reported 'Mr Lambert' being present when others were arrested. He was also believed to be responsible for a German raid in 1942 which led to the arrest of dozens of Belgian officers and soldiers and the man who financially supported the resistance in Antwerp; many were executed or imprisoned and some died in captivity.*

On 31 August 1944, a week before Belgium was liberated on 6 September, Harold and Suzanne Marteau left his chateau at La Hulpe and escaped to nearby Brussels and then moved to Kassel, where they stayed until October. Back at the chateau, his mistress Marguerite Anciaux made a bonfire of their papers before setting off on her bicycle on 2 September to hide out with a Dutch friend of Harold's who was a notorious collaborator. Anciaux was arrested on 6 September, insisting that she knew nothing of Harold's activities, but was sentenced to twenty years' forced labour for handing over three people to the Germans, one of whom died in captivity.

Harold and Suzanne then went to Berlin, where he approached

---

* A friend of mine was discussing this case in Ieper (Ypres) in 2008 when he was overheard by an elderly man whose ears pricked up when the name de T'Serclaes was mentioned. This man, Dr De Moeren, remembered his mother, a member of the Antwerp resistance, being visited by a 'Mr Lambert' who was looking for himself and his two brothers, who were also members. Dr De Moeren's mother was deeply suspicious of de T'Serclaes and would eventually be a witness at his trial.

Prince Josias zu Waldeck und Pyrmont, an SS general whose only son had Heinrich Himmler as a godfather.* Harold was so trusted by the Germans that they instructed him to spy on other Belgian collaborators in Hamburg and Kassel. In April 1945, when zu Waldeck surrendered to General Patton's forces at Buchenwald, de T'Serclaes and Marteau left for Munich, where they were given new identities and German passports. In the chaos at the end of the war it was easy to disappear, especially with friends in the right places, and they hid in Ebensee in Austria for three years, where he worked for Siemens. In August 1948 they moved to Goldegg, also in Austria, where he worked for Baroness Wiener-Welten, and a year later crossed the border into Italy, arriving in Rome in November 1949.

Harold's death sentence was commuted to life imprisonment but he did not return to Belgium; although Marteau handed herself in to the Belgian authorities in January 1950. Stripped of his title, his First World War decorations and medals except for the Croix de Guerre, Harold de T'Serclaes died in Rome in the 1950s. It seems very unlikely that Elsie ever knew anything about Harold's Second World War activities, that the man she had married, for whom she had had such hopes, had joined the enemy which shot down her only child. And yet he carried their marriage certificate to prove his loyalty to the Allied cause. He betrayed his past, his country, his comrades who had died between 1914 and 1918, and many resistance workers.

Eleven years' voluntary work with the Royal Air Force Benevolent Fund started for Elsie in 1949. She was sixty-five and travelled on public transport (there was no money for a car), visiting the families of servicemen and women who had recently been bereaved to

---

* In 1947 zu Waldeck would be convicted of crimes against humanity in connection with Buchenwald concentration camp and sentenced to life imprisonment, but was released after serving three years in prison.

see if they needed any help. She was also welfare officer for the Royal Air Force Homes at Morden in Surrey until 1959, when a bus strike proved the last straw 'walking and hitch-hiking to and from work made me very tired, and I felt I could no longer keep up the pace'. Elsie retired at the age of seventy-five.

During the Festival of Britain in 1951 there was a gathering of the Clan Chisholm Society at Murrayfield in Edinburgh; Mairi agreed to become honorary general secretary, and her nephew Alastair became clan chief of the re-formed society that her grandfather had founded at the end of the previous century. For nearly thirty years Mairi conducted a vast correspondence with Chisholms round the world, and organised clan meetings twice a year and the gatherings of the clan in Scotland and London. When she retired in 1980 the clan journal paid her a warm tribute: she had a 'genuine interest in people of all sorts and conditions, and in all walks of life and in every country'.

In 1964 George Harrap and Co. published Elsie's autobiography *Flanders and Other Fields*, a dramatic, sketchy and sometimes misleading account of her life. It was well received, although one reviewer thought, 'It is a sad reflection that after a dramatic and exciting life, including active service in world wars, Baroness de T'Serclaes has come to the conclusion that only in time of war has she found any real sense of purpose and happiness.' The *Sunday Express* critic thought it 'one of the best First World War books to have come out in this fiftieth anniversary year'. Eighty-year-old Elsie, an 'elegant old lady', gave interviews at Pervyse Cottage nursing her chihuahua to those who marvelled at her account of the 'grim and gay years' in Flanders. She said that Harold had been killed shortly after their 'lightning' honeymoon and treated interviewers to her view of danger: 'Why worry – it's quite useless. Go over the top smiling.'

In Argyllshire Mairi read the book and typed a single-spaced three-page foolscap response: 'for the record I would like to stress the actual facts'. She corrected some of Elsie's errors but did not complain about her own shadowy presence in the text. The references to her are scattered around the book like fifteen pieces of confetti, and never give Mairi her due. Elsie described a handful of their exploits in which Mairi featured briefly and gave two descriptions of her: she was 'strong, healthy and willing to learn, an excellent driver and mechanic' and 'brave, steady as well as being an excellent driver'. Mairi concluded her response: 'Unlike her I have found much happiness and sense of purpose in peace time. I have been blessed with friendships of both men and women, and although my health has not always been good it has never justified self-pity. What more can one say?'

In the summer of 1968 Elsie was honoured several times for her work in both world wars: there was a special press conference hosted by the Ministry of Defence and she was introduced to the Queen Mother at a reception for Princess Mary's Royal Air Force Nursing Services and the WRAF fiftieth anniversary at St James's Palace. At eighty-four she was still going strong and recording her life in press cuttings, as she had been doing for more than half a century.

In 1973, aged eighty-nine, Elsie was interviewed at Pervyse Cottage. Her taped voice is clipped but suggests weariness and some bitterness at the way her life has turned out. No longer the hearty and high-spirited baroness of the scrapbooks, she sounds physically and mentally frail, her memory porous. Halfway through the interview Elsie was shown a photograph of Mairi, whom she does not recognise. She is begrudging and dismissive about the young girl with whom she set off for war and who got her a place in Munro's corps: 'I never looked upon her as anything but a stooge . . . a cleaner-up, and she was quite a good driver . . . but she didn't know anything about wounds . . . She looked upon me as a very superior officer. She had to because I knew exactly the answers to every question.'

On 24 March 1977 the Imperial War Museum's exhibition *Women at War* was opened by Princess Anne, to whom Mairi Chisholm was introduced, and in November the documentary *Women at War: The Two Women of Pervyse* was screened on BBC2. Mairi loaned her diaries, medals, memorabilia and her khaki coat, breeches and headscarf, and donated them when the exhibition ended. Elsie's nephew loaned his aunt's mementoes, which were also donated to the museum. Elsie was too unwell to attend.

On the 26 April 1978 the Baroness Elizabeth Blackall de T'Serclaes died in a nursing home in Epsom, aged ninety-three, of pneumonia and senile dementia.

Three years later, on 22 August 1981, Mairi Lambert Gooden-Chisholm of Chisholm died of lung cancer. She was eighty-five years old and died at Cnoc-an-Fhurain in Barcaldine, Argyllshire in the home she shared with Edith May Davidson, Catherine Bridget 'Bird' Partridge and Grace Barbara 'John' Johnstone, with whom she had lived for almost sixty years.

When she died the Madonnas of Pervyse were gone. Elsie's indomitable spirit, which sent her on a horse up the stairs of a Devon haberdashery for a bet, scrambling and skidding on hairpin bends on a spluttering motorbike and sidecar, and up in the air with the man of the moment, Gustav Hamel, drove her for the rest of her life. She would not let go of her finest hour; she never felt more alive than when she was close to death. Mairi, also intrepid, made a different life for herself. She never spoke of the past unless asked about it; she always looked forward. However, Mairi never forgot the close friendships she made with the Belgian orderlies who had been with her and Elsie – once or twice she returned to Pervyse and had them to stay at Cnoc.

End Piece

When I saw an interview on television with a neat Scottish lady in her eighties talking about her war work in Belgium during the First World War I knew I wanted to write about Mairi Chisholm. In a modest, funny and matter-of-fact way Mairi described how she had done her bit. As I watched I became proud of that eighteen-year-old girl who had given up her safe life to roar away to London on her motorbike after a furious row with her mother, who had sold her machine to pay her way, and who had gone on to nurse right behind the front line in Belgium for most of the Great War. Then I heard about Elsie Knocker, her leader and friend, who got married during the war and became a baroness.

Everything I have learned makes me wish I had known them. Elsie was bossy and in later years tricky; her attitudes and vocabulary never moved on from Edwardian England. Mairi, recently a schoolgirl, twelve years younger than her fellow biker, was able to rebuild her life after the war and be happy in a way that Elsie was unable to do. Drawn to each other by their tomboyish ways and a shared love of taking life at full throttle, together Elsie and Mairi had had the time of their lives.

To put it in a contemporary context, imagine yourself and a

friend rushing off to Helmand Province in Afghanistan and staying there for three and a half years until calamity strikes. Mairi and Elsie did something very similar without thinking twice.

Elsie and Mairi's story has a resonance today in the brave and selfless who work for aid agencies and charities all round the world, risking their lives to help others live theirs. Meeting Mairi on the television that evening started to reveal to me a story of courage, suffering and love.

Sources

The sources in this book have not been footnoted. However I would like to help readers find out more about Elsie and Mairi and the people who came into their lives.

The starting point for the book was the two women's diaries, photograph albums and scrapbooks. The Imperial War Museum has the three diaries Elsie wrote during the war, and her visitors' book and War Album. They also have Mairi's three diaries, her photograph albums and scrapbooks are held by the National Library of Scotland in Edinburgh. Mairi and her father wrote dozens of letters to her aunt Lucy, his sister; these are a private collection owned by the family, who kindly let me use them.

The Imperial War Museum has two taped interviews with Mairi conducted in 1976 and 1977. Elsie and Mairi's diaries stopped in the spring of 1916, so these tapes were invaluable in filling many gaps in the story. I enjoyed meeting members of Mairi's family, who told me about her years after the end of the war.

The Imperial War Museum's collections also revealed nuggets of information about parts of the women's lives for which there are no other sources. For example, although Elsie and Mairi did not know Mr R. G. Plint, his file contained two of the

Crumps' concert programmes with photographs of the men who performed in Elsie and Mairi's hut at Steenkerke as pierrots and in drag.

A large number of British armed forces officers and other ranks appear in this story. I have been able to find out about their service careers, and a little of their lives before they met Elsie and Mairi, by consulting their service records in the War Office and Admiralty files at the National Archives at Kew. The Commonwealth War Graves Commission website revealed the fate of some of the men with whom Elsie and Mairi had fun. School archivists were able to provide details about some of these men when they were boys, which made their journey to the war, from which some of them did not return, all the more poignant.

A number of bigwigs in the diaries who signed the visitors' book at Pervyse appear in the obituary columns of *The Times*, and some are in the *Oxford Dictionary of National Biography*.

I wanted to find out about Elsie's handsome husband and his pals – who and what they were before the war, and what became of them. Two Belgian friends located them for me in the Belgian army and aviation archives in Brussels. Wounded Belgian soldiers, brave orderlies and playful officers played a big part in Elsie and Mairi's life.

The Cellar-House of Pervyse, edited by Geraldine Mitton and published in 1916, is a compilation of Elsie and Mairi's diaries and gives a strong sense of the lives they led. It also benefits from stories of events Mitton gleaned from interviews with them that do not appear in the diaries.

Kelly's Directories and local newspapers were helpful in finding out about the places where the women grew up and went to school.

Elsie's autobiography *Flanders And Other Fields* (1964) is a vivid account of her life, and although sketchy in places, especially about Mairi's role at Pervyse, which is not fully described, it does convey Elsie's forceful personality. It provides clues as to what it must have been like for Mairi to have lived with such an inspiring woman under such extraordinary circumstances for nearly four years.

The gritty and oil-smeared world of motorbiking before the First World War is evoked in the pages of *Motor Cycling* and *Motor Cycle*, where characters like Elsie and Mairi, Rosa Hammett, Muriel Hind and Mrs Mabel Hardee were making their presence felt in a most unladylike way.

The UK Census provides basic material for anyone interested in almost any aspect of British history. The J series files at the National Archives in Kew contained the divorce papers of some of the characters in this book.

Some of the minor characters with whom I became fascinated, such as the actresses and music-hall stars who appeared at the Alhambra in Leicester Square to raise money for Elsie and Mairi, have had their parts reduced and ended up on my cutting-room floor. *The Times* digital archive is the best online newspaper resource I know. I spent many hours immersed in another world with some creative and naughty ladies.

The Bank of England inflation calculator helps make sense of the cost of things and the value of money.

If you would like to know more about the content of this book please contact me via my website www.dianeatkinson.co.uk. I'd be happy to answer any comments and enquiries.

While every effort has been made to contact copyright holders, the author and publisher would be grateful for information about any material where they have been unable to trace the source, and would be glad to make amendments in further editions.

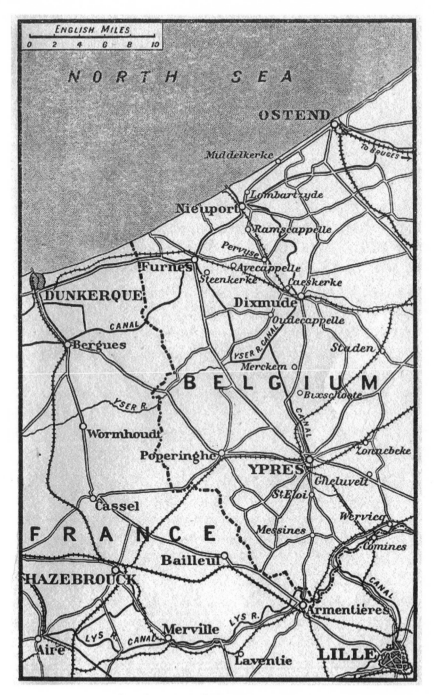

Sketch map of the Pervyse area,
taken from the cellar-house of Pervyse.

Bibliography

All books were published in London unless stated otherwise.

Adie, Kate, *Corsets to Camouflage: Women and War*, Hodder and Stoughton in association with the Imperial War Museum, 2003

Anon., *War Sites of the 1914–1918 Campaign of the Belgian Army*, War Office Department, Brussels, 1918

Anon., *Tonbridge School and the Great War of 1914–1918*, Whitefriars Press, 1923

Anon., *Strangers In A Strange Land: Belgian Refugees 1914–1918*, catalogue of exhibition at Flanders Fields Museum, Ieper, Davidsfonds/Leuven, Ghent, 2005

Anon., *The Yser and the Belgian Coast*, Michelin & Co., France, 1920, facsimile edition, 1985

Anon., *Ypres and the Battle of Ypres*, Michelin and Co., France, 1919

Barton, Peter, *The Battlefields of the First World War: The Unseen Panoramas of the Western Front*, Constable and Robinson Ltd, 2005

Bleyaert, Walter, *De Groote Oorlog In Pervyze: Vroeger Is Niet Voorbij*, Emiel Decock, Dixmuide, undated

Breton, Willy, *The Belgian Front and Its Notable Features*, Chatto & Windus, 1918

Brownlow, Kevin, *The War, the West and the Wilderness*, Secker and Warburg, 1979

Carmichael, Jane, *First World War Photographers*, Routledge, 1989

Carr, Kent, *Women Who Dared: Heroines of the Great War*, S. W. Partridge and Co. Ltd, 1920

Clutterbuck, L. A, *The Bond of Sacrifice: A Biographical Record of All the British Officers Who Fell in the Great War*, Volume II, January–June 1915, Anglo African Publishing, undated

Condell, Diana and Liddiard, Jean, *Images of Women in the First World War 1914–1918*, Routledge and Kegan Paul Ltd, 1987

Cook, Chris and Stevenson, John, *The Longman Handbook of Modern British History 1714–1980*, Longman, 1983

Crawford, Elizabeth, *The Women's Suffrage Movement: A Reference Guide 1866–1928*, University College Press, 1999

Davis, Paul, *The Dickens A–Z*, Checkmark Books, New York, 1998

Demoen, Herman, *Het Diksmuide Van Toen*, Marc Van de Wiele, Bruges, undated

De Ruvigny's, Roll of Honour, 1914–1918, reprint, Naval and Military Press, Uckfield, Sussex, 2001

De T'Serclaes, the Baroness Elizabeth Blackall, *Flanders and Other Fields: The Memoirs of the Baroness de T'Serclaes*, George Harrap and Co., 1964

De Vere Stacpoole, Horace, *The Crimson Azaleas*, Philip Allan, 1908, 1935 edition

D'Udekem D'Acoz, Marie-Pierre, *Voor Koning En Vaderland: De Belgische Adel In Her Verzet*, Tielt, Lannoo, Brussels, 2003

De Wilde, Robert, *Mon Journal de Campagne: De Liège à l'Yser*, Plon-Nourrit et Cie, Paris, 1918

Dunlop, Jean, *The Clan Chisholm*, W. & A. K. Johnston & G. W. Bacon Ltd for the Clan Chisholm Society, Edinburgh, 1953

Escott, Beryl E., *Women in Air Force Blue: The Story of Women in the Royal Air Force from 1918 to the Present Day*, Patrick Stephens Limited, Wellingborough, 1989

Ferro, Mark, Brown, Malcolm, Cazals, Remy, and Meuller, Olaf, *Meetings in No Man's Land: Christmas 1914 and Fraternization in the Great War*, Constable Ltd, 2007

Furley H. D. (ed.), *Tonbridge School Register 1861–1945*, Rivington's, 1951

Gibbs, Philip, *The Soul of War*, Heinemann, 1915

Gilbert, Martin, *First World War*, Weidenfeld and Nicolson, 1994

Gilbert, Martin, *The Somme: the Heroism and the Horror of War*, John Murray, 2007 edition

Gleason, Arthur, *Young Hilda at the Wars*, Frederick A. Stokes, New York, 1915

Hanna, Martha, *Your Death Would Be Mine: Paul and Marie Pireaud in the Great War*, Harvard University Press, Cambridge, Massachusetts 2006

'Ixion', *Motor Cycle Cavalcade*, Iliffe & Sons Ltd, 1950

Jones, Simon, *World War 1 Gas Warfare Tactics and Equipment*, Osprey Publishing Ltd, Oxford, 2007

Kelly's Post Office Directories

Lake, Deborah, *Smoke and Mirrors: Q-Ships Against the U-Boats in the First World War*, Sutton Publishing Ltd, Stroud, 2006

Lee, Janet, *War Girls: The First Aid Nursing Yeomanry in the First World War*, Manchester University Press, Manchester, 2005

Lekeux, Father Martial, *Mes Cloîtres Dans la Tempête*, Plon-Nourrit et Cie, Paris, *c*.1919

Levine, Joshua, *On a Wing and a Prayer*, Collins, 2008

Macdonald, Lyn, *The Roses of No Man's Land*, 1980, Michael Joseph, Papermac edition, 1984

Mackenzie, Alexander, *History of the Chisholms*, privately published, 1891

Macnaughtan, Sarah, *My Wartime Experiences in Two Continents*, John Murray, 1919

Mitchell, David, *Women on the Warpath: The Story of Women of the First World War*, Jonathan Cape, 1966

Mitton, G. E. (ed.), *The Cellar-House of Pervyse: A Tale of Uncommon Things from the Journals and Letters of the Baroness T'Serclaes and Mairi Chisholm*, A & E Black, 1916

Moore, Eva, *Entrances and Exits*, Frederick A Stokes, New York, 1923

Moran, Lord, *The Anatomy of Courage*, 1945, London, Carroll and Graf Publishers, New York edition, first published by Constable and Company Ltd, London, 1945

Morgan, Kenneth O. (ed.), *The Oxford History of Britain*, Oxford University Press, Oxford, 1999

Nouvelle Biographie Nationale, Volume 9, Académie Royale des Sciences, des Lettres at des Beaux-Arts de Belgique, Brussels, 2007

Palmer, Alan, *The Salient: Ypres, 1914–1918*, Constable, 2007

Parker, Peter, *The Old Lie: the Great War and the Public-School Ethos*, Hambledon Continuum edition, first published by Constable and Company Ltd, 1987

Parry, Melanie (ed.), *Chambers Biographical Dictionary of Women*, Chambers, 1996

Pieters, Walter E, *Above Flanders' Fields: A Complete Record*

of the Belgian Fighter Pilots and Their Units During the
Great War *1914–1918*, Grub Street, 1998

Raitt, Suzanne, *May Sinclair: A Modern Victorian*, Oxford
University Press, Oxford, 2000

Robertshaw, Andrew, *Somme 1 July 1916: Tragedy and
Triumph*, Osprey Publishing Ltd, Oxford, 2006

Schepens, Luc, en Vandewoulde, Émile, *Albert & Elisabeth
1914–1918: Albums Van De Koningin, Nota's Van De
Koning*, Gemeentekrediet, Brussels, undated

Sheldon, James, *Veteran and Vintage Motor Cycles*, B. T.
Batsford, 1961

Sinclair, May, *A Journal of Impressions of Belgium*,
Macmillan, New York, 1915

Souttar, Henry, *A Surgeon in Belgium*, Edward Arnold, 1915

Vanleene, Patrick, *Op Naar de Grote Oorlog: Mairi, Elsie e
de Anderen in Flanders Fields*, de Klaproos, Koksijde,
undated

Winter, Jay and Baggett, Blaine, *1914–1918: The Great War
and the Shaping of the Twentieth Century*, BBC Books,
1996

Zuckerman, Larry, *The Rape of Belgium*, New York University Press, New York and London 2004

Acknowledgements

I am so happy and grateful that Trevor Dolby asked me to write this book. I have enjoyed every moment of the research and every word of the writing. Thanks to John Kelly for his faith in me and for introducing me to Trevor. Special thanks go to Lilias Atkinson, Ruari Chisholm of Chisholm, Susan Chisholm of Chisholm and Mairi-Angela Foster, who told me so much about Mairi and allowed me to reproduce photographs from their family albums and quote from family letters. And for the wonderful time I spent with Lilias. For the use of the Baroness de T'Serclaes' copyright material at the Imperial War Museum, and permission to use her words, I would like to thank Paul Knocker. I am also grateful for his permission to reproduce the photograph of her taken at home in the 1960s, and for the insights he shared with me about his extraordinary grandmother. Thanks also to Mrs Elizabeth Edwards, with whom I spent a day immersed in her Petre family papers and photograph albums, which showed me how important Mairi and Jack Petre had been to each other. She also wined and dined me in the most hospitable way.

To Julian Putkowski for his extraordinary expertise. He told me about Elsie and Mairi and repeatedly went over the top, across no-man's-land and into Hellfire Corner (his study) to locate some of the army who appear in this story. Dominiek Dendooven and Piet Chielens for their exemplary research, encyclopedic knowledge of the First World War and translation of documents they unearthed for me in Belgium. Walter Pieters, who generously allowed me to see the material on Belgian airmen from his forthcoming book.

Annice Collett is a wonderful librarian and biker at the Vintage Motor Cycle Club, Burton-on-Trent. She never tired of my endless enquiries about women on motorbikes and sent me splendid material. Thanks to the Trustees of the National Library of Scotland for their permission to use Mairi's photographs and words; Sheila Mackenzie of the Department of Manuscripts could not have been more helpful. Thanks go to Dr Terry Rogers, Honorary Archivist at Marlborough College, for the fine day he spent showing me round the town where Elsie grew up and married, and for sending me a copy of the one of the three pictures that survive of Elsie before the First World War. To Sylvia Ospina and Paul Hammond for their super translations of newspaper articles, letters and official documents. To David Baldwin for the wonderful pictures of lady motorcyclists' accessories he supplied me with from the archives of Alfred Dunhill Ltd of London. To Dr Nick Hiley at the University of Kent for sharing his knowledge of Ernest Brooks with me. To Kevin Brownlow for so cheerfully rummaging though his vast collection for a picture of Frank Bassill. Lennie Maiden is the best computer doctor I know.

I have been fortunate to have written this book at a time when the Internet makes it possible to 'meet' so many kind and helpful people. School archivists have pored over their school magazines and researched their rolls of honour; their work has enabled me to broaden my view of some of the young English officers who knew Elsie and Mairi and went to their parties, enjoying each other's company in the most unlikely of circumstances. Many old boys did not survive to tell their own tales. Thanks go to: Mrs Ann Wheeler at Charterhouse School, Jill Barlow at Cheltenham College, who told me so much about Mairi's brother's education, to Pamela Taylor at Mill Hill School, David Knight at Stonyhurst College and Mary Dobson at Westminster City School.

Thanks also to John Pulford and his team at Brooklands Museum, Weybridge; Peter Liddle, who interviewed Elsie and Mairi in the 1970s; and Karen Mee at the Brotherton Library, University of Leeds. I am grateful to the Trustees of the Imperial War Museum for their permission to use Elsie and Mairi's photographs and words, and thanks to the staff in the film archive, photographic, printed books, sound and document departments who are always so obliging. To Peter Elliott and Peter Devitt at the Royal Air Force Museum, Hendon, and Anna Clark at the Fleet Air Arm Museum at Yeovilton. To the librarians at Cedar Rapids Public Library in Iowa for the material they sent to me on Helen Gleason. To François de Broqueville and Guy Van der Ghinst, who answered so many questions about their fathers' friendships with Elsie and Mairi and the Munro corps. To Jean Munro, who knew Mairi for the last thirty years of her life and whose book on the Clan Chisholm was so helpful. To Patrick Vanleene for writing such a good book in Flemish about Elsie and Mairi and the Munro corps.

Friends play a big part in the writing of books. Pauline Tanner accompanied me on many research trips in Elsie and Mairi's footsteps; Deborah Cherry put me straight on a lot of things, not least the identities of mystery ladies in sidecars; and Debby Murphy was always there to translate some Flemish if I needed her to; Nicola Gooch always listens and is full of ideas.

To my agent David Godwin, whose interest in and care of his authors is impeccable. The greatest thanks go to Patrick Hughes, without whose love and support and criticism this book could not have been written. To him I owe the most.

Place Names, Then and Now

Alveringhem	Alveringem
Avecapelle	Avekapelle
Berlaare	Berlare
Bruges	Brugge
Caeskerke	Kaaskerke
Coxyde	Koksijde
Dixmude	Diksmuide
Furnes	Veurne
Ghent	Gent
Lokeren	Lokeren
Melle	Melle
Nieuport	Nieuwpoort
Oostkerke	Oostkerke
Oudecapelle	Oudekapelle
Passchendaele	Passendale
Pervyse	Pervijze
Poperinghe	Poperinge
Ramscapelle	Ramskapelle
Stuyvenskerke	Stuivenkenskerke
La Panne	De Panne
Wulveringhem	Wulveringem
Ypres	Ieper
Yser	Ijzer
Zele	Zele

List of Illustrations

List of Illustrations and sources of quotations used in captions:

Plate Section 1:
Page 1: Elsie and Mrs Emily Upcott, Marlborough College Archives; Mairi, her mother and Uailean, private collection; Mairi's school photograph, private collection; Ruari, private collection.

Page 2: Pervyse, Imperial War Museum, quote from *The Times,* 14 November 1914, p.8; first-aid post, National Library of Scotland, quote from Robert de Wilde, *De Liège A L'Yser, Mon Journal de Campagne, 1915.*

Page 3: Helen Gleason, Lady Dorothie Feilding, Mairi and unknown officers, private collection; Elsie and Georges Frederic Gilson, Imperial War Museum.

Page 4: Gardening, Imperial War Museum; Elsie against sandbags, National Library of Scotland; Elsie swigging from bottle of wine, National Library of Scotland; tin hats, private collection.

Page 5: Posing in a shell hole, private collection, quote from Geraldine Mitton (ed.), *The Cellar-House of Pervyse: A Tale of Uncommon Things From The Journals and Letters Of The Baroness de T'Serclaes And Mairi Chisholm,* p.209; Henry Halahan, private collection, quote from Baroness de T'Serclaes, *Flanders And Other Fields,* p.88; Mairi portrait, Imperial War Museum.

Page 6: Baron de T'Serclaes, National Library of Scotland; Elsie and Harry on their wedding day, National Library of Scotland, quote from *Marlborough Times,* 28 January 1916; romance in a war-zone, National Library of Scotland.

Page 7: Fund-raising trip, National Library of Scotland.

Page 8: John Joseph Petre, Stonyhurst College Archives; Mairi with Petre and Teddy Gerard, National Library of Scotland.

Plate Section 2

Page 1: Elsie, Mairi and 'Tecky', Imperial War Museum; punting, National Library of Scotland, quote *Flanders And Other Fields,* p.87.

Page 2: The Crumps, Imperial War Museum (R. G. Plint); most photographed women of the First World War, Imperial War Museum.

Page 3: Photograph with Shot, private collection; first-aid post, private collection; the New Ladies of the Lamp, National Library of Scotland.

Page 4: Taking cover, private collection; family group, private collection.

Page 5: Elsie recovering from gas attack, National Library of Scotland, recovery in Chelsea; National Library of Scotland; engagement photograph, National Library of Scotland.

Page 6: Cantray House, private collection; Uailean, private collection; Jersey, private collection.

Page 7: Elsie in the 1960s, private collection.

Page 8: Mairi at her desk, private collection.

Text Picture credits

Page 27: Elsie in *Motor Cycling* magazine, Vintage Motorcycle Club; chic motoring attire and leather smock, Alfred Dunhill Ltd.

Page 37: Ladies' motor cycling overalls, Alfred Dunhill Ltd.

Page 38: The Bijou bonnet, Harem veil and Amherst muff, Alfred Dunhill Ltd.

Index